THE GIGALAW GUIDE
TO INTERNET LAW

The

GigaLaw

GUIDE TO INTERNET LAW

Doug Isenberg

RANDOM HOUSE TRADE PAPERBACKS

NEW YORK

2002 Random House Trade Paperback Edition

Library of Congress Cataloging-in-Publication Data
Isenberg, Doug.
The GigaLaw guide to Internet law / Doug Isenberg.
p.   cm.
Includes index.
ISBN 0-8129-9198-2 (trade pbk.)
1. Internet—Law and legislation—United States. 2. Computer networks—Law
and legislation—United States. I. Title.
KF390.5.C6 I84 2002
343.7309'944—dc21   2002023119

For Leslie, my love, whose patience and support
always are invaluable

Foreword

by Dave Baker, Vice President,
Law and Public Policy, EarthLink

In the days immediately following the September 11, 2001, attacks on the World Trade Center and the Pentagon, federal law enforcement authorities approached EarthLink and other Internet service providers (ISPs) with court-ordered authorizations to collect information about the online activities of certain customers. This provoked great interest from the media, which asked: Were such requests unusual? And could attempts to collect such information compromise the privacy and security of other customers?

The answers were rather less dramatic than some might have anticipated. Yes, we received requests for information, but no, these were not unusual. In fact, we (and other ISPs) handle such requests on a regular basis. Despite the extraordinary events that gave rise to these demands, both law enforcement authorities and ISPs already knew their obligations and their limits in intercepting and retrieving online information, as established in the Electronic Communications Privacy Act of 1986.[1] These rules were subsequently clarified in the USA PATRIOT Act of 2001.[2]

What then about all our other customers and users of our network? Was their privacy in jeopardy? Before the terrorist attacks, online privacy had been discussed most often in a commercial context: Did websites sell users' personal information? Did customers have adequate notice of a company's privacy policy? Could users choose whether or not to receive further information, or should their choice be preselected by default? While not unimportant, these questions suddenly took a backseat to concerns about governmental intrusions into personal information and communications. As James K. Glassman had stated some months earlier, "Privacy advocates should stop wasting their time beating up on DoubleClick and focus on the real privacy debate—a debate about the power of government in the digital age."[3]

Fortunately, we at EarthLink had addressed this as well. In an earlier case, concern over possible interception of communications by persons other than those named as targets of investigations led us to resist attempts by federal authorities to install on our network the brashly named "Carnivore" system, the FBI's software application that allows it essentially to eavesdrop on e-mail.[4] Even in the wake of the terrorist attacks, we were able to comply with valid law enforcement requests for information without installing Carnivore and compromising the privacy and security of our nearly five million other customers.

But privacy concerns, whether commercial or governmental, are but one example of legal issues surrounding the Internet. Others include: How can we protect intellectual property rights such as copyrights, trademarks, and patents? How can we fight "spam," the electronic junk mail that clogs users' in-boxes and ISPs' servers? How should we tax (or not tax) e-commerce transactions, which often involve multiple jurisdictions? How do we protect children from indecency and exploitation while preserving free speech? And does supporting free speech mean tolerating hate on the Internet?

The Internet law issues we at EarthLink continually face—the issues discussed in-depth in *The GigaLaw Guide to Internet Law*—are the same issues that every businessperson, every entrepreneur, and every Internet user should know about.

As the Internet has grown and developed, so, too, have the laws surrounding it. No longer an information "wild, wild west," the Internet increasingly is influenced by legal considerations. Some of these considerations are unique to the Internet, its architecture, and its capabilities. Others present the issue of "whether new wine can be poured into an old bottle"[5] (as one court said in a 1994 case on on-line software piracy)—that is, well-established principles merely applied to a new medium. And some issues, such as those raised by Napster, present entirely new clashes between preexisting law and modern technology.

Napster provides a great example of a "killer app" killed by its failure to address legal realities. A brilliantly simple application, it took full advantage of the Internet's very nature as an information service to create a means of distributing music far more efficiently than the conventional process of pressing a CD, wrapping it, boxing it, shipping it, unloading it, and displaying it in a store just so a customer could drive to that store, buy the CD, take it home, and put it in a player to decode the CD's digital information in order to finally hear music. But as good as its peer-to-peer file-sharing technology was, Napster failed to address vital legal issues such as copyrights, licenses, and royalty payments. Rock stars, songwriters, and music publishers are entitled to be paid for their work, as the federal courts in the Napster lawsuits repeatedly ruled. Napster will always serve as a reminder that just because you can do something online doesn't mean you can ignore existing laws.

This is not to say that laws inhibit growth or stifle innovation. Just the opposite. The "dot-com" boom may be over, but the Internet is here to stay. MTV's first music video twenty years ago had it wrong: Video didn't kill the radio star; it made him bigger than ever. So, too, a coherent body of law won't kill the Internet; instead, it will create a framework upon which the Internet can continue to flourish and grow.

CONTENTS

INTRODUCTION

WHY YOU NEED TO KNOW ABOUT INTERNET LAW

In January 2000, when the GigaLaw.com website was launched and began providing information about important legal issues for conducting business on the Internet, I wrote in a welcome letter[1] on the site that Internet law, like the Internet itself, had grown at an incredible pace. At the time, I noted that the U.S. court system did not address any Internet issues until 1994, but that by 1999, more than 550 published court opinions had made reference to the Internet. Then, that seemed like a significant figure worth citing. Now, even despite the significant bursting of many Internet bubbles, the growth continues: In 2001, U.S. state and federal courts issued more than 1,100 published opinions referring to the Internet in some capacity—twice as many as just two years earlier.

While not all of these cases involve substantive issues of Internet law such as those covered in this book, the point is clear: Internet law is a vital topic about which anyone who conducts business online must become educated. This is true regardless of your online activities if you fall into any of the following categories:

- a self-employed businessperson or independent contractor, creating content for the World Wide Web, designing websites, or authoring software applications;
- an entrepreneur who wants to launch an online business;
- a consumer who engages in e-commerce;
- an information technology professional for a company of any size;
- a business executive for a company that exists solely on the Internet or simply has a promotional website; or
- a lawyer who regularly fields high-tech legal questions from clients or simply needs to be prepared for the occasional Internet legal issue.

Regardless of what role you play online—in your personal or professional life, as a sole proprietor, or as an employer or an employee—Internet law affects you. This book explains how.

"Internet law" is a very broad term. In the beginning (that is, in the mid-1990s), lawyers who practiced Internet law primarily had backgrounds in intellectual property law—copyrights, trademarks, and patents. However, as the Internet has grown, Internet law has grown, too. Today, Internet law applies to a very wide body of legal issues, including not only intellectual property but also privacy, the First Amendment, contracts, employment law, and more. Unfortunately, as this topic has grown larger and more sophisticated, non-lawyers and even many lawyers have become increasingly confused by the complicated and evolving legal issues that apply in cyberspace.

At the same time, Internet law is becoming more mainstream. As GigaLaw.com Daily News[2] illustrates, not a day has passed in recent years without at least several significant developments in Internet law. And many of these issues—such as Napster's copyright lawsuits, domain name disputes, monitoring of employees' Internet use, widespread "spamming," and much more—often are reported in the mainstream media, sometimes even on the front page. Therefore, even if your goal is not to launch an e-business that stays within the relevant legal boundaries, knowing about Internet law has become just as significant as knowing about other important issues in the news, from politics to education to health (and, not surprisingly, Internet law affects them all).

Whether you read this book from cover to cover or merely use it as a reference, you'll find that Internet law is a very interesting but also very tricky subject. Because Internet law is still developing— only a few years ago most judges knew very little about the Internet, let alone how to use it—many of the rules are in flux. As a result, although this book explains the basics of Internet law and discusses many of the emerging issues (primarily in the United States, unless otherwise noted), it's very important that you learn about the current status of any legal issue and how other countries' laws could apply before acting. As the disclaimer on page vii notes, you should not rely on this book for any legal advice, not only because of the budding nature of many Internet legal issues, but because every legal situation is unique. The best way to make sure you understand the legal relevance of your actions online is to consult with an attorney. Of course, if you consult this book first, you'll probably do yourself a favor, by identifying the legal issues that apply to your situation and educating yourself about the fundamental issues, thereby maximizing the value of the time you spend with a lawyer—and minimizing your legal fees.

THE SEVEN MAJOR PARTS OF INTERNET LAW

Most of the seven major parts to this book introduce an important Internet law topic with a "case study," an example of a particularly interesting or key legal case. By reading these case studies, you'll quickly gain an understanding of the importance of Internet law and how significantly it could affect you. The following chapters of each part then provide the basic legal concepts and further details on specific laws that apply to conducting business online. Here's what you'll learn in this book:

The first three parts—Chapters 1 through 14—address the three basic aspects of intellectual property law: copyrights, trademarks, and patents. Specifically, **Part I (Copyright Law)** opens with a discussion of a copyright lawsuit filed by Playboy against a man who allegedly published nearly 7,500 of the magazine's photos online without permission. A court awarded Playboy more than $3.7 million in damages for the man's copyright infringement. But you don't have to work for (or against) Playboy to understand the relevance of copyright law to the Internet. Because so much online content—photos, text, graphics, music, and software—is protected by copyright law, you need to know how to protect it and how not to violate it.

Part II (Domain Names and Trademarks) introduces two vital and often interconnected topics. A domain name is an Internet company's online address, but "cybersquatters"—people who register another's trademark as a domain name—often have created significant roadblocks for reaching the address. In early domain name disputes, trademark owners had to rely on existing laws, which often failed to provide protection, but Congress and the Internet's governing body have since stepped in, creating new laws and rules that have helped trademark owners and hurt cybersquatters. Still, cybersquatting persists. In addition, trademarks have taken on a new importance on the Internet. After reading Part II, you'll learn what trademarks are, how to protect them, and how to use them in cyberspace.

Part III (Patent Law) discusses one of the most controversial—and, often, rewarding—sets of intellectual property laws online. Patents have received a lot of attention on the Internet, particularly as companies have sought and obtained protection for "business methods," such as Amazon.com's infamous "1-click" patent. Although patents have existed for much longer than the Internet itself, they have taken on new importance in recent years, not only for business methods but also for software, to which the courts have only recently extended patent protection. The chapters in this part of the book explain the fundamental issues of patent law, including how to obtain a patent and what it protects, as well as more sophisticated topics such as how to enforce and license them.

Part IV (Privacy) explains an issue that has become one of the most sensitive for consumers and businesses online. Should Internet companies be able to use information about consumers they collect online? Are there any limits? Does every website need a privacy policy? Should children's information be protected by additional laws because of children's vulnerability and innocence? What about privacy laws in countries other than the United States—how do they apply? The chapters in this part of the book answer all of these questions and also discuss why privacy has become such a hot topic. After reading these chapters, you'll know better how to protect your privacy on the Internet as a consumer and how to avoid legal problems over privacy issues as a business.

Part V (Free Speech and the First Amendment) explains the only Internet laws thus far that have reached the U.S. Supreme Court: portions of the Communications Decency Act and the Child Online Protection Act. These laws, designed to limit the distribution of what many consider to be inappropriate material online—such as pornography—were popular with Congress but not with the courts, which generally have found them to violate the First Amendment. But, as the other chapters in this part illustrate, free speech is not just about pornography on the Internet; it's also about junk e-mail and hate speech—communications that most of us despise but that the First Amendment protects.

Part VI (Contract Law and High Technology) discusses some high-tech twists to negotiating and entering into contracts on the Internet. As we all know, the Internet has transformed the way in which business transactions are conducted. E-mail and Web-based communications are essential tools for companies that want to conduct business at "Internet speed," but understanding how contracts work in cyberspace is vital for every party to a transaction. The chapters in this part explain the U.S. "electronic signatures" act, "click-wrap" agreements, and the important issues to look for in any website development agreement.

Finally, **Part VII (Employment Law)** explains the often-overlooked issues that are with increasing frequency causing many legal headaches among Internet and high-tech employers without an understanding of the risks. For example, as one chapter discusses, any company could face a lawsuit from an employee based on sexually oriented comments and/or photos distributed via e-mail in the office. Technology is also changing the way employers must address disabilities in the workplace. Additionally, this part of the book explains the increasing importance of "noncompete" agreements that limit who an employee can work for after leaving a company and the contentious issue of monitoring employees' Internet usage.

THE GIGALAW.COM WEBSITE

Despite the breadth of this book, it is—like the Internet itself—incomplete. This book covers the most important and fundamental Internet legal issues, but there are many others that are not addressed in these pages, including antitrust law, cybercrime, and taxation of e-commerce. For these issues and many more, you can turn to the GigaLaw.com website for articles and other information about their background and current developments.

Like any good website, GigaLaw.com also offers much more than any book ever could. In addition to its ever-expanding database of articles on Internet law, GigaLaw.com offers updates on many of the issues in this book, daily Internet law news via e-mail,[3] a law library containing many important cases and statutes, a bookshelf[4] of other helpful books on topics relating to Internet law, and a discussion list[5] where you can talk about the issues in this book—as well as new developments in Internet law—with the author and contributors, other attorneys, and others who share an interest in this important topic.

A NOTE ABOUT ENDNOTES

Throughout this book, many cases, laws, and news items, as well as other important information, are linked through endnotes to the World Wide Web. By exploring the websites listed in the endnotes, you'll find significantly more detail about all of the topics in this book. Where an important topic does not contain an endnote, it probably means that additional information about it was not available online (at least as of this writing); this is true for many of the older cases cited in this book (which are important to Internet law but were decided before the Web existed) and for many of the district court judicial opinions (which are available only sporadically online). Also, given the ever-changing nature of the Internet, some of the websites listed in the endnotes may no longer be valid (although they were all valid as of this writing) because most of them are not maintained by GigaLaw.com or this book's authors. Please check the GigaLaw.com website for updated information about the endnotes.

Finally, I hope you'll let me know what you think of this book and the issues in it. Feel free to contact me via my website, DougIsenberg.com.

Doug Isenberg
Atlanta

PART I

COPYRIGHT LAW

CHAPTER ONE

Case Study: An Introduction to Copyright on the Internet, *Playboy* v. *Sanfilippo*

Playboy Enterprises, Inc.—yes, *that* Playboy—is one of the more active participants in Internet law, filing numerous lawsuits against people and companies that use the well-known adult entertainment publisher's intellectual property in cyberspace without obtaining permission. Intellectual property includes copyrights (such as photographs of nude models) and trademarks (such as the "Playboy" and "Playmate" names); clearly, Playboy has a lot to protect online.

There's no denying that, on the Internet, the sex industry is quite popular. And in many ways the sex industry has been at the forefront of important Internet developments, including online payment systems, affiliate programs, innovative advertising techniques, and more. Playboy is among the tamer players in the online adult world, but its name is certainly among the best known, and it has a large library of high-quality content—which is important for the success of any publisher, particularly on the Web. But popularity has a downside, too. While imitation may be the greatest form of flattery, Playboy (like other publishers) is not in business to give away its content for free. So, when individuals and other companies have copied Playboy's photos for their own websites—either by scanning images from the printed *Playboy* magazine or by copying images from Playboy's site—Playboy has not hesitated to enforce its rights.

One case in particular is especially interesting and enlightening and serves as a great introduction to the issue of copyright law and the Internet. The following facts are based on an opinion written by a federal judge in California and Playboy's allegations in a case decided in 1998.[1]

In the case, *Playboy* v. *Sanfilippo,* Playboy filed a lawsuit against Francesco Sanfilippo and his company, Five Senses, for copyright infringement. According to Playboy, Sanfilippo operated a website through which he provided and sold access to thousands of copyrighted photographs owned by Playboy. Sanfilippo's website, like many adult sites with pornographic content, was divided into public and private sections. The public, or free, section advertised images available in the private area, which was accessible to those who bought a password from Sanfilippo.

Playboy said it sent Sanfilippo a "cease and desist" letter in October 1996. These letters are often sent by copyright owners or their lawyers to people or companies who they believe have committed copyright infringement. The letters, sometimes known as "demand letters," typically inform a person or company that it is committing copyright infringement and demand that the action come to an immediate stop. Sending a cease and desist letter is usually, but not always, a wise precursor to filing a lawsuit, because doing so often scares the recipient into complying without incurring the costs, angst, and uncertainty of courtroom litigation.

Two days later, Playboy's attorney sent another demand letter to Sanfilippo. According to Playboy, Sanfilippo immediately acknowledged that some of the images on his website were scanned directly from Playboy's magazine; he did not dispute that Playboy owned the copyright in the images; and he agreed to promptly remove them from his site. However, Sanfilippo did not do so, and Playboy's attorney later sent another cease and desist letter, after which Sanfilippo said he would remove the images within twenty-four hours—which he did not do. Instead, by February 1997, the site still displayed Playboy's photos and even offered for sale CD-ROMs containing the pictures.

Fed up with Sanfilippo's continued defiance of Playboy's legal demands, Playboy filed a federal lawsuit in April 1997. Playboy alleged that Sanfilippo's website contained twenty-seven files of its images, for a total of 7,475 pictures! Playboy sought and obtained from the court a temporary restraining order and an order of seizure; within two weeks, Playboy and Sanfilippo agreed to a preliminary injunction—a court requirement that prevented Sanfilippo from using the images until the lawsuit was resolved. Playboy then filed a motion with the court asking for a "summary judgment," a court order that there are no genuine issues of material fact to be decided in a lawsuit and that one party is entitled to judgment as a matter of law. In other words, a court will grant a summary judgment motion only in an obviously lopsided case.

To prevail on a claim for copyright infringement, the court in the Sanfilippo case noted that a plaintiff must prove two things: (1) that it owns a valid copyright, and (2) that the defendant violated one of the copyright owner's "exclusive rights" listed in the U.S. Copyright Act.[2] As to the first requirement, the court found that there was no factual dispute that Playboy owned the copyright rights in the images on Sanfilippo's website, because even he admitted as much. As to the second requirement, the court said Sanfilippo admitted copying sixteen files directly from a third-party source onto his hard drive without Playboy's permission and that the additional eleven files were uploaded to his hard drive by someone else with Sanfilippo's authorization. Because copying is clearly one of the exclusive rights listed in the U.S. Copyright Act (they don't call it *copy*right law for nothing!), the court quickly concluded that Playboy was entitled to summary judgment for the 7,475 images.

The court then turned to the issue of damages—that is, how much money Sanfilippo should be ordered to pay Playboy. Damages are an interesting concept in copyright law and, depending upon the facts, can serve a number of purposes: to take away any profit a defendant may have made by committing copyright infringement, to compensate a plaintiff for money he lost as a result of having his property infringed, or to punish a defendant for having broken the law. According to one provision of the U.S. Copyright Act, under certain circumstances a plaintiff is entitled to "statutory damages" for each act of infringement in an amount from $500 to $20,000, "as the court considers just."[3] And in cases where the defendant's conduct was "willful," that is, where he acted with knowledge that his conduct constituted copyright infringement, the court may "in its discretion" increase the damages amount to as much as $100,000 per infringement. (These figures, which applied at the time of the court's opinion in 1998, since have been increased, as noted in Chapter 2.)

Playboy argued that, with respect to nine of the twenty-seven files containing its images on Sanfilippo's site, Sanfilippo's copyright infringement was willful (and Playboy was therefore entitled to the higher statutory damages) because, among other things, Sanfilippo allegedly admitted in a deposition that he knew the copying and sale of Playboy's photos amounted to copyright infringement. The court agreed.

Playboy requested that the court enter an award in the staggering amount of $285,420,000! This figure was based on 1,699 images at $100,000 each (the maximum amount for "willful" copyright infringement) and 5,776 images at $20,000 each (the maximum amount for nonwillful statutory damages). Ultimately, the court found that an award of only $500 per image was "sufficient to adequately compensate [Playboy] and deter any future infringement by [Sanfilippo]"— but that still totaled $3,737,500.

The lessons from this case should be clear:

• Under U.S. copyright law, it is illegal to copy someone else's photographs, without permission, and publish them on your website. As we'll see in later chapters in this book, copyright law protects many other types of works, too, in addition to photographs.

• If you commit copyright infringement by publishing some-one else's property on your website, you are exposing yourself to the world. In the past, some people may have been able to get away with copyright infringement because the copyright owner was unaware of what was happening—such as if someone copied photos and used them in a newspaper advertisement in one city. Because the World Wide Web is, as its name implies, available worldwide (except, of course, in those countries where the tech-nology is unavailable or the government forbids it), copyright scofflaws are less likely to go undetected.

• If you are a copyright owner, you can successfully sue a cyber-space infringer.

• If you are a copyright infringer, you should respond to a de-mand letter—and take appropriate steps to right your wrong. If you don't, a copyright lawsuit could prove quite expensive.

CHAPTER TWO

The Basics of Copyright Law

Copyright law traces its roots to a document called the Statute of Anne, adopted by England in 1710.[1] While many people may have learned about copyright law only in recent years—thanks to high-profile Internet lawsuits such as those involving Napster—the general concept is nothing new. A sophisticated, workable legal system for protecting original creations has existed for a long time. But because most U.S. copyright laws were written before the arrival of the World Wide Web, it is often difficult, though not impossible, to apply these pre-Internet laws in cyberspace.

A basic understanding of copyright law in general is necessary to understand the particular issues that apply to copyright and the Internet. Therefore, let's begin by answering the most basic copyright questions.

WHAT DOES COPYRIGHT LAW PROTECT?

As stated in the U.S. Copyright Act[2] (a recodification of laws passed by Congress, for the most part, in 1976, but amended through the years to take into account, among other things, new technologies such as the Internet), copyright protects "original works of authorship fixed in any tangible medium of expression, now known or later developed, from which they can be perceived, reproduced, or otherwise communicated, either directly or with the aid of a machine or device." In particular, the Copyright Act lists the following as some examples of original works of authorship:[3]

- literary works;
- musical works, including any accompanying words;
- dramatic works, including any accompanying music;
- pantomimes and choreographic works;
- pictorial, graphic, and sculptural works;
- motion pictures and other audiovisual works;
- sound recordings; and
- architectural works.

As you can see, this list does not specifically refer to any particular works on the Internet, but keep in mind that the list is not complete and that many kinds of high-tech creations qualify as original works of authorship. So, while traditionally copyright law may have protected written words such as newspaper and magazine articles as well as books, copyright law also protects written words that appear on a website and the software programs that run them (software also can be protected by patents, as discussed in Chapter 13); while traditionally copyright law has protected photographs published in art books and displayed in fancy frames on museum walls, it also protects photographs in digital formats such as JPG and GIF; while traditionally copyright law has protected sheet music and, later, music distributed on albums and cassettes, today it also protects music in the popular MP3 format; and while traditionally copyright law has protected artwork created with oils on canvas, it also protects art-work created with Adobe Illustrator as well as, under some circum-stances, the actual Web pages on which that artwork is published.

WHAT RIGHTS DOES A COPYRIGHT OWNER HAVE?

Typically, when many people think about copyright, they immedi-ately think the law makes it illegal to *copy* someone else's work with-out permission. And, assuming the work is indeed protected by copyright law in the first place, that is usually true (although there are exceptions, including the "fair use" doctrine, discussed later in this chapter). But copyright law makes it illegal to do many other things, too. The U.S. Copyright Act specifically says that a copyright owner has the exclusive right to do the following (that is, to do the following himself and to prevent others from doing any of them):[4]

- to reproduce the copyrighted work in copies or phonorecords;
- to prepare derivative works based upon the copyrighted work;
- to distribute copies or phonorecords of the copyrighted work to the public by sale or other transfer of ownership, or by rental, lease, or lending;
- in the case of literary, musical, dramatic, and choreographic works, pantomimes, and motion pictures and other audio-visual works, to perform the copyrighted work publicly;
- in the case of literary, musical, dramatic, and choreographic works, pantomimes, and pictorial, graphic, or sculptural works, including the individual images of a motion picture or other au-diovisual work, to display the copyrighted work publicly; and
- in the case of sound recordings, to perform the copyrighted work publicly by means of a digital audio transmission.

If someone does any of the above things without the copyright owner's permission, he could be liable for committing copyright in-

fringement. Certainly, the first item in the list—the right to reproduce a copyrighted work—is the most common right violated in a
copyright infringement dispute or lawsuit. When Francesco Sanfilippo and his company published 7,475 Playboy photos on a website
without Playboy's permission, as discussed in Chapter 1, a court
found that he had committed copyright infringement by violating
Playboy's exclusive right to reproduce the photos.

Probably the second most frequently violated right is the next
item above, the right to prepare derivative works. A derivative work
is one that is *derived* from another. To quote the Copyright Act
again, a derivative work is specifically "a work based upon one or
more preexisting works, such as a translation, musical arrangement,
dramatization, fictionalization, motion picture version, sound recording, art reproduction, abridgment, condensation, or any other form
in which a work may be recast, transformed, or adapted. A work
consisting of editorial revisions, annotations, elaborations, or other
modifications which, as a whole, represent an original work of authorship, is a 'derivative work.' "5 So, for example, finding a useful
article on a website, making some changes by rearranging a few items
and editing a few sentences, and then distributing it to an e-mail
subscription list could violate the exclusive right to prepare derivative
versions of the article, a right held by the author of the article (or,
perhaps, by the author's employer, or by someone else to whom the
copyright ownership has been transferred).

While some of the exclusive rights in copyright law rarely apply
to online activity, many of them often do. Because photographs,
graphic images, text, music, software, and much more can be protected by copyright law, the owner's rights can be violated when
someone else reproduces them or creates derivative versions of them
on the Internet.

HOW DO YOU GET COPYRIGHT PROTECTION?

Many people are surprised to learn that, under U.S. law, the creator of an original work of authorship does not need to do anything to obtain a copyright: As soon as the work is created and fixed in a tangible medium, it is automatically protected. Note that this is very different from other forms of legal protection, such as patents (see Chapter 12), which require filing an application and overcoming significant obstacles before you can obtain protection.

If you're confused because you've heard something about registering with the U.S. Copyright Office, there's good reason. While it's not necessary to file a copyright application to obtain protection, you may file an application, and there are advantages to doing so. Unlike filing patent and trademark applications, filing a copyright application is usually a rather straightforward process (although some applications, such as for software and multimedia works, including websites, pose more complicated issues). The U.S. Copyright Office has an entire website devoted to filing a copyright application, and most applications require only a modest fee.[6]

By filing an application for your copyrighted work, you obtain the following advantages, according to the Copyright Office:[7]

- Registration establishes a public record of the copyright claim.
- Before an infringement suit may be filed in court, registration is necessary for works of U.S. origin.
- If made before or within five years of publication, registration will establish prima facie evidence in court of the validity of the copyright and of the facts stated in the certificate.
- If registration is made within three months after publication of the work or prior to an infringement of the work, statutory damages and attorneys' fees will be available to the copyright owner in court actions. Otherwise, only an award of actual damages and profits is available to the copyright owner.

• Registration allows the owner of the copyright to record the registration with the U.S. Customs Service for protection against the importation of infringing copies.

DO YOU NEED TO HAVE A REGISTERED COPYRIGHT TO USE THE COPYRIGHT SYMBOL?

You do not need to have a registered copyright to use the copyright symbol, ©. Nor do you need to use the copyright symbol to ensure your protection, although there are some advantages for using the symbol, such as putting others on notice that you are claiming copyright protection in your work.

In any event, it's important to keep in mind that the copyright symbol is just one part of a proper copyright "notice." A copyright notice is simply a few words that provide the public with useful information about copyright ownership in the work to which the notice is attached. Although it looks simple, care should be taken when composing a copyright notice, because the wording can have legal consequences. Under U.S. copyright law, a valid copyright notice generally consists of three elements:[8]

• the symbol ©, the word "Copyright" or the abbreviation "Copr.";
• the year of first publication of the work; and
• the name of the copyright owner, or a recognizable abbreviation or generally known alternative designation.

So, for example, this is a proper copyright notice for this book: "Copyright 2002 Douglas M. Isenberg." And this is *not* a proper notice—"(c) Douglas M. Isenberg"—because it fails to use the correct copyright symbol, word, or abbreviation and because it omits the year.

The law states that the notice may be placed "on publicly distributed copies from which the work can be visually perceived, either directly or with the aid of a machine or device." The law also states that the notice should be "affixed to the copies in such manner and location as to give reasonable notice of the claim of copyright." While including a proper copyright notice on traditional works such as books is relatively easy, it becomes a little trickier on some high-tech works such as software and websites. This is discussed in further detail in Chapter 3.

HOW LONG DOES COPYRIGHT PROTECTION LAST?

Copyright law, like patent law, is actually mentioned in the U.S. Constitution, which states: "The Congress shall have power to . . . promote the progress of science and useful arts, by securing for limited times to authors and inventors the exclusive right to their respective writings and discoveries." So, according to the Founding Fathers, copyright (and patent) protection should last only for "limited times." Although the U.S. Copyright Act indeed sets limits, the limits are very generous to copyright owners:[9]

- For a copyrighted work owned by an individual and created on or after January 1, 1978 (the date of the most current U.S. Copyright Act), copyright protection endures for the life of the author plus an additional seventy years after the author's death.
- For a copyrighted work prepared by two or more authors and owned by them jointly, the protection lasts until seventy years after the death of the last surviving author.
- For a "work made for hire" (a special category of works, discussed next), copyright protection lasts for either 95 years from the year of first publication or 120 years from the year of its creation, whichever occurs first.

(A 1998 law had extended the term of copyright protection for twenty years to the limits described above. That law, formally known as the Copyright Term Extension Act of 1998 but informally known as the Sonny Bono Copyright Term Extension Act, was challenged by a group of plaintiffs—including an online book publisher—as unconstitutional. In February 2001, the U.S. Court of Appeals for the District of Columbia upheld the act.[10] The U.S. Supreme Court agreed to hear the case challenging the act, *Eldred* v. *Ashcroft,* during its 2002–03 session.)

WHAT IS A "WORK MADE FOR HIRE"?

Typically, the person who creates a work subject to copyright protection is, by law, deemed to be the owner of the copyright in the work. However, under some circumstances, another person or a company could be the copyright owner. One common circumstance is the "work made for hire" doctrine.[11]

If a work is made for hire, then the person who created it is not the owner of the copyright in the work. This can arise in either of two ways:[12]

• If the work is prepared by an employee within the scope of his or her employment. In this case, the employer will be the copyright owner.

• If (1) the work is specially ordered or commissioned for use as a contribution to a collective work, as a part of a motion picture or other audiovisual work, as a sound recording, as a translation, as a supplementary work, as a compilation, as an instructional text, as a test, as answer material for a test, or as an atlas, and (2) the parties agree in writing that the work is a work made for hire. In this case, the person or company for whom the work was prepared will be the copyright owner.

In the world of Internet law, it is very important to understand the work-made-for-hire concept to ensure that you retain, or obtain, the ownership rights you expect. For example, if you are an employee who creates Web-based application services for your company's clients, you may spend a lot of time creating software programs using Perl or another language, but ultimately you do not own any rights to the programs you create; instead, they will be owned by your employer (unless your employer's client has a contract for the creation of the programs in which the employer assigns, or transfers, copyright ownership to the client itself—this is discussed further in Chapter 3). As a result, you cannot take copies of the programs you create with you to another job when you leave or use them in any way for yourself or anyone else, without your employer's permission.

WHAT IS THE "FAIR USE" DOCTRINE?

The "fair use" doctrine is probably one of the most misunderstood concepts in copyright law. In general, this doctrine says that certain limited uses of a copyrighted work for purposes such as criticism, comment, news reporting, teaching, scholarship, and research do not constitute copyright infringement. However, determining whether a particular use qualifies as fair is often not an easy task. The U.S. Copyright Act provides some guidance, by telling us that the following four factors must be considered:[13]

- the purpose and character of the use, including whether such use is of a commercial nature or is for nonprofit educational purposes;
- the nature of the copyrighted work;
- the amount and substantiality of the portion used in relation to the copyrighted work as a whole; and
- the effect of the use upon the potential market for or value of the copyrighted work.

Plenty of courts, including the U.S. Supreme Court, have struggled with how to apply the factors listed above. So, if you can't immediately read them and understand whether a particular use of a copyrighted work is fair, don't worry: Even most lawyers who practice in this area of the law struggle with this question. On the other hand, if you think the answer to a particular fair use question is immediately clear, think again, because it probably isn't.

The fair use doctrine has many applications in the context of Internet law. In the Napster online music litigation, for example, Napster argued that it should not be liable for copyright infringement because any copying of music that occurred as a result of its service was "fair," largely because of the last factor listed above. Napster tried to convince the courts that people who downloaded free music would not have bought the relevant CDs anyway (or that some people, after sampling a few songs on Napster, then went out and bought the CDs), so its service did not damage the "potential market for or value of the copyrighted work." (An interesting argument, perhaps, but the trial court didn't buy it.) In another case, *Kelly* v. *Arriba Soft*, the U.S. Court of Appeals for the Ninth Circuit in February 2002 ruled that an online image-searching site was allowed under the fair use doctrine to reproduce small or "thumbnail"-sized images of a professional photographer's photos (but not full-sized images).[14] In other contexts, when publishing a website you may want to publish some information written by someone else (such as a favorable review of your company) but cannot obtain—or don't want to go through the trouble of asking for—permission from the person or company who owns the copyright in the information; if your use qualifies as "fair," you can publish it without getting permission.

Typically, though, if you have any questions about whether your use of someone else's work qualifies as fair, you will want to get a formal legal opinion from an attorney. Wrongly assuming that the use is fair could prove to be costly if the copyright owner decides to sue for infringement.

WHAT ARE THE CONSEQUENCES
OF COPYRIGHT INFRINGEMENT?

As the Playboy case discussed in Chapter 1 illustrates, copyright infringement can be very expensive. (In that case, a court ordered the defendant to pay Playboy more than $3.7 million for publishing more than seven thousand of Playboy's photos on his website without Playboy's permission.) Though this case may be extreme, any person or company that is found liable for having committed copyright infringement is certainly going to regret its actions. The U.S. Copyright Act says that an infringer of copyright is liable for either (1) the copyright owner's actual damages and any additional profits of the infringer, or (2) "statutory damages" (as happened in the Playboy case) in an amount ranging anywhere from $750 to $30,000 (or $150,000 if the infringement was "willful," that is, if the defendant knew he was committing copyright infringement) per work infringed, "as the court considers just."[15] (These figures represent increases made in the Copyright Act since the Playboy case was decided in 1998.)

In addition to paying damages, a losing defendant in a copyright lawsuit also will have to stop making use of the copyrighted work.[16] In the context of Internet law, this can be devastating to a company. For example, a company using software to power order-processing functions on its website without a proper software license could be ordered to stop using the software; as a result, the company suddenly may find itself unable to continue accepting orders. And the public relations fallout from copyright infringement can be damaging, too. The Business Software Alliance, an international organization representing leading software and e-commerce developers (including such well-recognized names as Adobe, Apple, Intel, Macromedia, and Microsoft) in sixty-five countries, often fights software "piracy" (shorthand for committing copyright infringement of software) by publicizing settlements with companies accused of using its members' programs without permission or adequate licenses. "While the Internet vastly increases opportunities to sell products and services, it also creates new opportunities to steal software," BSA says on its website.[17] "Until recently, unauthorized copying of software required physical exchange of floppy disks, CDs or other hard media. But, as the Internet continually gets easier, faster and less expensive, software piracy does the same." The organization estimates that $12 billion was lost because of illegal software in 1999. With the stakes so high, copyright infringement is certainly to be taken seriously.

Finally, in addition to paying monetary damages and suffering from bad publicity, a copyright infringer can, under some circumstances, be sentenced as a criminal, too. In 1997, the U.S. Congress passed the No Electronic Theft (or NET) Act, establishing under some circumstances criminal penalties of up to three years in jail for illegally copying software, even if the defendant did not profit financially from doing so.[18]

WHAT IS THE DIGITAL MILLENNIUM COPYRIGHT ACT?

As discussed more fully in Chapter 4, in 1998 Congress passed the Digital Millennium Copyright Act (DMCA), which, among many other things, allows for criminal prosecutions with imprisonment for up to ten years of those who circumvent technological measures that protect copyrighted works.[19] The DMCA is a lengthy set of amendments to the general U.S. Copyright Act and is a complex law that came about as a direct result of the Internet and other forms of high technology. The DMCA also was a response to a worldwide movement to provide better protection for copyrights in cyberspace through the World Intellectual Property Organization's Copyright Treaty[20] and Performances and Phonograms Treaty.[21] Among other things, the DMCA establishes protections for Internet service providers under certain circumstances where a service provider's customers may commit copyright infringement online.

The DMCA also increases protection for devices controlled by certain technological measures by making it illegal (and in some circumstances, a crime) to circumvent—or avoid—the protections. In one very interesting case, the FBI arrested a Russian computer programmer, Dmitry Sklyarov, in July 2001 for allegedly publishing a software program that made it possible to get around the built-in security protections of the Adobe e-book reader.[22] The FBI said Sklyarov's actions violated the DMCA, although the U.S. Attorney's Office for the Northern District of California agreed in December 2001 to drop the charges against Sklyarov in exchange for his cooperation in the government's case against his employer.[23]

CHAPTER THREE

CREATING A COPYRIGHT-FRIENDLY WEBSITE

Building and maintaining a website requires careful planning and regular diligence to avoid infringing on anyone else's copyrights and to protect your own. This chapter addresses some of the most important issues to keep in mind when publishing on the Internet.

USE A GOOD WEBSITE DEVELOPMENT AGREEMENT

Unless you or your employees are building your website yourselves, you'll probably turn to another company or person—a website developer—to create your online presence. While locating, interviewing, and selecting a developer who can meet your needs and whom you can trust is often a project in and of itself, it's vital to remember that, no matter how good you feel about the company or person who will design your site, you should enter into a written contract. Failure to do so could cause many headaches and cost you a lot of money for something you won't even own!

That's right. Believe it or not, by failing to use a website development agreement—that is, a contract—many companies fail to obtain the copyright ownership of their own website. The consequences, of course, are quite significant. A company that does not own the copyright rights to its own website remains at the mercy of the party who *does* own them. And if that party decides to stop the company from continuing to use its own website, the company may find itself in a very awkward position, trying to assert rights to something it does not own outright. Or if the company and its original developer part ways, the company may not later have the legal right to update its own website, because doing so could create a "derivative work" under the U.S. Copyright Act.

If you or your employees create your company's website, you have much less reason to worry, because, as discussed in Chapter 2, when an employee creates a copyrightable work in the course of his employment, copyright ownership vests *by law* (that is, without the need for a contract) in the employer under one part of the "work made for hire" doctrine. Just be certain that the employees are indeed employees and not independent contractors (typically working on a part-time or temporary basis and not receiving company benefits) and that creating the company website or content for it is a part of their jobs (not something they volunteered to do at home on their own time). If you have any doubts, you may want to consider requiring them to enter into a contract with the company for development of the website.

A good website development agreement contains many terms and typically will run for many pages and often will contain attached exhibits. Such agreements address many issues other than just copyright. Among other things, it will include details about the scope of the website to be created, deadlines to be met, fees to be paid, obligations for ongoing maintenance, and much more. For a website of any sophistication, a form agreement is rarely suitable. Rather, drafting a good agreement requires intensive discussions among the company for whom the site will be created, the company or person creating it, and, ideally, lawyers for both sides.

As to copyright issues, typically a company will want the agreement to contain provisions granting it ownership rights in the site and its content. A website can contain many copyrightable elements, including the "look and feel" of the overall site itself, powerful software applications or simple scripts powering it that run behind the scenes, images and photographs that appear on it, and, of course, the text that visitors will read on its pages. Some or all of these elements will be created by the website designer or developer, who, by default under the U.S. Copyright Act, will become the copyright owner unless the contract properly states otherwise. Depending upon the nature of the copyrighted material involved, a simple "work for hire" acknowledgment may be sufficient for the company (rather than the designer or developer) to be the copyright owner. A typical provision says something such as:

> All copyrightable works created by Developer and delivered to Company shall be deemed "works made for hire," as that phrase is defined in Section 101 of the United States Copyright Act, 17 U.S.C. § 101, and used in 17 U.S.C. § 201, on behalf of Company, and Company shall own all right, title, and interest, including the worldwide copyright, in and to such materials.

However, as discussed in Chapter 2, only certain types of copyrightable works can qualify as "works made for hire." Specifically, the work must be "specially ordered or commissioned for use as a contribution to a collective work, as a part of a motion picture or other audiovisual work, as a sound recording, as a translation, as a supplementary work, as a compilation, as an instructional text, as a test, as answer material for a test, or as an atlas."[1] As a result, many if not most elements of a website will not qualify as a work made for hire.

So, how does the company become the copyright owner of content that does not qualify as a work made for hire? Simple: The creator assigns, or transfers, copyright ownership to the company. A typical provision states:

> Developer hereby assigns and agrees to assign to Company all of the right, title, and interest, including intellectual property rights, in all copyrightable works created by Developer and delivered to Company under this Agreement.

Although this provision may appear simple, a number of related issues often complicate it. For example, what if the developer includes some content that is in the public domain, such as open-source software, in the website? Or what if the developer wants to retain copyright ownership for itself, so it can reuse some of the content, and grant the company only a license to use it? Or what if the developer, inadvertently or on purpose, includes some content on the website that it did not create and that is actually owned by someone else? All of these issues can and should be addressed through other provisions in the website development agreement, to ensure the company obtains the copyright ownership and protection it needs.

Chapter 28 discusses additional issues other than copyright that should be included in a website development agreement.

DON'T PUBLISH ANYTHING ON YOUR WEBSITE UNLESS YOU ARE, OR HAVE PERMISSION FROM, THE COPYRIGHT OWNER

This may sound obvious, but it's amazing how many people and even successful companies don't bother to determine whether they have the right to publish something on their websites. For example, a company pleased that a flattering article was written about it in the local newspaper may want to post the article on its website for the world to see; but unless the company has obtained permission from the newspaper in which the article was originally published, doing so would probably constitute copyright infringement. Or a company that publishes a hard-copy brochure about itself may want to put the brochure's contents online, including a fancy photograph that appears on the cover and was licensed by the company. But unless the company obtained a broad license or one that specifically allows for online reproduction, posting it on the company website could constitute copyright infringement. Obviously, the law can be easily broken.

There's a simple rule to follow that can help you avoid online copyright infringement problems like these: Don't publish anything on your website unless you know who created it. If it was created by a company employee during the course of his or her employment, then it may be a "work made for hire" in which the company owns the copyright and can publish it online without concern for copyright issues. If it was created by a nonemployee specifically for the company, then, unless it qualifies as a work for hire under the special categories discussed above and in the previous chapter, someone else may own the copyright in it and the company should not publish it online without a copyright assignment (a transfer of the rights to the company) or a license (permission from the copyright owner).

The most difficult issues to address often concern those works that don't fall into either of the categories just discussed. These are often previously existing original works of authorship identified by a company that may be useful for incorporating into a website. The works may be any element of the site—text, images, software, or music files. Sometimes the copyright owner may be identified easily, and in that case the company will need to obtain an assignment of the work or a license to use it. But often the copyright owner cannot be easily identified, because the work does not contain a copyright notice, or the copyright notice fails to provide enough information.[2] If you cannot identify or locate the copyright owner and obtain permission, the safest route is simply not to publish the work on your site. Although, in some circumstances, your use may be protected either because the work is so old it's in the public domain (that is, copyright protection has expired) or because your use would qualify as "fair" (as discussed in Chapter 2), you'll probably want to consult with a copyright attorney before using someone else's work on your site without permission.

DON'T ALLOW ANYONE ELSE TO POST INFRINGING CONTENT ON YOUR WEBSITE

Under the theory of indirect copyright infringement, a person or company can be held legally responsible for direct copyright infringement committed by someone else. This was the primary legal issue in dispute in the Napster litigation, in which the music industry sought to hold Napster liable for copyright infringement committed by its customers, who used Napster's software to exchange music in the MP3 format with millions of others. There are two theories of indirect copyright infringement:

- "Contributory" copyright infringement. This exists when a defendant has knowledge of the infringing activity and induces, causes, or materially contributes to the infringing activity of another.
- "Vicarious" copyright infringement. This exists when a defendant has the right and ability to supervise the infringing activity and also has a direct financial interest in the activity.

As Napster learned very well after repeated rulings against it by the courts, indirect copyright infringement can be quite costly to a company that conducts business on the Internet. However, a company need not flout the law as visibly as Napster to be found liable for copyright infringement committed by someone else. Any company that allows visitors to its website to post content—such as in a discussion forum or chat room or on a hosted website—runs the risk that the visitors will, purposefully or innocently, post content to which someone else owns the copyright. As a result, a company would be wise to regularly police all sections of its site where others can post content and promptly respond to complaints from copyright owners that their rights are being infringed. However, because it is often impossible to determine who the real copyright owner is or whether a particular action really constitutes infringement, some online service providers can shield themselves from legal liability by taking certain actions, thanks to the Digital Millennium Copyright Act, discussed in Chapter 4.

BE SENSITIVE TO "FRAMING" AND "LINKING" ISSUES

In 1997, as websites were growing and the technology behind them was evolving, The Washington Post and a number of other publishers (including CNN, the Los Angeles Times, and Time) filed a lawsuit against a website called TotalNews, which included links on its site to news articles published on other sites. TotalNews used frames— a common and sometimes annoying, sometimes useful technique by which a Web browser displays content from more than one Web page simultaneously, including the different pages in "frames" within a Web surfer's single browser and on one screen. So, while one frame remained fixed with the TotalNews logo, navigational links, and advertising, another frame displayed content (specifically, news articles) from another website. The Washington Post and the other publishers alleged in their complaint that this technique was "the Internet equivalent of pirating copyrighted material from a variety of famous newspapers, magazines, or television news programs."[3] The news industry plaintiffs said that TotalNews's framing cost them advertising revenue because, "by juxtaposing advertising sold by Defendants against advertising sold by Plaintiffs on their own sites, and by obscuring the advertising on Plaintiffs' sites, Defendants directly compete against Plaintiffs and interfere with Plaintiffs' contractual relationships with their advertisers."

The TotalNews case was watched very closely because, at the

time, no one was certain about the legal issues related to framing. (In addition to a claim of copyright infringement, the publishers in the TotalNews case also alleged eight other legal violations, including trademark infringement and trademark dilution.) Lawyers and Web publishers saw the TotalNews case as a potentially precedent-setting lawsuit that could provide guidance for how websites would be created in the future. However, as often happens, the parties ultimately settled their lawsuit, so the court never had an opportunity to issue an opinion about the legality of framing. (Following the settlement, TotalNews stopped framing content from the publishers that sued it, but it continued to present content from some other publishers in frames.) Although other lawsuits have addressed the legal issues of framing, this issue has never been resolved clearly.

In addition to framing, a number of lawsuits also have raised the issue of whether merely linking to another website (even without frames) is illegal. In the best-known case, Ticketmaster sued a company called Tickets.com because Tickets.com provided "deep links" to the Ticketmaster website, that is, links to pages on the Ticketmaster site other than its home page (as is commonly done on the Web). Ticketmaster did not appreciate the deep-linking because it wanted users looking to buy tickets from its site to start at its home page and navigate through the site—by doing so, users presumably would be exposed to other content and valuable advertising. As a result, Ticketmaster sued Tickets.com for several causes of action, including copyright infringement. However, in March 2000, the U.S. District Court for the Central District of California dismissed a number of the claims. Among other things, it said: "[H]yperlinking does not itself involve a violation of the Copyright Act (whatever it may do for other claims) since no copying is involved. The customer is automatically transferred to the particular genuine web page of the original author. There is no deception in what is happening. This is analogous to using a library's card index to get reference to particular items, albeit faster and more efficiently."[4] And, in a later ruling, in August 2000, the court said that Tickets.com's transitory copying of data from the Ticketmaster website to create the data for its links was protected by copyright's "fair use" doctrine.[5]

Ticketmaster is not the only company that has tried to control how others link to its website. In 2001, KPMG Consulting Inc. wrote a letter to a website owner attempting to get him to remove a link to the company's site. The letter reportedly said that "such links require that a formal Agreement exist between our two parties, as mandated by our organization's Web Link Policy."[6] The Better Business Bureau (BBB) has tried to control who can link to its website.[7] And, the International Trademark Association (INTA) has an extensive list of conditions that it wants others to meet when linking to its site.[8]

Despite the court's ruling allowing deep-linking in the Ticketmaster case, at least one other court apparently sees the practice differently. In the *Universal City Studios* v. *Reimerdes* case discussed in Chapter 4, a federal district court judge in August 2000 ordered a defendant who provided access to DeCSS (a program that allows the copying of copy-protected DVDs) to stop linking to any website containing the program,[9] a judgment affirmed by the U.S. Court of Appeals for the Second Circuit in November 2001.[10] And, in early 2002, the owner of the *Dallas Morning News* website tried to stop a Web publisher from deep-linking to articles on its site.[11] In addition to alleging that deep-linking could violate copyright law, the *Dallas Morning News* site contains a notice in its "Terms of Service"[12] that forbids deep-linking or framing, but the notice is not necessarily legally enforceable because visitors can view some limited content on the website without even seeing or agreeing to the terms— potentially creating what one court has called, in the July 2001 case *Specht* v. *Netscape,*[13] an unenforceable "browse-wrap" agreement. (For more about the questionable enforceability of some online agreements, see Chapter 29.) In July 2002, a Danish court ordered a news site to stop hyperlinking,[14] although it is unclear what impact, if any, the decision will have on other sites.[15]

Of course, as in all legal matters, the particular facts of each situation are extremely important. So, while the trial court in the Ticketmaster case did not find copyright infringement, another case with slightly different facts could turn out differently. And while the parties in the TotalNews case reached a settlement agreement, another website that uses frames differently may find itself unable to settle a lawsuit. The DeCSS case presents a unique situation. And the assertions by KPMG, BBB, and INTA probably amount to no more than chest-thumping. However, despite the lack of more definitive legal rulings, some cautious guidance is probably appropriate:

• If you're using frames to display content from different pages of your own website, you should have nothing to worry about, so long as you own all rights to the content.

• If you want to display content from another website in a frame, the safest bet is to obtain permission from the publisher of the other site, preferably in writing.

• If you do not want to ask permission to frame another site, or if you have asked for permission but were denied, you still may be able to do so. However, you should proceed cautiously, preferably with the advice of an attorney who has reviewed your use of frames. Among other things, you probably should avoid framing sites in a manner that obscures their advertising, and you should take additional steps to make it clear to users who is responsible for content in various frames. Certainly, do not create frames in a manner that makes it appear as if someone else's content is your own.

• Similarly, if you want to include a link to another website (without using frames), the safest approach is to ask permission from the other site.

• However, in practice, links are created on the Web all the time without permission. So, if you don't have permission to link to another site, be sure the link does not mislead users, such as by confusing them with a link stating or implying that the linked page is something other than what it really is.

• Also, for both framing and linking, be certain you are not bound by any contractual obligations before creating the frames or links. For example, if you have a preexisting relationship with another website, your current contract may limit or prevent your ability to frame or link to it.

USE PROPER COPYRIGHT NOTICES ON YOUR WEBSITE

As discussed in Chapter 2, it is not necessary to use a copyright notice, but there are advantages in doing so. Although, as previously noted, a copyright notice is usually quite simple, using one on a website can become a bit more complicated. Here are some of the most important issues to keep in mind when writing and publishing a copyright notice on a website:

• Make sure the copyright owner's name is correct. Because a single Web page may contain multiple copyrighted elements, a single copyright notice in the footer of the page may not be sufficient. For example, a page that contains a photograph, text, and a unique "look and feel" could have three different copyright owners. If that's the case, and if the copyright owners find it desirable, three separate copyright notices, each identifying which work it belongs to, may need to be included.

• Make sure the year of first publication is correct. Typically, simply using a copyright notice in a website template that reflects the current year is not necessarily correct. Remember, the year in a copyright notice should state the year in which the copyrighted work was *first published.* In practice, many websites include a range of dates in their copyright notices (such as "1999–2002") to reflect the various dates on which various elements were first published, but the U.S. Copyright Act doesn't specifically address this.

• Make sure the copyright notice is placed properly. The Copyright Act says: "The notice shall be affixed to the copies in such manner and location as to give reasonable notice of the claim of copyright."[16] The Copyright Office has issued guidelines for proper placement of copyright notices on traditional works such as books and sculptures,[17] but it has not specifically said what is acceptable for websites. The common practice is to include a copyright notice in the footer of every page of a website, and this makes sense; a notice appearing only on certain pages could be overlooked.

REGISTER YOUR WEBSITE WITH THE U.S. COPYRIGHT OFFICE

As discussed, registering a copyright is a pretty simple process, but the nature of websites can complicate it. The complications arise because a website may be copyrightable itself, but it also may be composed of many separate copyrightable elements (such as images, text, and software). As a result, it may be desirable to file multiple copyright applications relating to a company's website. Also, unlike traditional copyrighted works such as paintings or books, many sophisticated websites are dynamic in nature and therefore include content that frequently changes. Thus, new copyright applications may need to be filed as the site evolves. And many websites are composed of copyrightable elements that cannot be submitted via traditional forms designed for tangible works. As a result, a copyright application for a website may need to contain a compact disc with the site's contents.

The U.S. Copyright Office's website is a great source of information about filing copyright applications. Among the documents particularly helpful to copyright protection for websites are the following:

- Circular 55, "Copyright Registration for Multimedia Works," which explains that a "multimedia kit" such as a CD-ROM may be filed with a copyright application;[18]
- Circular 61, "Copyright Registration for Computer Programs";[19]

- Form TX, the most common form for filing a copyright application, typically covering text-based copyrighted material and computer programs;[20]
- Form PA, the application used for works of the performing arts, such as musical works, motion pictures, and other audiovisual works;[21]
- Form SR, the application used for sound recordings;[22] and
- Form VA, the application for works of visual arts such as photographs and other images.[23]

The Copyright Office also publishes the circular "Copyright Registration for Online Works," which explains many of the issues unique to filing an application for a website.[24] Among other things, this document explains that one of the following items must be submitted along with an application for an online work such as a website:

- A computer disk (clearly labeled with the title and author) containing the entire work, and, in addition, representative portions of the authorship being registered in a format that can be examined by the Copyright Office (printout, audiocassette, or videotape). If the work is short (five pages of text or artwork, or three minutes of music, sounds, or audiovisual material), deposit the entire work and confirm that it is complete. If the work is longer, deposit five representative pages or three representative minutes. This identifying material should include the title and author, and the copyright notice, if any.
- A reproduction of the entire work, regardless of length. Send the format appropriate for the authorship being registered, for example, a printout, audiocassette, or videotape. No computer disk is required.

Finally, the Copyright Office has introduced a program known as CORDS, for Copyright Office Electronic Registration, Recordation and Deposit System, which it describes as a fully automated, innovative system to receive and process digital applications and digital deposits of copyrighted works for electronic registration via the Internet.[25] CORDS accepts copyright applications and deposits in a number of common file formats (including HTML, ASCII, PDF, and MP3) for several different types of works, including computer programs and e-books, and has been developing a system for websites, too. However, CORDS is available only on a small scale with a limited number of test partners.

CHAPTER FOUR

THE DIGITAL MILLENNIUM COPYRIGHT ACT

The Digital Millennium Copyright Act[1] (DMCA) is one of the few laws enacted by the U.S. Congress in recent years in direct response to new legal issues created by the Internet and other forms of high technology. The DMCA—a set of amendments to the existing U.S. Copyright Act—is in some respects also one of the most confusing and controversial laws in this area.

The DMCA was signed into law by President Clinton in October 1998 in response to two treaties passed by the World Intellectual Property Organization[2] (WIPO), a specialized agency of the United Nations to which the United States belongs. In 1996, as the Internet was emerging as a mainstream medium, WIPO adopted two important treaties, the Copyright Treaty[3] and the Performances and Phonograms Treaty.[4] In the United States, the ninety-four-page DMCA implements these two treaties and also takes a number of other important actions related to copyright law; in all the DMCA is divided into the following five titles:

• Title I, the "WIPO Copyright and Performances and Phono-grams Treaties Implementation Act of 1998," implements the WIPO treaties.

• Title II, the "Online Copyright Infringement Liability Limi-tation Act," creates limitations on the liability of online service providers for copyright infringement when engaging in certain types of activities.

• Title III, the "Computer Maintenance Competition Assur-ance Act," creates an exemption for making a copy of a computer program by activating a computer for purposes of maintenance or repair.

• Title IV contains six miscellaneous provisions, relating to the functions of the Copyright Office, distance education, the excep-tions in the Copyright Act for libraries and for making "ephe-meral" recordings, "webcasting" of sound recordings on the Internet, and the applicability of collective bargaining agreement obliga-tions in the case of transfers of rights in motion pictures.

• Title V, the "Vessel Hull Design Protection Act," creates a new form of protection for the design of vessel hulls.

Clearly, some of these titles are more relevant to Internet law than others. This chapter will focus on parts of the first two, specifically, those relating to technological protection and copyright manage-ment systems (in Title I) and liability for online copyright infringe-ment (Title II).

TECHNOLOGICAL PROTECTION AND COPYRIGHT MANAGEMENT SYSTEMS

As a result of the ease with which property in digital formats—such as software, photographs, music, e-books, and, to a limited extent, movies—can be copied, artists, authors, and publishers have sought new ways to protect their property via technology. In the past, the sheer difficulty involved in reproducing and distributing someone else's property, at least on a scale of any significance, posed a real hurdle to widespread copyright infringement. For example, although it may be simple to open up a book on a photocopy machine and copy a page or two, copying an entire book is not very practical. To do so would be time-consuming and costly and result in an end product that's not as attractive as the original. While copying a compact disc of music or software on a floppy may be much quicker and inexpensive, anyone who did so before the mid-1990s could not distribute his copies to too many others very easily because typically he had to come face-to-face with someone else for the hand-off to occur. Of course, now the Internet has changed all of that.

An entire industry is growing up around something called "digital rights management," or DRM. Although DRM means different things to different people, essentially it refers to the ways in which authors and publishers use technology to track, manage, or prevent copying of their digital works. In one version, some companies have created a "digital watermarking" system that enables photographers to alter their digital images in a way that is invisible to the human eye but creates an imbedded code to identify their product. Theoretically, these digital watermarks—so named because of their tenuous similarity to the traditional, visible watermarks in high-quality stationery—enable photographers to locate their photos on websites when used without permission and to easily identify the photos as their own. (However, the effectiveness of digital watermarks has been questioned by those who claim the protections afforded by the technology can be easily thwarted.) In another version, DRM allows the publishers of music CDs to build in certain copy-protection software that prevents users from making high-quality copies; a copy is marred by distracting noises when someone tries to play it. And, in another, much more common version, software companies require users to enter a key code or serial number, without which the associated application will not run.

Although the reasons for creating all of these copy-protection schemes are understandable, copy protection is sometimes controversial. For example, should a photograph distributor be entitled to track or prevent the copying of photos in the public domain, that is, photos for which the copyright has expired? Should a music publisher be able to prevent a consumer from making a single copy of its new CD for his or her own, noncommercial use at home? And should a software publisher have the right to render an expensive program useless simply because a purchaser may have misplaced the original manual on which the serial number was printed? In all of these cases, the copyright owner or someone else is placing greater restrictions on the copying of a digital work than even U.S. copyright law has created.

These issues are at the crux of an important section of the Digital Millennium Copyright Act. You should know about them because, as a copyright owner or publisher, you may want to take advantage of the additional legal protections the DMCA can give you. And as a consumer or user of someone else's copyrighted material, you need to know about this aspect of the DMCA to ensure that you don't violate this additional layer of legal protection, which carries criminal penalties as well as civil fines. This controversial section of the DMCA makes it illegal to "circumvent"—that is, to decrypt, avoid, bypass, remove, deactivate, or impair—certain technological measures that control access to copyright-protected works.[5] The section also makes it illegal to manufacture, import, offer to the public, or otherwise traffic in any technology, product, service, device, or component that is primarily designed or produced for circumventing technological protections under certain circumstances.

Why is this section of the DMCA so important? A real-life example explains it best. In July 2001, a Russian computer programmer by the name of Dmitry Sklyarov was attending Defcon, a Las Vegas convention of computer hackers. According to news reports, Sklyarov, an employee of a Moscow-based company called ElcomSoft, was making a presentation related to completion of his Ph.D. at Moscow State Technical University. His presentation was titled "E-Book Security: Theory and Practice." ElcomSoft offered a program, Advanced eBook Processor, that converts copy-protected e-books in the Adobe Acrobat eBook Reader format to a format that allows them to be opened in any PDF viewer without restrictions. For obvious reasons, publishers of e-books have been concerned that their products could be easily copied and redistributed, so they have created technologies that make the copying more difficult.

As a result of the ElcomSoft software, representatives from Adobe met with the FBI. And following Sklyarov's presentation at Defcon, he was arrested for violating the DMCA. Specifically, a criminal complaint was filed against him in U.S. District Court in California, charging him with "willfully and for financial gain import[ing], offer[ing] to the public, provid[ing], and otherwise traffick[ing] in a technology, product, service, and device that is primarily designed or produced for the purpose of circumvention [of] a technological measure that effectively controls access to a work protected under [the U.S. Copyright Act], namely books distributed in a form readable by the Adobe eBook Reader, in violation of [the DMCA]."[6] Sklyarov faced a fine of up to $500,000 and imprisonment of up to five years for charges of violating the DMCA.

Following significant protests by a number of groups and individuals, including the Electronic Frontier Foundation, an Internet civil liberties group, Adobe eventually called for the charges against Sklyarov to be dropped. "We strongly support the DMCA and the enforcement of copyright protection of digital content," Adobe's senior vice president and general counsel, Colleen Pouliot, said in a press release.[7] "However, the prosecution of this individual in this particular case is not conducive to the best interests of any of the parties involved or the industry. ElcomSoft's Advanced eBook Processor software is no longer available in the United States, and from that perspective the DMCA worked. Adobe will continue to protect its copyright interests and those of its customers." In exchange for Sklyarov's cooperation with the U.S. government—including his agreement to testify against ElcomSoft—the U.S. Attorney's Office for the Northern District of California eventually agreed to drop the charges against Sklyarov.[8]

In another early application of the DMCA, not involving its criminal provisions, eight major motion picture studios in January

2000 sued a number of defendants, including Eric Corley, a computer hacker known as Emmanuel Goldstein who publishes a magazine and website about hacking. The movie studios in that case, *Universal City Studios* v. *Reimerdes,* alleged that Corley violated the DMCA by offering for download on his website a software application called DeCSS, a program that allows the copying of DVDs protected by the technology CSS (Content Scramble System), which the movie studios use to prevent the widespread copying of movies on DVDs. (Unlike movies on VHS tapes, movies on DVDs are in digital format and therefore can be copied without any loss in quality and distributed over the Internet.) The existence of the DMCA was crucial to the studios' legal claims, because they did not allege that Corley and the other defendants (or anyone) had *actually copied* any movies on DVD; they only alleged that *distribution* of the DeCSS program that made copying possible was illegal under the DMCA's anticircumvention protections. After a trial, U.S. District Court Judge Lewis Kaplan in August 2000 ruled that Corley and his company had violated the anticircumvention provisions of the DMCA[9] and ordered them to stop distributing the DeCSS program.[10] The U.S. Court of Appeals for the Second Circuit affirmed the order in November 2001,[11] and in July 2002 the defendants elected not to ask the U.S. Supreme Court to review the case.[12]

Although the movie studios' concerns are legitimate, the case is quite controversial, because without the DMCA and the studios' copy-protection technology, the Copyright Act would permit some limited copying of movies on DVD, such as for personal use or otherwise pursuant to the "fair use" doctrine. Indeed, in a landmark 1984 case, *Sony* v. *Universal City Studios,*[13] the U.S. Supreme Court rejected claims that the manufacturer of the Betamax video recorder should be held liable for copyright infringement even though the machines obviously could be used to copy movies and TV programs. The Supreme Court in that case said the Betamax machines had "commercially significant noninfringing uses"—that is, they could be used by consumers to make recordings that were protected by the fair use doctrine. Had the DMCA been in existence two decades earlier, the entire home video recording industry might never have gotten off the ground.

Because of the courts' rulings in the *Reimerdes* case, another company filed a declaratory judgment action in April 2002 in U.S. District Court for the Northern District of California, asking the court to rule that the DMCA does not prevent it from selling its own DVD-copying software. In that case, *321 Studios* v. *MGM Studios,* the plaintiff said in its complaint that "[t]he DMCA prohibits legitimate conduct, including the fair use of copyrighted works permitted under the Copyright Act."[14]

As these early cases under the DMCA demonstrate, this new Internet-age law is controversial but also has very sharp teeth, and you do not want to break it by breaking a "technological measure" that protects a copyrighted work. And if you make copyrighted works available to others online or elsewhere, the DMCA provides you with a strong incentive to create a copy-protection scheme to safeguard them.

LIMITING LIABILITY FOR ONLINE COPYRIGHT INFRINGEMENT

Another very important section of the Digital Millennium Copyright Act addresses the issue of when Internet service providers should be legally responsible for copyright infringement committed by their customers online. Here's why this is important: Suppose John Doe creates a website on which he offers visitors the ability to download, for free, a high-priced software application created by your company and for which your company owns the copyright. Apparently, John Doe simply purchased a legitimate copy of the software at the local computer store and, for whatever reason, decided to upload all of the disk's content to his website and announce to the world that anyone could come and get your program for free.

There's little, if any, doubt that John Doe is committing copyright infringement by reproducing and distributing your company's software on the Internet without permission. Your first thought might be to send him a cease and desist letter, demanding that he immediately remove the software application from his website. Or you may want to go right ahead and file a copyright infringement lawsuit against him, asking the court to issue a temporary restraining order preventing him from offering your software to the world until the lawsuit can be heard. Either action would be wise, but each could have its disadvantages. Filing a lawsuit is often a time-consuming and expensive process. As for the cease and desist letter, it may or may not be as effective as filing a lawsuit. And in either case, you may face a significant obstacle if you don't know how to reach John Doe—or if you don't even know John Doe's name! How could this be? Suppose the website offering your company's software has been created by someone using any one of the free Web hosting services on the Internet, such as Yahoo GeoCities, homestead, Tripod, or Angelfire. In that case, John Doe was able to build his site without identifying himself on it or even revealing his true identity to the company that hosts it for him.

Although you can file a lawsuit against someone who's anonymous (it's actually called a "John Doe suit"), the DMCA may be your best bet. Under the DMCA, you can, under certain circumstances, contact a copyright infringer's Internet service provider and have it delete the infringing content. And if you or your company is an Internet service provider that receives a proper request from a copyright owner asking you to delete someone else's content, the DMCA can protect you from liability if the alleged copyright infringer pursues you for disrupting his or her online activity. In either event, while the DMCA can prove very useful, it is also complex and requires adherence to many technical legal requirements.

If you are the copyright owner of a work that has been infringed by being published on someone else's website, you may act under the DMCA procedures only if the Internet service provider hosting the content has designated a specific agent, or person, to receive notifications of claimed infringement. (Because the DMCA creates a special exemption—sometimes called a "safe harbor"—from legal liability for service providers who designate an agent, many providers have chosen to do so. The process for designating an agent is discussed a little bit later in this chapter.) You can identify the provider's designated agent either by locating the contact information on the provider's own website (follow the links to the host's "copyright policy," "terms of use," "terms of service," or similar document) or by viewing the list of designated agents registered with the U.S. Copyright Office.[15] Once you've identified the designated agent, the DMCA says that you must provide substantially the following information in writing:[16]

- a physical or electronic signature of a person authorized to act on behalf of the owner of an exclusive right that is allegedly infringed;
- identification of the copyrighted work claimed to have been infringed, or, if multiple copyrighted works at a single online site are covered by a single notification, a representative list of such works at that site;
- identification of the material that is claimed to be infringing or to be the subject of infringing activity and that is to be removed or access to which is to be disabled, and information reasonably sufficient to permit the service provider to locate the material;
- information reasonably sufficient to permit the service provider to contact the complaining party, such as an address, telephone number, and, if available, an electronic mail address at which the complaining party may be contacted;
- a statement that the complaining party has a good faith belief that use of the material in the manner complained of is not authorized by the copyright owner, its agent, or the law; and
- a statement that the information in the notification is accurate, and, under penalty of perjury, that the complaining party is authorized to act on behalf of the owner of an exclusive right that is allegedly infringed.

Once an Internet service provider acting within the DMCA's safe harbor provision receives a notice containing this information, it must "expeditiously" remove or disable access to the allegedly infringing material.

From the service provider's perspective, electing to abide by the safe harbor requirements is a relatively easy task that carries a great benefit: Qualifying providers generally will not be liable for copyright infringement for hosting content that violates the rights of a copyright owner. Otherwise, a service provider that does not choose to participate in the DMCA safe harbor program could face liability for direct or indirect copyright infringement, even though it was the service provider's customer that actually posted the allegedly infringing content. (A similar exemption is available to online service providers for defamation lawsuits under the Communications Decency Act, discussed in Chapter 21. However, unlike the DMCA, the exemption for defamation does not require the service provider to take specific steps to qualify.)

To qualify for the exemption from legal liability for removing content stored by one of its customers, a service provider must, under the DMCA's definition, be "a provider of online services or network access, or the operator of facilities therefor." It also must appoint a designated agent, that is, a person to whom copyright owners can submit the notice discussed above. To designate an agent, a service provider must list the name, address, phone number, and e-mail address of the agent on a publicly accessible portion of its site and also provide it to the U.S. Copyright Office.[17] Also, the Register of Copyrights (the top official at the U.S. Copyright Office in Washington, D.C.) may require additional contact information. To provide the information to the Copyright Office, service providers may fill out a form and are required to pay a small fee.[18]

Once a service provider has designated an agent, the DMCA says it will generally be exempt from liability for copyright infringement if it[19]

• does not have actual knowledge that the material or an activity using the material on the system or network is infringing;

• in the absence of such actual knowledge, is not aware of facts or circumstances from which infringing activity is apparent; or

• upon obtaining such knowledge or awareness, acts expeditiously to remove, or disable access to, the material;

and if it

• does not receive a financial benefit directly attributable to the infringing activity, in a case in which the service provider has the right and ability to control such activity; and

• upon notification of claimed infringement . . . , responds expeditiously to remove, or disable access to, the material that is claimed to be infringing or to be the subject of infringing activity.

As you can see, the Digital Millennium Copyright Act is not a simple law, and even the descriptions in this chapter are general. Therefore, before sending a notice under the DMCA or attempting to qualify as a service provider under the safe harbor provisions, you should consult with an attorney who is experienced and familiar with the latest developments of this important Internet law.

PART II

DOMAIN NAMES AND TRADEMARKS

CHAPTER FIVE

CASE STUDY: AN INTRODUCTION TO DOMAIN NAMES AND

TRADEMARK DISPUTES, *ELECTRONICS BOUTIQUE* v. *ZUCCARINI*

John Zuccarini has been described as a "notorious cybersquatter," that is, someone who deliberately and in bad faith registers domain names in violation of the rights of trademark owners. He has been sued multiple times and, according to the courts, has registered hundreds of domain names that are similar to many famous brands. He also has been hit with the largest monetary award against a cybersquatter— $500,000 for registering five domain names that were found to violate the rights of an international video game store. His story provides an interesting and informative introduction to the legal wrangling between domain name registrants and trademark owners.

The facts in this chapter are based upon those described by a U.S. District Court judge in Pennsylvania in two rulings against Zuccarini, in October 2000[1] and January 2001.[2] Zuccarini's is not the first reported case of cybersquatting, but his story is too remarkable and timely to ignore.

Electronics Boutique is a specialty retailer in video games and personal computer software that, at the time of a court hearing in October 2000, operated more than six hundred retail stores, mostly in malls. Electronics Boutique also sells products on the Internet at websites associated with the domain names electronicsboutique.com and ebworld.com. The video game and software retailer has used the service mark "Electronics Boutique" since 1977 and has obtained several registrations with the U.S. Patent and Trademark Office, including "Electronics Boutique," which was registered in 1987. It uses the marks in print, trade literature, and advertising and on the Internet. On advertising alone, it has spent tens of millions of dollars using its trademarks.

In 1997 and 1996, respectively, Electronics Boutique registered the domain names electronicsboutique.com and ebworld.com and it sells products on the Internet at websites associated with these domain names. Electronics Boutique invested heavily in its website to attract customers. In the last fiscal year before the judge's October 2000 ruling, the store had revenues of $273 million, averaging $1.1 million in sales from its website, which attracted 2.6 million visitors over eight months.

Zuccarini registered the domain names electronicboutique.com, electronicbotique.com, ebwold.com, and ebworl.com in May 2000. According to one of the court's rulings: "When a potential or existing online customer, attempting to access [Electronics Boutique's] website, mistakenly types one of Mr. Zuccarini's domain misspellings, he is 'mousetrapped' in a barrage of advertising windows, featuring a variety of products, including credit cards, Internet answering machines, games, and music. The Internet user cannot exit the Internet without clicking on the succession of advertisements that appears. Simply clicking on the 'X' in the top right-hand corner of the screen, a common way to close a web browser window, will not allow a user to exit. Mr. Zuccarini is paid between 10 and 25 cents by the advertisers for every click. Sometimes, after wading through as many as 15 windows, the Internet user could gain access to [Electronics Boutique's] website."[3] On one occasion, a visitor sent an e-mail to the webmaster at EBWorld.com stating, "I do not know if you are affiliated with www.electronicbotique, but I believe you are."

As a result of Zuccarini's actions, Electronics Boutique sued him, alleging that he had committed trademark infringement and trademark dilution, that he had engaged in illegal unfair competition, and that he had violated the Anticybersquatting Consumer Protection Act[4] (ACPA), a 1999 amendment to the U.S. trademark laws that, as its name implies, addresses the growing practice of registering domain names identical or similar to someone else's trademarks. In response, Zuccarini "embarked on a campaign orchestrated to avoid involvement" in the lawsuit, according to the court. When Electronics Boutique attempted to serve Zuccarini with the lawsuit, he took elaborate steps to avoid it, allegedly hiding at a local hotel, returning mail sent to his apartment, refusing to pick up certified mail, and ignoring phone messages from Electronics Boutique's lawyer and the U.S. Marshals Service.

On the same day Electronics Boutique filed its lawsuit, it also sought and the court granted a temporary restraining order (commonly known as a TRO) forbidding Zuccarini from using the misspelled Electronics Boutique domain names he had registered (as well as any others identical or confusingly similar to any registered trademarks owned by Electronics Boutique) and ordering him to deactivate the domain names. Four days later, the company that maintained the servers on which Zuccarini's domain names were hosted notified him via e-mail that they were being disabled because of the TRO. Zuccarini replied, asking his host to "please reactivate the domains as soon as possible." The TRO was valid for only ten days, but after Electronics Boutique informed the judge that it had been unable to serve Zuccarini with the lawsuit, the TRO was extended. Nineteen days after the lawsuit was filed, the judge held a hearing, and although Zuccarini did not attend, the judge later noted that Zuccarini was obviously aware of the lawsuit because of his e-mail correspondence with his Web host. As a result, the judge entered a preliminary injunction against Zuccarini based on Electronics Boutique's claims under the Anticybersquatting Consumer Protection Act. Zuccarini also failed to show up for a later hearing on the case, and it was not until after the judge issued a permanent injunction and large monetary award against him that Zuccarini sent a lawyer to court on his behalf, at which point he failed to persuade the judge to set aside the judgment.

In issuing the permanent injunction and fine, the judge found that Zuccarini had violated the ACPA by registering and using the domain names that were similar to those used by Electronics Boutique. Specifically, the court found that Zuccarini had used domain names that were confusingly similar to Electronics Boutique's trademarks with a bad-faith intent to profit from doing so. Violations of the ACPA are not the same as typical trademark infringement cases— indeed, that's why Congress passed the ACPA, to fill the gap created by difficult cases that do not amount to trademark infringement or trademark dilution, all of which are discussed in greater detail in subsequent chapters in this book. But violating the ACPA amounts to violating U.S. trademark law, and that's exactly what Zuccarini did.

In brief, here's what the court found in evaluating whether Zuccarini violated the first U.S. law on domain names:

• The Electronics Boutique trademarks are distinctive and famous. Although any type of trademark can be infringed, only distinctive or famous trademarks can be protected by the ACPA. In this case, the court found that Electronic Boutique's lengthy (twenty-year) use of its trademarks, the millions of dollars it had spent on promoting goods and services associated with the trademarks, and the fact that no other entity uses similar trademarks all led to the trademarks being both famous and distinctive.

• The domain misspellings used by Zuccarini are confusingly similar to Electronics Boutique's trademarks. The "confusingly similar" language in the ACPA is also applicable in traditional trademark infringement cases and is required for any court to find that the cybersquatting law has been violated. As the court noted, "the profitability of Mr. Zuccarini's enterprise is completely dependent on his ability to create and register domain names that are confusingly similar to famous names. As the similarity in the spellings of Mr. Zuccarini's domain names to popular or famous names increases, the likelihood that an Internet user will inadvertently type one of Mr. Zuccarini's misspellings (and Mr. Zuccarini will be compensated [because of the pop-up advertisements]) increases."[5]

• Zuccarini had bad-faith intent to profit from the Electronics Boutique trademarks. The judge said: "Mr. Zuccarini's bad-faith intent to profit from the domain misspellings is abundantly clear. Mr. Zuccarini registered the domain misspellings in order to generate advertising revenue for himself, despite being aware of the Electronics Boutique stores and website. . . . I find that Mr. Zuccarini specifically intended to prey on the confusion and typographical and/or spelling errors of Internet users to divert Internet users from [Electronic Boutique's] website for his own commercial gain."[6] In another case in which Zuccarini was involved, he allegedly admitted that, by registering thousands of domain names in similar fashion, he received between $800,000 and $1 million a year.

The court then turned to the issue of damages, that is, what amount of money Zuccarini should be required to pay to Electronics Boutique. The ACPA allows for damages of anywhere from $1,000 to $100,000 per domain name, "as the court considers just." The court here was obviously angry at Zuccarini's cybersquatting, noting that he had "victimized a wide variety of people and entities" by registering hundreds of domain names that were misspellings of famous people's names, famous brands, company names, television shows, and movies. In addition to Electronics Boutique, among those that had alleged similar misconduct by Zuccarini were Radio Shack, Office Depot, Nintendo, Hewlett-Packard, the Dave Matthews Band, and The Wall Street Journal. In addition, the judge apparently was not pleased that Zuccarini had ignored the court's rulings and the lawsuit for so long. As a result, the judge ordered Zuccarini to pay the maximum damages allowed by the ACPA: $100,000 per domain name, for a total of $500,000. In addition, because the judge found this case to be "exceptional," he also ordered Zuccarini to pay Electronics Boutique's attorneys' fees and costs of litigation, which amounted to more than $30,000.

The Electronics Boutique case is not a typical trademark lawsuit, nor is Zuccarini a typical cybersquatter. (Indeed, in October 2001, Zuccarini was charged by the Federal Trade Commission with violating federal laws for "more than 5,500 copycat Web addresses to divert surfers from their intended Internet destinations to one of his sites, and hold them captive while he pelted their screens with a barrage of ads."[7] The FTC said Zuccarini had been sued sixty-three times for domain name disputes in the previous two years.) But the Electronics Boutique case highlights the importance of trademarks on the Internet. Although Electronics Boutique ultimately prevailed on its claim under the new Anticybersquatting Consumer Protection Act, it also brought claims based on traditional trademark infringement and trademark dilution, causes of action that have allowed many trademark owners to prevail against domain name squatters. And these long-standing trademark laws have application to many other aspects of conducting business online other than in the context of domain names. In any event, at least one thing is clear: Trademarks are at least as important in cyberspace as they are in the "real world," if not even more important, so it's vital to learn how to protect yourself (or your company) by using, registering, and enforcing trademarks properly and to respect trademarks owned by others.

CHAPTER SIX

The Basics of Trademark Law

Cybersquatting is probably the most prominent form of trademark violation on the Internet, but it is not the only type. One company can infringe another's trademark in cyberspace even if domain names are not an issue. Just as one company can defy trademark law simply by choosing the wrong name for its business, products, or services in the physical world, the same thing can occur in the virtual world of the Internet.

A basic understanding of the essentials of trademark law is necessary to appreciate the legal issues of cybersquatting or any other type of trademark violation on the Internet.

WHAT IS A TRADEMARK?

According to the Lanham Act,[1] the set of U.S. laws relating to trademarks, a trademark includes any word, name, symbol, or device, or any combination thereof used by a person . . . to identify and distinguish his or her goods, including a unique product, from those manufactured or sold by others and to indicate the source of the goods, even if that source is unknown.[2]

While trademarks identify "goods"—usually, tangible products—service marks identify, predictably, services. Often trademarks and service marks are interchangeably referred to as trademarks, or simply marks.

Many trademarks are very well known, such as Coca-Cola carbonated beverages, Fireman's Fund insurance, Honda automobiles, and UPS package delivery services. Of course, trademarks are well known in cyberspace, too. EBay identifies online auction services, Yahoo identifies directory services, EarthLink identifies Internet access services, WebTV identifies certain hardware components that can be used to access the Internet, Cisco identifies telecommunications equipment, and BlackBerry identifies a handheld device for accessing e-mail.

In addition to words, as the Lanham Act's definition of trademarks makes clear, a symbol can also function as a trademark. Popular trademark symbols on the Internet include the Microsoft windowpane logo; Apple Computer's high-tech, one-bite-taken fruit; the Ask Jeeves butler; the Monster.com eye; the AOL triangle; and even the Gateway computer cow pattern.

"Trade dress" is similar to trademarks and refers to the overall appearance of a product. Interestingly, some cases indicate that high-tech product designs are protected by trade dress law. For example, Apple has asserted trade dress rights in the design of its iMac computer. And many other popular overall product appearances probably serve to identify and distinguish the products, qualifying them for trade dress protection—such as the successful Palm V handheld computer, Iomega's Zip drives, and the Sony VAIO series of laptops.

WHAT ARE THE DIFFERENT TYPES OF TRADEMARKS?

Not every word, name, symbol, or device can function as a trademark, and some words, names, symbols, or devices are stronger than others. Generally, the courts have described trademarks as falling into the following categories, listed in decreasing level of strength:

• Arbitrary or fanciful. Fanciful trademarks are those that have been made up, such as newly coined words. Examples include Xircom, Avaya, Lucent, Equant, Accenture, and Intel. Arbitrary marks are those that in no way describe the goods or services with which they're used, such as Google for search services, Egghead for electronic sales, eBay for online auctions, Apple for computers, and BlackBerry for handheld wireless e-mail devices. Arbitrary and fanciful trademarks are very strong, but they usually require those who use them to expend considerable amounts of money to create an association in the public's mind between the mark and the associated goods or services.

• Suggestive. Suggestive trademarks are those that indirectly describe the goods or services they identify. Examples include Win-Book for notebook computers running the Windows operating system; LinkSys for cables and software that link together two computer systems; and ViewSonic for monitors.

• Descriptive. Descriptive trademarks are those that describe the goods or services they identify. Examples include MapQuest for mapping services; The Weather Channel for information about the weather; and Travelocity for travel services. Descriptive trademarks are not entitled to registration as federal trademarks without what lawyers call "secondary meaning," that is, whether the relevant audience has created an association between the trademark and the goods and services with which the mark is used.

• Generic. A generic term is the name of a particular good or service, such as "personal computer," "cell phone," "modem," or "e-book." Generic terms are not entitled to trademark protection and therefore can be used by anyone. As one judge wrote in March 2002 in the case *Microsoft* v. *Lindows.com,* a trademark dispute over the names used by two software companies that raised the question of whether the mark "Windows" is generic for a graphical computer operating system: "[W]hen a trademark's primary significance is to describe the type of product rather than the producer or source, the mark is a generic term."[3]

HOW DO YOU APPLY FOR A TRADEMARK REGISTRATION?

Trademark rights arise from use, not from registration. That means that it is unnecessary to file a trademark application and obtain a registration to gain rights to a trademark. However, there are a number of advantages in obtaining a U.S. (also known as a "federal") trademark registration. The following is a list of some advantages prepared by the U.S. Patent and Trademark Office:[4]

• Constructive notice nationwide of the trademark owner's claim.
• Evidence of ownership of the trademark.
• Jurisdiction of federal courts may be invoked.
• Registration can be used as a basis for obtaining registration in foreign countries.
• Registration may be filed with the U.S. Customs Service to prevent importation of infringing foreign goods.

You also may file for a trademark registration at the state level, which is often a simpler and less expensive process, but the advantages are not as great. Therefore, this discussion focuses on federal trademark registrations.

The U.S. Patent and Trademark Office[5] (PTO) is the government entity that supervises the federal trademark registration process. Applying for a trademark is not difficult, and the PTO's website offers useful information about how to do so, including an online application system. However, because all applications are reviewed by the PTO and often require follow-up work by the applicant, the process is not always simple and, in any event, is rarely quick; an "easy" application may take one year or more from the date of filing until the date the trademark becomes registered.

In deciding whether to issue a federal trademark application, the PTO will compare the trademark in your application against those already registered at the PTO and those for which registration is pending. The PTO also will compare the goods and services stated in your application with the others. Often, the PTO will find identical or similar marks and issue what is known as an "office action," a nonfinal rejection of the application to which you can respond, attempting to convince the trademark examining attorney that your application should be approved despite other trademarks. Another common reason for the PTO's issuing an office action is if the examining attorney determines that your mark is not entitled to registration because the mark is either generic or descriptive. Depending upon the nature of the office action, responses to it can range from a mere formality to a well-researched, well-written legal argument. Many applications fail to mature into registrations because trademark owners choose to apply for the marks themselves rather than use an attorney with knowledge and experience in this area of the law.

Once registered at the U.S. Patent and Trademark Office, a trademark must be maintained or the registration—and all of the time, effort, and money that went into it—could be lost. Among other things, a trademark owner must file, by specified dates following the trademark's registration, affidavits that the mark is still being used and applications for renewal.

There are two common types of trademark applications: use-based and intent-to-use. In a use-based application, the trademark owner already has begun using the trademark. If an applicant has not yet begun using a trademark but wants to go ahead and attempt to secure rights, he may file an intent-to-use (ITU) application, if he has a bona fide intent to use the trademark in commerce. The advantage of filing an ITU application is that the applicant may obtain an earlier priority date for his mark than if he waited until actual use began.

HOW DO YOU CONDUCT A TRADEMARK SEARCH?

Searching for trademarks is an important thing to do either because you're evaluating whether to adopt a particular trademark of your own (and want to ensure that others are not already using the same or similar marks in connection with the same or similar services) or because you're defending a trademark lawsuit and want to show that the plaintiff's trademark is weak in light of a number of other similar or identical uses by others. U.S. trademark law does not require an applicant to conduct a trademark search before applying for a registration, but doing so is a wise move.

If you ask a trademark lawyer to conduct a search for you, he or she will need to know at least two pieces of information: What trademark do you want to use, and with what goods or services do you want to use it? Then the trademark lawyer will likely first perform what is commonly known as a "knockout search," that is, a search of federally (U.S.) registered trademarks to see whether someone else already is using or has applied for a mark that is identical or appears to be confusingly similar. If he finds such a mark, he probably will recommend that you go back to the drawing board to select a new one. If he does not find a knockout, he may then recommend that you authorize him to conduct a fuller search, one that will look at additional federal registrations as well as trademarks registered at the state level (every state maintains a separate system), "common law" trademarks (that is, trademarks used but never registered), and, perhaps, domain names.

Except for the knockout search, a lawyer probably will turn to an outside trademark service to conduct the search and prepare a report (though the lawyer will interpret it for you, either verbally or in writing). Many lawyers use one of two popular companies to conduct the search: Thomson & Thomson[6] or CCH CORSEARCH.[7] In addition, there are a number of other companies that have entered the trademark search business in recent years, though their track records are unproven.

Many people wonder whether the expense of a trademark search is really worthwhile. The answer is yes, but there are some things you can do yourself to help reduce your legal fees, thanks to the Internet. For example, at the U.S. Patent and Trademark Office's website, you can conduct your own simplified knockout search—something that was not possible only a few years ago. However, you should be aware that the PTO's Web-based search service has a number of limitations. Among them:

- Searches are limited to text marks only. If you want to search for a logo or other design, you cannot do so at the PTO website.
- The search structure will not look for alternative spellings. For example, a search for "Adobey" or "Adobie" will not locate "Adobe."
- The database of trademarks is not current. The database is updated regularly, but there's always some delay between the time an application is filed and the time it is entered into the PTO's records.
- The database is limited to U.S. federal registrations and applications. It does not include trademarks at the state level, common law trademarks, or domain names. It also does not include trademarks from other countries, an increasingly important issue given the borderless nature of the Internet.

• Of course, any search you conduct yourself will not be accompanied by an informed legal opinion from a lawyer who can interpret the results.

Despite these limitations, using the PTO's website is usually a smart first step in the trademark application process, because it can be useful in learning whether another existing trademark would prevent you from proceeding with yours.

In addition to searching the PTO's trademark database, it's always wise to do some additional online searching at some of the popular search engines by seeing whether any websites contain references to your trademark. And you can search for domain names using various search tools—usually known as the "WHOIS" interface—maintained by the different domain name registrars. A popular site that searches WHOIS databases at multiple registries is known as Allwhois.[8]

If your own informal trademark search does not indicate any problems, you probably should proceed next to use the services of a professional. A lawyer experienced in conducting and interpreting trademark searches is a worthwhile expense.

WHAT ARE THE TRADEMARK REGISTRATION SYMBOLS?

Three different symbols are often used to denote a trademark: ®, ™, and ℠. They serve similar but not identical purposes.

The ® symbol—sometimes known as the "circle-R" symbol—is used to identify a trademark or service mark that has been registered at the U.S. Patent and Trademark Office. (Some other countries also use the ® symbol to denote marks registered pursuant to their national laws.) The Lanham Act also says that either of the following is an acceptable alternative: "Registered in the U.S. Patent and Trademark Office" or "Reg. U.S. Pat. & Tm. Off."[9] However, use of any of these notices by a trademark owner is entirely optional, and failing to use any of them will not affect the validity of the trademark, although the Lanham Act provides an incentive for doing so: If a trademark owner uses one of these notices, he or she does not need to prove that a defendant had actual notice of the registration to recover damages and profits in a trademark lawsuit. The ® symbol should not be used if the trademark is not registered at the U.S. Patent and Trademark Office, unless it is registered in another country that uses the ® symbol.

The ™ symbol is used to designate trademarks that are not protected by a federal registration. It can be used on trademarks registered at the state level or even common law trademarks, that is, those that are in use but not registered anywhere. By using the ™ symbol, a trademark owner is putting others on notice that he or she claims trademark rights. However, because no law governs the use of this symbol, it is of only limited significance.

Finally, the significance of the ᔢᴹ symbol is exactly the same as for the ™ symbol, the only difference being that the ᔢᴹ symbol is used only in connection with service marks, not trademarks.

On your website, you should use all of these trademark symbols appropriately. By doing so, you will put others on notice about your trademark rights, perhaps warning them not to adopt trademarks similar to yours. The Lanham Act does not specify exactly where the symbol should be used, other than "with the mark." That raises an interesting question: If a trademark appears multiple times on a single Web page, should the symbol be used with each instance of the mark? Lawyers are divided about the answer to this question, although many advise that the appropriate symbol can be used only upon the initial or most prominent occurrence of the mark, avoiding excessive page clutter.

WHAT IS TRADEMARK INFRINGEMENT?

According to the Lanham Act, trademark infringement occurs when someone[10] uses in commerce any word, term, name, symbol, or device, or any combination thereof, or any false designation of origin, false or misleading description of fact, or false or misleading representation of fact, which—

(A) is likely to cause confusion, or to cause mistake, or to deceive as to the affiliation, connection, or association of such person with another person, or as to the origin, sponsorship, or approval of his or her goods, services, or commercial activities by another person, or

(B) in commercial advertising or promotion, misrepresents the nature, characteristics, qualities, or geographic origin of his or her or another person's goods, services, or commercial activities. . . .

The key phrase here is "likely to cause confusion." Trademark law is designed to protect consumers, to prevent someone from becoming confused and thinking that a product or service is provided by a particular company when it isn't.

However, deciding when this likelihood of confusion exists is not always an easy thing to do. Through the years, the courts have developed a number of factors to consider when evaluating the likelihood of confusion. Although the factors vary by jurisdiction—that is, the court that is actually hearing the dispute—they generally include the following:

• The strength of the trademark allegedly infringed. Typically, stronger trademarks—that is, those that are arbitrary or fanciful as opposed to descriptive, as discussed above—are entitled to a greater degree of protection.

• The similarity between the plaintiff's trademark and the mark used by the defendant. Usually, the more similar the marks, the more likely a court will find a likelihood of confusion. However, the two marks need not be identical, and even if they are, likelihood of confusion is not necessarily a given.

• The similarity of the goods or services. Because trademarks must be used in connection with a particular good or service, others sometimes may be free to use the same trademark in connection with different goods or services (although this is less likely for stronger marks). For example, online retailer Amazon.com would have a difficult time alleging trademark infringement against Aquion Partners, which uses the Amazon trademark to identify water-softening units for domestic use.

• Evidence of actual confusion. Trademark infringement does not require that anyone actually be confused about the source of two different goods or services, only that someone is *likely* to be confused. However, it is often said that evidence of actual confusion—that is, evidence that someone already has been confused—is perhaps the most important factor for a court in a trademark infringement case.

• The degree of care likely to be exercised by consumers. Typically, more sophisticated consumers are thought to be less likely to be confused.

• The marketing channels used. Historically, this factor has looked at such things as whether a trademark owner and an alleged infringer promoted their goods or services in the same media, such as television, newspapers, trade magazines, etc. On the Internet, this factor appears to have become less significant, because often both parties have an online presence.

• The defendant's intent in selecting the mark. Although trademark law is designed primarily to protect the consumer and not necessarily to punish those who act in bad faith, the courts do not look favorably on a defendant who purposefully selects a trademark because he intends to woo another trademark owner's customers.

Some courts evaluate additional factors, and others do not always evaluate each of these factors. Interestingly, because these factors have been developed by the courts and are not a part of the Lanham Act itself, it is impossible to know how any court will balance them. Often, in a trademark infringement case, a court will analyze each factor, indicating which factors favor which party, the plaintiff or the defendant, and then summarize its position, such as: "A majority of these factors weigh in favor of finding a likelihood of confusion." However, not every factor necessarily carries the same weight as the other factors, so the process is more complicated than simply adding them up and declaring a winner.

WHAT IS TRADEMARK DILUTION?

Trademark dilution is a legal theory that has existed at the state level for a number of years but was only made a part of the federal Lanham Act in 1995. Trademark dilution is a separate legal cause of action from trademark infringement. A defendant in a trademark lawsuit may be found liable for trademark infringement and/or trademark dilution (or neither).

In general, whereas trademark infringement protects against a likelihood of confusion, trademark dilution protects the strength of famous trademarks from being diluted even if there is no likelihood of confusion: for example, "Microsoft" to describe pillows. Probably no one would think that the pillows were manufactured by the software company, but use of this trademark in this way could dilute the trademark's ability to identify the company's computer products and services.

Typically, dilution can occur in two ways. Under one theory, a defendant's use of a plaintiff's trademark tarnishes the trademark by creating an association with the trademark that is contrary to the image the trademark has acquired. For example, think of "Hewlett-Packard" to describe a brand of toilet paper or "Handspring" to describe enemas. Under the other theory, a defendant's use of a plaintiff's trademark whittles away at the distinctive quality of the trademark by diluting the strong association the public has between the mark and the plaintiff, as in the Microsoft pillows example.

Under the U.S. Anti-Dilution Act,[11] only "famous" marks qualify for protection. To determine whether a mark is famous, the act says a court may consider the following factors (but it is not limited to these):

- the degree of inherent or acquired distinctiveness of the mark;
- the duration and extent of use of the mark in connection with the goods or services with which the mark is used;
- the duration and extent of advertising and publicity of the mark;
- the geographical extent of the trading area in which the mark is used;
- the channels of trade for the goods or services with which the mark is used;
- the degree of recognition of the mark in the trading areas and channels of trade used by the mark's owner and the person against whom the injunction is sought;
- the nature and extent of use of the same or similar marks by third parties; and
- whether the mark was registered under the [Lanham Act].

Although these factors may seem difficult to achieve, the truth is that courts have found many trademarks to be famous that are not nearly so well known as Coca-Cola or Microsoft. Often, it seems that, especially in Internet cases, some courts have gone out of their way to find a trademark famous (and therefore protected by the anti-dilution law) if the defendant using the trademark appears to be acting in bad faith.

CHAPTER SEVEN

TRADITIONAL TRADEMARK LAW AND DOMAIN NAMES

Although a number of relatively new legal tools, such as the Anti-cybersquatting Consumer Protection Act (introduced in Chapter 5 and discussed in detail in Chapter 8) and the Uniform Domain Name Dispute Resolution Policy (discussed in Chapter 9), have made cybersquatting more difficult, it was only a few years ago that neither of these existed and trademark owners had to rely on traditional, preexisting trademark laws to pursue cybersquatters.

THE IMPORTANCE OF DOMAIN NAMES

The short history of domain names and trademarks is very interesting. The courts, trademark owners, and domain name registrants have come a long way since one of the first reported domain name cases, in 1994, between MTV Networks and video disc jockey Adam

Curry, over rights to mtv.com. In that early case, the court devoted lengthy footnotes to explain what the Internet is and what a domain name is! In what would prove to be an understatement, the court said: "A domain name mirroring a corporate name may be a valuable corporate asset, as it facilitates communication with a customer base."[1]

Domain names are important for at least one obvious reason: Companies want to provide an easily identifiable address for themselves online. And consumers expect to find companies they're seeking at the evident address. Although the addition in late 2001 of seven new top-level domains may be changing the landscape somewhat, consumers have learned that the easiest way to locate a website is often to search for it at the URL consisting of "www." plus the company, product, or service name plus ".com." Thus, for example, a consumer is likely to look for information about FedEx at www.fedex.com, for Microsoft at www.microsoft.com, for Toyota at www.toyota.com, and so forth. If someone else has registered the company's name (or the name of its product or service) as a domain name, then consumers may be less likely to find the information they're seeking—or, they may become confused about the information they find if it is associated with someone else. It is precisely this type of situation—known as "trademark infringement"—that U.S. trademark law is designed to prevent. A number of cases have been decided under the legal theory of "trademark dilution," which can protect famous marks.

DOMAIN NAMES AND TRADEMARK INFRINGEMENT

U.S. courts have now decided numerous domain name cases based on traditional trademark infringement. As in other trademark cases, courts in domain name disputes will evaluate the same legal factors to determine whether a defendant's use of a domain name creates a likelihood of confusion. Although, as discussed in Chapter 6, the exact factors can vary depending upon where the lawsuit is heard, they typically include at least the following:

- the strength of the trademark;
- the similarity of the parties' services;
- the similarity of the trademark to the domain name;
- evidence of actual confusion;
- the degree of care likely to be exercised by consumers; and
- the domain name registrant's intent in choosing the domain name.

However, as in any trademark infringement case, evaluating these factors is not always an easy or predictable process. Because domain name disputes are relatively new, courts are still struggling with how to apply traditional trademark infringement law in this new context. As a very general rule, courts appear especially eager to find trademark infringement where the domain name registered is identical or very similar to a well-known trademark. And courts also appear eager to find trademark infringement where the registrant is purposefully using the domain name to attack or otherwise damage a trademark owner.

For example, one court ruled against an active participant in the antiabortion movement who registered the domain name plannedparenthood.com and created a website at that domain name with information contrary to that espoused by Planned Parenthood Federation of America, Inc., the well-known reproductive health organization known as Planned Parenthood.[2] In evaluating the legal factors for trademark infringement, the court found in favor of Planned Parenthood on most all of them, ultimately issuing a preliminary injunction against the defendant's use of the plannedparenthood .com domain name. Among other things, the court found that Planned Parenthood's trademark was strong because it had been in use for more than fifty years. And the court found evidence of actual confusion—often the most damaging finding in any trademark infringement case—based on Internet users who arrived at the website at www.plannedparenthood.com by typing in the URL directly and also via a search engine using "Planned Parenthood" as a search term.

In another case, a court ruled in favor of a company called Cardservice International in a trademark infringement suit against Webster R. McGee, the registrant of the domain name cardservice.com.[3] As in the Planned Parenthood case, the court evaluated the usual factors for trademark infringement cases and noted:

> Because of McGee's use of "cardservice.com", Cardservice International has no access to an internet domain name containing its registered mark, and must use a different domain name. Cardservice International's customers who wish to take advantage of its internet services but do not know its domain name are likely to assume that "cardservice.com" belongs to Cardservice International. These customers would instead reach McGee and see a home page for "Card Service". They would find that McGee's internet site offers advertisements for and provides access to the same services as Cardservice International—credit and debit card processing. Many would assume that they have reached Cardservice International or, even if they realize that is not who they have reached, take advantage of McGee's services because they do not otherwise know how to reach Cardservice International. Such confusion is not only likely, but, according to McGee, has actually occurred at least four or five times since he began using "cardservice.com. . . ."

> Such a result is exactly what the trademark laws were designed to protect against. Cardservice International has obtained a trademark to ensure that the name "cardservice" will be associated by consumers only with Cardservice International.

However, not all trademark infringement cases are decided in favor of trademark owners in domain name disputes. In one case, a court ruled in favor of a domain name registrant defending his registration of home-market.net against a plaintiff who had registered and used the domain name home-market.com.[4] In that case, the court said that the plaintiff had failed to establish that it possessed a valid trademark for "home-market," which the court said was a descriptive mark without secondary meaning. In addition, the court said that even if the plaintiff had a valid trademark, it would not prevail on a trademark infringement claim because only one of the relevant factors (the similarity of the marks) weighed in its favor. The court said that the domain name registrant defendant did not intend to deceive consumers and that there was only the "barest evidence of actual confusion."

Ultimately, any domain name lawsuit based on trademark infringement is highly fact-specific. In other words, the actual circumstances of the case must be evaluated closely and compared with the "likelihood of confusion" factors. And still, the judge or jury will decide how to balance the factors, because trademark law does not dictate how to do so.

Of course, these are just a few of the many cases that have been decided, and many more lawsuits have been settled or threatened that did not result in a reported opinion from a court. Though the cases may seem confusing, at least one thing is clear: Purposefully registering and using a domain name that is identical to a strong trademark will almost certainly motivate a trademark owner to take action. And, depending on the other facts involved and the court that hears the case, the domain name registrant could be found liable for trademark infringement.

DOMAIN NAMES AND TRADEMARK DILUTION

Interestingly, about the same time domain name lawsuits became common, in 1996, the U.S. Anti-Dilution Act[5] came into effect. As a result, a number of lawsuits also have been decided under this law, which can sometimes be more useful than a claim of trademark infringement because it does not require a court to find a likelihood of confusion by evaluating the typical factors previously discussed. Instead, a domain name registrant commits trademark dilution simply by making "commercial use in commerce" of a "famous mark" if the use "causes dilution of the distinctive quality of the famous mark."

One of the first domain name cases to receive widespread legal attention was decided in 1996 under the brand-new Anti-Dilution Act. The defendant was Dennis Toeppen, whose name quickly became synonymous with "cybersquatter," since he had registered the names of some rather well-known companies as domain names, including deltaairlines.com, crateandbarrel.com, ramadainn.com, and neiman-marcus.com. He also had registered intermatic.com, although "Intermatic" was protected by five U.S. trademark registrations owned by a manufacturer and distributor of a wide variety of electrical and electronic products that began business in 1941. Although "Intermatic" is probably not as well known to the general public as many other trademarks, the court apparently had little trouble finding it to be famous because it had been used exclusively by the electronics company for more than fifty years. And, according to the court, Toeppen's use of the domain name diluted Intermatic's trademark rights because he "lessen[ed] the capacity of Intermatic to identify and distinguish its goods and services by means of the Internet."[6] The court then entered a permanent injunction against Toeppen from using the intermatic.com domain name.

Another important trademark dilution case involving Toeppen concerned the domain name panavision.com, equivalent to the trademark owned by Panavision International for use in connection with the motion picture and television industry.[7] According to the court, Toeppen offered to sell the domain name to Panavision for $13,000 and tried to persuade the company that he had rights to the domain name despite Panavision's trademark. "If your attorney has advised you otherwise, he is trying to screw you," Toeppen allegedly stated. "He wants to blaze new trails in the legal frontier at your expense. Why do you want to fund your attorney's purchase of a new boat (or whatever) when you can facilitate the acquisition of 'PanaVision.com' cheaply and simply instead?" Though colorful,

Toeppen's tactics apparently did little to please the court, which ultimately found that the Panavision trademark was famous and that Toeppen's use of the domain name amounted to dilution, in part because it put the company's "name and reputation at his mercy."

While some in Congress clearly intended that the Anti-Dilution Act would apply to this new practice of cybersquatting when it debated the proposed law in 1995, the Toeppen cases and others decided on dilution grounds generated a lot of controversy among lawyers, some of whom believed the courts were flouting the law's requirement that a trademark be "famous" before it can be protected. Some lawyers said the courts were even twisting this new law simply to achieve a predetermined result because the cybersquatters' actions were appropriate for condemnation.

Also, in domain name cases under the dilution law as well as those under trademark infringement, the courts have wrestled with how to handle those cases where the domain name registrant has only registered the domain name and not actually created a website in connection with it. Because trademark infringement and trademark dilution require that a defendant actually "use" the trademark "in commerce," it is not always clear whether a true cybersquatter—that is, someone who registers a domain name and does nothing else—violates traditional trademark law. For example, in the district court's opinion in the panavision.com case, the court wrote, "Registration of a trade-[mark] as a domain name, without more, is not a commercial use of the trademark and therefore is not within the prohibitions of the [Trademark] Act."[8] Other courts have reached similar conclusions— in cases involving rights to domain names containing "Oscar" (brought by the Academy of Motion Picture Arts and Sciences), "Skunk Works" (the name for a Southern California–based group of engineers that developed the first American jet plane in 1943),[9] and "Juno" (in a dispute between a lighting company and the free e-mail/Internet access provider).[10]

However, in other similar cases, some courts have found the necessary "use in commerce" requirement, though some have labeled the legal ruling a stretch. For example, in the Toeppen cases, the courts found that he had used the domain names intermatic.com and panavision.com in commerce. In the intermatic.com case, Toeppen argued that his use of the domain name was not in commerce because he never used it to sell any goods or services, but the court said that the "Supreme Court has held that the in commerce requirement should be construed liberally."[11] And in the panavision.com case, the court found that Toeppen's use of the domain name was in commerce because his "business" involved trying to sell the domain name.

Fortunately for trademark owners, the "use in commerce" requirement is now much less important today than it was in the mid to late 1990s, when the courts began struggling with this issue. The Anticybersquatting Consumer Protection Act[12]—an amendment to existing trademark law—creates a new legal cause of action in addition to trademark infringement and trademark dilution. And, unlike the other two legal theories, a claim under the ACPA does not require that the defendant actually use the domain name on which he or she is squatting; rather, under the ACPA, it is sufficient if a defendant "registers, traffics in, or uses a domain name." The ACPA is discussed in detail in the next chapter.

DOMAIN NAMES AND COMPETING TRADEMARK RIGHTS

Finally, domain names and trademarks pose some especially difficult issues in addition to those discussed already. Some of the most interesting cases involve domain names consisting of trademarks to which more than one entity can claim ownership. Typically, in such a situation, the "early bird gets the worm" theory prevails. Thus, for example, a court in 2000 refused to rule in favor of Nissan Motor Co. in a trademark infringement lawsuit over the domain names nissan .com and nissan.net, which had been registered by Nissan Computer Corporation in 1994 and 1996, respectively.[13] (Although the court's published opinion doesn't state whether the car company had filed a trademark infringement suit against the computer company even be-fore its registration of the domain names, it's worth remembering that many companies can peacefully coexist using the same trade-mark if they are engaged in providing different products or services. Also, interestingly in this case, the computer company's president was named Uzi Nissan.) After evaluating the trademark infringement factors, the court found a likelihood of confusion but allowed the computer company to keep nissan.com and nissan.net so long as it prominently displayed a disclaimer and offered no information about automobiles. As a result, the first words on the Web page at www.nissan.com state: "Not affiliated with Nissan Motor Co. Ltd. For Nissan vehicles see 'NissanDriven.com.' "

In another interesting situation in which two companies have rights to the same trademark, the parties simply took the approach favored by King Solomon. The home page of the website at www.scrabble.com displays a split screen that asks visitors to click on one side for U.S. and Canadian residents and the other side for everyone else. A note at the bottom of the page says: "SCRABBLE® is a registered trademark. All intellectual property rights in and to the game are owned in the U.S.A. by Hasbro Inc., in Canada by Hasbro Canada Corporation and throughout the rest of the world by J.W. Spear & Sons Limited of Maidenhead, Berkshire, England, a sub-sidiary of Mattel Inc. Mattel and Spear are not affiliated with Hasbro or Hasbro Canada."

Similarly, the home page of the website at www.playtex.com con-tains a split screen. On the left-hand side, visitors can click for prod-ucts from Playtex Apparel, Inc., a wholly owned subsidiary of the Sara Lee Corporation, which manufactures the Cross Your Heart bra and other lingerie and intimate apparel; this side links to a website at the domain name playtexnet.com. On the right-hand side, visitors can click for products from Playtex Products, Inc., a distributor of personal care products for infants and women; this side links to a website at the domain name playtexproductsinc.com.

CHAPTER EIGHT

The Anticybersquatting Consumer Protection Act

As illustrated by the domain name case brought by Electronics Boutique against John Zuccarini, described in Chapter 5, the U.S. Anticybersquatting Consumer Protection Act[1] (ACPA) is a useful legal tool for trademark owners to use against domain name registrants they believe have violated their rights. Not surprisingly, the ACPA is a new law, passed by Congress in November 1999. While relatively few cases have been decided under this act, that hasn't stopped trademark owners from successfully wielding it in numerous lawsuits.

The ACPA is not the only law that can be used against cybersquatters. Indeed, a number of lawsuits were decided before the ACPA was even on the books, typically under more traditional causes of action such as trademark infringement and trademark dilution, as discussed in the previous chapter. However, some clever cybersquatters quickly found loopholes in existing laws that enabled them to get away with registering others' trademarks as domain names, such as by refusing to sell the domain name (thereby avoiding the U.S. trademark act's requirement that a defendant use the trademark "in commerce"), posting disclaimers on websites associated with the domain name (thereby decreasing the odds of consumer confusion, as required for trademark infringement suits), or simply not creating any website associated with the domain name. As a result, Congress began seeking a way to nab cybersquatters who evaded existing trademark law.

THE U.S. CONGRESS ATTACKS CYBERSQUATTING

According to a report from the U.S. Senate's Judiciary Committee, the purpose of the ACPA is to "protect consumers and American businesses, to promote the growth of online commerce, and to provide clarity in the law for trademark owners by prohibiting the bad-faith and abusive registration of distinctive marks as Internet domain names with the intent to profit from the goodwill associated with such marks—a practice commonly referred to as 'cybersquatting.' "[2] A further excerpt from the report (with footnotes deleted) provides an excellent and informative background of the problems associated with cybersquatting prior to passage of the ACPA:

> Trademark owners are facing a new form of piracy on the Internet caused by acts of "cybersquatting," which refers to the deliberate, bad-faith, and abusive registration of Internet domain names in violation of the rights of trademark owners. For example, when Mobil and Exxon announced their proposed merger in December, 1998, a speculator registered every variation of the possible resulting domain name, i.e., mobil-exxon.com, exxon-mobil.com, mobilexxon.com, etc., ad infinitum. In another example of bad-faith abuses of the domain name registration system, Network Solutions—the domain name registry that administers the Internet's ".com," ".net," ".org," and ".edu" top level domains—pulled [the plug] on a London computer club in May, 1999, that had

registered over 75,000 domain names using an automated computer program. Their aim was to lock up all available four letter domains by systematically reserving every possible combination of letters, starting with aaaa.com, then aaab.com, aaac.com, up to zzzz.com, until every available combination had been reserved.

The practice of cybersquatting harms consumers, electronic commerce, and the goodwill equity of valuable U.S. brand names, upon which consumers increasingly rely to locate the true source of genuine goods and services on the Internet. Online consumers have a difficult time distinguishing a genuine site from a pirate site, given that often the only indications of source and authenticity of the site, or the goods and services made available thereon, are the graphical interface on the site itself and the Internet address at which it resides. As a result, consumers have come to rely heavily on familiar brand names when engaging in online commerce. But if someone is operating a web site under another brand owner's trademark, such as a site called "cocacola.com" or "levis.com," consumers bear a significant risk of being deceived and defrauded, or at a minimum, confused. The costs associated with these risks are increasingly burdensome as more people begin selling pharmaceuticals, financial services, and even groceries over the Internet. Regardless of what is being sold, the result of online brand name abuse, as with other forms of trademark violations, is the erosion of consumer confidence in brand name identifiers and in electronic commerce generally.

Cybersquatters target distinctive marks for a variety of reasons. Some register well-known brand names as Internet domain names in order to extract payment from the rightful owners of the marks, who find their trademarks "locked up" and are forced to pay for the right to engage in electronic commerce under their own brand name. For example, several years ago a small Canadian company with a single shareholder and a couple of dozen domain names demanded that Umbro International, Inc., which markets and distributes soccer equipment, pay $50,000 to its sole shareholder, $50,000 to an Internet charity, and provide a free life-time supply of soccer equipment in order for it to relinquish the "umbro.com" name. The Committee also heard testimony that Warner Bros. was reportedly asked to pay $350,000 for the rights to the names "warner-records.com", "warner-bros-records .com", "warner-pictures.com", "warner-bros-pictures[.com]", and "warnerpictures.com".

Others register well-known marks as domain names and ware-house those marks with the hope of selling them to the highest bidder, whether it be the trademark owner or someone else. For example, the Committee heard testimony regarding an Australian company operating on the Internet under the name "The Best Do-mains," which was offering such domain names as "911porsche .com," at asking prices of up to $60,911, with a caption that reads "PORSCHE: DO I NEED TO SAY ANYTHING?" The Committee also heard testimony regarding a similarly enterpris-ing cybersquatter whose partial inventory of domain names—the listing of which was limited by the fact that Network Solutions will only display the first 50 records of a given registrant—includes names such as Coca-Cola, Pepsi, Burger King, KFC, McDonalds, Subway, Taco Bell, Wendy's, BMW, Chrysler, Dodge, General Motors, Honda, Hyundai, Jaguar, Mazda, Mercedes, Nis-san, Porsche, Rolls-Royce, Saab, Saturn, Toyota, and Volvo, all of which are available to the highest bidder through an online offer sheet.

In addition, cybersquatters often register well-known marks to prey on consumer confusion by misusing the domain name to di-vert customers from the mark owner's site to the cybersquatter's own site, many of which are pornography sites that derive adver-tising revenue based on the number of visits, or "hits," the site receives. For example, the Committee was informed of a parent whose child mistakenly typed in the domain name for "dosney .com," expecting to access the family-oriented content of the Walt Disney home page, only to end up staring at a screen of hardcore pornography because a cybersquatter had registered that domain name in anticipation that consumers would make that exact mistake. Other instances of diverting unsuspecting consumers to pornographic web sites involve malicious attempts to tarnish a trademark owner's mark or to extort money from the trademark owner, such as the case where a cybersquatter placed pornographic images of celebrities on a site under the name "pentium3.com" and announced that it would sell the domain name to the highest bidder. Others attempt to divert unsuspecting consumers to their sites in order to engage in unfair competition. For example, the business operating under the domain name "disneytransportation .com" greets online consumers at its site with a picture of Mickey Mouse and offers shuttle services in the Orlando area and reservations at Disney hotels, although the company is in no way affiliated with the Walt Disney Company and such fact is not clearly indicated on the site. Similarly, the domain name address "wwwcarpoint.com," without a period following "www", was used by a cybersquatter to offer a competing service to Microsoft's popular Carpoint car buying service.

Finally, and most importantly, cybersquatters target distinctive marks to defraud consumers, including to engage in counterfeiting activities. For example, the Committee heard testimony regarding a cybersquatter who registered the domain names "attphonecard.com" and "attcallingcard.com" and used those names to establish sites purporting to sell calling cards and soliciting personally identifying information, including credit card numbers. We also heard the account of a cybersquatter purporting to sell Dell Computer products under the name "dellspares.com", when in fact Dell does not authorize online resellers to market its products, and a similar account of someone using the name "levis501warehouse.com" to sell Levis jeans despite the fact that Levis is the only authorized online reseller of its jeans. Of even greater concern was the example of an online drug store selling pharmaceuticals under the name "propeciasales.com" without any way for online consumers to tell whether what they are buying is a legitimate product, a placebo, or a dangerous counterfeit. . . .

Current law does not expressly prohibit the act of cybersquatting. The World Intellectual Property Organization (WIPO) has identified cybersquatting as a global problem and recognized in its report on the domain name process that "[f]amous and well-known marks have been the special target of a variety of predatory and parasitical practices on the Internet." Trademark holders are battling thousands of cases of cybersquatting each year, the vast majority of which cannot be resolved through the dispute resolution policy set up by Internet domain name registries.

Instances of cybersquatting continue to grow each year because there is no clear deterrent and little incentive for cybersquatters to discontinue their abusive practices. While the Federal Trademark Dilution Act has been useful in pursuing cybersquatters, cybersquatters have become increasingly sophisticated as the case law has developed and now take the necessary precautions to insulate themselves from liability. For example, many cybersquatters are now careful to no longer offer the domain name for sale in any manner that could implicate liability under existing trademark dilution case law. And, in cases of warehousing and trafficking in domain names, courts have sometimes declined to provide assistance to trademark holders, leaving them without adequate and effective judicial remedies. This uncertainty as to the trademark law's application to the Internet has produced inconsistent judicial decisions and created extensive monitoring obligations, unnecessary legal costs, and uncertainty for consumers and trademark owners alike.

In cases where a trademark owner can sue, the sheer number of domain name infringements, the costs associated with hundreds of litigation matters, and the difficulty of obtaining damages in standard trademark infringement and dilution actions are significant obstacles for legitimate trademark holders. Frequently, these obstacles lead trademark owners to simply "pay off" cybersquat-

[Senate Judiciary Committee Report on Cybersquatting]

ters, in exchange for the domain name registration, rather than seek to enforce their rights in court. Legislation is needed to address these problems and to protect consumers, promote the continued growth of electronic commerce, and protect the goodwill of American businesses. Specifically, legislation is needed to clarify the rights of trademark owners with respect to bad faith, abusive domain name registration practices, to provide clear deterrence to prevent bad faith and abusive conduct, and to provide adequate remedies for trademark owners in those cases where it does occur.

The resulting legislation was the Anticybersquatting Consumer Protection Act, which, although not always successful, is a helpful legal tool now wielded in many domain name lawsuits. The rest of this chapter explains how it works.

THE LEGAL REQUIREMENTS OF THE ANTICYBERSQUATTING CONSUMER PROTECTION ACT, AND SOME EXAMPLES

The ACPA expands traditional trademark law to apply specifically to cybersquatting, but its scope certainly is not unlimited. The act applies only under the following circumstances:

- The domain name registrant must have "a bad faith intent to profit from" a trademark, and
- The registrant must register, traffic in, or use a domain name that meets one of the following requirements:
    o in the case of a mark that is distinctive at the time of registration of the domain name, is identical or confusingly similar to that mark;
    o in the case of a famous mark that is famous at the time of registration of the domain name, is identical or confusingly similar to or dilutive of that mark; or
    o is a trademark, word, or name protected by certain sec-

tions of the U.S. Code (specifically, marks of the Red Cross and certain Olympic marks).

The key (and sometimes most controversial) element of any ACPA claim is contained in the first requirement listed above: bad-faith intent to profit from a trademark. This concept is new to trademark law, so the act itself provides some guidance. To determine whether a defendant has acted in bad faith, the ACPA lists nine factors a court may consider (and it may choose to consider others, too):[3]

• the trademark or other intellectual property rights of the domain name registrant, if any, in the domain name;
• the extent to which the domain name consists of the legal name of the person or a name that is otherwise commonly used to identify that person;
• the domain name registrant's prior use, if any, of the domain name in connection with the bona fide offering of any goods or services;
• the domain name registrant's bona fide noncommercial or fair use of the mark in a site accessible under the domain name;
• the domain name registrant's intent to divert consumers from the mark owner's online location to a site accessible under the domain name that could harm the goodwill represented by the mark, either for commercial gain or with the intent to tarnish or disparage the mark, by creating a likelihood of confusion as to the source, sponsorship, affiliation, or endorsement of the site;
• the domain name registrant's offer to transfer, sell, or otherwise assign the domain name to the mark owner or any third party for financial gain without having used, or having an intent to use, the domain name in the bona fide offering of any goods or services, or the person's prior conduct indicating a pattern of such conduct;
• the domain name registrant's provision of material and

misleading false contact information when applying for the registration of the domain name, the domain name registrant's intentional failure to maintain accurate contact information, or the domain name registrant's prior conduct indicating a pattern of such conduct;

• the domain name registrant's registration or acquisition of multiple domain names which he knows are identical or confusingly similar to marks of others that are distinctive at the time of registration of such domain names, or dilutive of famous marks of others that are famous at the time of registration of such domain names, without regard to the goods or services of the parties; or

• the extent to which the mark incorporated in the domain name registration is or is not distinctive and famous.

As you can see, there are quite a few ways that a domain name registrant can act in bad faith and violate the ACPA. However, the ACPA also says that a registrant can avoid a finding of bad faith if "the court determines that [he] believed and had reasonable grounds to believe that the use of the domain name was a fair use or otherwise lawful."

The courts have not yet had many opportunities to weigh these factors and provide guidance about when "bad faith" actually exists. But in one egregious case, a court found that a cybersquatter had violated all of the "bad faith" factors listed in the ACPA. In that case, the defendant made the mistake of registering domain names similar to the name of Morrison & Foerster, a well-known international law firm with a prominent intellectual property practice![4] Among other things, the court said, the defendant had no intellectual property rights to the Morrison & Foerster name; he was not known by either Morrison or Foerster; he had never used the name to conduct any business before registering the domain names; he obviously intended to divert the firm's clients by registering morrisonandfoerster.com (the firm operated under the whimsical mofo.com); he implied that the domain name was for sale by linking it to a website at

NameIsForSale.com; he supplied false contact information in his registration record and even changed a contact name to "DefaultData
.com"; and he had registered the names of more than 90 law firms.
As if those factors weren't enough, the court said it was most con-
vinced that the defendant had acted in bad faith based on a reason
not listed in the ACPA: He testified that he went "on a rampage" to
target law firms and the corporate community after a company re-
neged on a contract with him.

In the Morrison & Foerster case, the court ordered the defendant
to transfer the disputed domain names to the law firm and pay its
costs. But, as the Electronics Boutique case discussed in Chapter 5
showed, cybersquatting can prove quite costly: Courts have leeway
to award damages of anywhere from $1,000 to $100,000 per domain
name.

After a finding of "bad faith" under the ACPA, many of the additional requirements of the act are interpreted according to traditional
trademark law, as discussed in Chapter 6. For example, the requirement that a trademark be "distinctive" means that it must be arbitrary, fanciful, suggestive or, with sufficient use, descriptive; generic
marks would not qualify. The requirement that a trademark be "famous" is interpreted according to the factors listed in the U.S. Anti-
Dilution Act,[5] listed in Chapter 6.

Also, the requirement that a domain name must be either identical
or "confusingly similar" to the trademark involved is interpreted according to longstanding applications used in trademark infringement cases; for example, one court held in an ACPA case that
ernestandjuliogallo.com was sufficiently similar to the trademark
"Ernest & Julio Gallo" (despite the domain name's use of the word
"and" in lieu of the ampersand—a limitation of domain names because of the requirement that they use only alphanumeric characters
and the hyphen).[6]

Finally, to prevail under an ACPA claim, a trademark owner must
show that the defendant has registered, trafficked in, or used the domain name. This requirement is much broader than some courts had
applied in traditional trademark lawsuits involving domain names

before the ACPA, because now a defendant can be found liable for merely registering a domain name, even if he has not otherwise used it.

The ACPA has gone a long way toward reducing cybersquatting, although the practice still proliferates. And, while trademark owners have applauded this new trademark law, some critics have objected that it goes too far and tramples on people's rights to use others' trademarks in criticism or parody, uses that typically have been categorized as "fair" and legal under trademark law. Regardless, the ACPA is a formidable law that domain name registrants must respect.

CHAPTER NINE

The Uniform Domain Name Dispute Resolution Policy

Trademark owners who believe they have been wronged by someone registering a domain name identical or similar to their trademark can take advantage of the Uniform Domain Name Dispute Resolution Policy (UDRP), an administrative, out-of-court dispute process.[1] The UDRP was adopted by ICANN, the Internet Corporation for Assigned Names and Numbers, and, although it is used quite frequently, it is often criticized by those who believe it unfairly favors large companies over small, sometimes individual, domain name registrants. The truth is, the UDRP clearly favors trademark owners, but trademark owners can be individuals or multibillion-dollar corporations. And, it typically offers a quick, cost-efficient alternative to filing a lawsuit.

APPLICATION OF THE UNIFORM DOMAIN NAME DISPUTE
RESOLUTION POLICY

The UDRP applies to all "global" or "generic" top-level domains (gTLDs)—for a long time, mostly ".com," ".net," and ".org," but ICANN's seven new gTLDs (".aero," ".biz," ".coop," ".info," ".museum," ".name," and ".pro") are subject to the UDRP, too. The UDRP also has been adopted by the managers of a few country-code top-level domains (ccTLDs), including ".nu," ".tv," and ".ws," although—unlike the gTLDs—these managers are free to stop following the UDRP at any time. The majority of the two-hundred-plus ccTLD managers do not follow the UDRP. In addition, the UDRP is not applicable to the other popular gTLDs, such as ".gov," ".mil," and ".int," but these are not typically open to registration by most entities anyway.

You may wonder how it is possible that the UDRP is legally binding on domain name registrants. The answer is, usually, through a "click-wrap" agreement. (For more on the legal status of click-wrap agreements, see Chapter 29.) Most registrars inform anyone registering a new domain name that the registration is subject to the UDRP. This typically occurs during the online domain name registration process, where new customers are required to indicate their acceptance of various terms and conditions relating to the domain name. If customers do not click to agree, registrars will not allow them to continue with the registration process and obtain their domain name. For example, when registering a domain name with VeriSign's Network Solutions, a registrant must check a box that states: "I have read the service agreement and agree to its terms." The words "service agreement" are linked to a Web page containing a long list of terms applicable to the registration. Among many other things, the service agreement says: "The registrant acknowledges having read and understood and agrees to be bound by the terms and conditions of the following documents, as they may be amended from time to time, which are hereby incorporated and made an integral part of this Agreement . . . The Uniform Domain Name Dispute Policy. . . ."

So, like it or not, you have no choice when registering most domain names: You must agree to the terms of the UDRP.

WHAT THE UNIFORM DOMAIN NAME
DISPUTE RESOLUTION POLICY IS

The UDRP is a complicated document that is not always interpreted consistently. As a result, if you are a trademark owner and want to enforce your rights under the UDRP, or if you are a domain name registrant and have a UDRP complaint filed against you, you should immediately consult with an attorney familiar with this domain name dispute procedure. And although the UDRP has not changed since the current version was adopted in October 1999, it is subject to modification on thirty days' notice, so it's very important to keep up with any changes (including any that may have occurred since this chapter was written).

In general, the UDRP is an administrative process that can be used, in lieu of filing a lawsuit (such as one based on trademark infringement, trademark dilution, or the Anticybersquatting Consumer Protection Act), to obtain the transfer or cancellation of a domain name. The UDRP is usually much faster and less expensive than filing and pursuing a lawsuit and, for trademark owners, is often the preferable way of proceeding against a stubborn domain name registrant. Filing a UDRP action can cost as little as $1,500, which, although more than the cost of filing a lawsuit in federal court, is often the only substantial expense involved, because UDRP proceedings do not entail follow-up legal briefs and motions, depositions, or courtroom hearings. And unlike federal lawsuits, which can drag on for years, many UDRP proceedings are often resolved in a few months or less.

THE UNIFORM DOMAIN NAME DISPUTE RESOLUTION POLICY'S REQUIREMENTS

If you are a trademark owner who wants to file a UDRP complaint against a domain name registrant, you must first determine whether you meet the threshold requirements for doing so. To invoke the UDRP, at least three requirements must exist:

- The domain name in dispute must be identical or confusingly similar to a trademark or service mark in which you have rights.
- The domain name registrant must have no rights or legitimate interests in the domain name.
- The domain name must have been registered and be used in bad faith.

As stated in the UDRP, during the administrative proceeding, it will be your burden to prove that each of these elements exists. If you can prove these points to an administrative panel and if you meet the UDRP's other technical requirements, the panel may order that the domain name be canceled or transferred to you.

Despite its controversy, the UDRP is much better than a previous domain name dispute procedure employed by Network Solutions when it was the sole registrar of ".com," ".net," and ".org" domains. Under that now-outdated policy, a trademark owner could persuade Network Solutions to place a domain name "on hold," making it unavailable to the domain name registrant—but also making it unavailable to the trademark owner who filed the complaint! And under a loophole that existed for a while, some domain name registrants sought quick trademark registrations in the country of Tunisia, because the policy afforded certain protections to owners of federal trademarks. Tunisia, unlike the United States and most countries with sophisticated intellectual property laws, reportedly would grant a trademark registration in as little as twenty-four hours. Fortunately, domain name registrants and trademark owners need not play such games any longer, because the UDRP has closed some of these earlier loopholes.

To file a UDRP complaint, you will first need to select one of the approved dispute resolution service providers. As of mid-2002, four ICANN-approved services were in operation: the Asian Domain Name Dispute Resolution Centre;[2] the CPR Institute for Dispute Resolution;[3] the National Arbitration Forum;[4] and the World Intellectual Property Organization[5] (a fifth, eResolution, stopped accepting cases as of November 30, 2001[6]). Some lawyers and litigants have strong opinions about which provider is best or most favorable to a particular cause, and although panelists are required by the UDRP's rules to be "impartial and independent," you or your lawyer may want to spend some time evaluating how a particular provider—and even a specific panelist working for that provider—has ruled in previous domain name disputes. Either one or three panelists will review and decide each dispute. Although the providers are required to follow certain rules approved by ICANN,[7] the providers also may supplement the rules, so it's important to review all applicable documents before initiating a complaint. The rules discussed in this chapter do not include any specifically adopted by a particular provider.

The complaint must be submitted in hard copy and electronic format and must conform to a long list of requirements. Among many other things, the complaint must describe the following:

• the manner in which the domain name(s) is/are identical or confusingly similar to a trademark or service mark in which the complainant (that is, the person or company filing the complaint) has rights;

• why the domain name holder should be considered as having no rights or legitimate interests in respect of the domain name(s) that is/are the subject of the complaint; and

• why the domain name(s) should be considered as having been registered and being used in bad faith.

The complaint may include documentary or other evidence, but in-person hearings are forbidden unless the panel decides that the dispute is "exceptional" and a hearing is necessary.

The party filing a UDRP complaint also must undertake certain sometimes rigorous steps to ensure that the domain name registrant is notified of the action. Although all domain name registrants are required to provide accurate contact information when registering, many fail to do so, especially if they are purposefully trying to register a domain name they know is identical or confusingly similar to someone else's trademark. While this kind of false information actually can be used as evidence of the "bad faith" necessary to prevail under a UDRP action, it does not relieve the trademark owner of attempting to notify the registrant that a complaint has been filed. So, to help ensure that the domain name registrant is notified, the complainant must use "reasonably available means calculated to achieve actual notice." The UDRP rules specify a number of ways in which this can be accomplished.

The domain name registrant who has a UDRP complaint filed against him must respond to the complaint promptly—within twenty days of the start of the proceeding. If he fails to respond, the administrative panel likely will simply decide the dispute based on the complaint alone, which probably will be sufficient to rule against him. If the respondent does choose to reply, the UDRP requires the response, like the complaint, to be filed in hard copy and electronic format. Among many other requirements, the response must "[r]espond specifically to the statements and allegations contained in the complaint."

HOW PANELISTS DECIDE CASES UNDER THE
UNIFORM DOMAIN NAME DISPUTE RESOLUTION POLICY

So, how does an administrative panel make its decision? After ensuring that the technical formalities of the process have been met, the panel will review the complaint and response as well as any evidence submitted and decide whether the complainant has met the three UDRP requirements listed above.

The first UDRP requirement is that the domain name be "identical or confusingly similar to a trademark or service mark in which the complainant has rights." As simple as this language may seem, it contains a number of issues that need to be examined. It may be easy to determine when a domain name is "identical" to a trademark, as in the UDRP case involving microsoft.org[8]—but what about microoosoft.com (with two o's)? (A panel awarded the domain name be transferred to Microsoft because it was "both phonetically and visually the same as [Microsoft's] trademark.")[9] While plenty of decisions have found nonidentical domain names to be "confusingly similar," it is sometimes unclear what a particular panel will deem to be confusingly similar. In one case, for example, a WIPO panel found that aolteen.com was not confusingly similar to the AOL trademark owned by America Online, even though it acknowledged that some people would associate the domain name with AOL.[10] A second complicating issue in this first UDRP factor is whether the complainant "has rights" in a particular trademark or service mark. In one interesting case, for example, a WIPO panel found that Backstreet Boys Productions, Inc., did not have rights to the trademark BACKSTREET BOYS because, although that mark had been registered with the U.S. Patent and Trademark Office, it was owned by Backstreet Productions Inc., a different legal entity.[11] A case such as this emphasizes the importance of proper trademark management.

The second UDRP requirement is that the respondent have "no rights or legitimate interests in respect of the domain name." The UDRP lists three factors for panelists to consider, and if any one is present, then the respondent will prevail:

• before any notice to the Respondent of the dispute, the Respondent's use of, or demonstrable preparations to use, the domain name or a name corresponding to the domain name in connection with a bona fide offering of goods or services; or

• the Respondent (as an individual, business, or other organization) has been commonly known by the domain name, even if the Respondent has acquired no trademark or service mark rights; or

• the Respondent is making a legitimate noncommercial or fair use of the domain name, without intent for commercial gain to misleadingly divert consumers or to tarnish the trademark or service mark at issue.

The panel also may consider other factors.

Finally, the third and usually most difficult UDRP requirement is whether the domain name "has been registered and is being used in bad faith" by the respondent. Fortunately, the UDRP itself provides some guidance here. It says that any of the following is evidence of bad faith:

• circumstances indicating that the Respondent has registered or acquired the domain name primarily for the purpose of selling, renting, or otherwise transferring the domain name registration to the complainant who is the owner of the trademark or service mark or to a competitor of that complainant, for valuable consideration in excess of the Respondent's documented out-of-pocket costs directly related to the domain name; or

• the Respondent has registered the domain name in order to prevent the owner of the trademark or service mark from reflecting the mark in a corresponding domain name, provided that the Respondent has engaged in a pattern of such conduct; or

• the Respondent has registered the domain name primarily for the purpose of disrupting the business of a competitor; or

• by using the domain name, the Respondent has intentionally attempted to attract, for commercial gain, Internet users to its website or other online location, by creating a likelihood of confusion with the complainant's mark as to the source, sponsorship, affiliation, or endorsement of Respondent's website or location or of a product or service on Respondent's website or location.

The panel also may consider other factors in addition to those listed above.

SOME ODD RESULTS

You may be surprised to learn what various UDRP panels have found to be "bad faith" or not. Here are just a few examples, drawn from the more than five thousand proceedings involving nearly ten thousand domain names:

• In a dispute filed by the musician Bruce Springsteen against the registrant of the domain name brucespringsteen.com, a WIPO panel ruled that the registrant did not have "bad faith" because, among other things, the singer had a website at bruce springsteen.net, so the registrant did not prevent Springsteen from reflecting his trademark (that is, his name) in a "correspond-ing" domain name.[12]

• In a dispute filed by computer seller Gateway, Inc., over the domain name gateway-computer.com, a WIPO panel found bad faith because the registrant attempted to sell the domain name to "the logical targets" on eBay—Gateway and its competitors.[13] The panel noted that the respondent in that case also had registered compaq-computer.com and hp-computer.com.

• In a dispute filed by Time Warner Entertainment Company, L.P., against the registrant of numerous domain names containing "harrypotter"—including harrypottersstore.com, harrypottertwo .com, and theharrypottermovie.com—a WIPO panel ruled for Time Warner after the registrant failed to respond.[14] In finding bad faith, the panel said it "believes that the registration of over one hundred such [Harry Potter] domain names is sufficient to constitute a pattern of conduct."

• In a dispute filed by Victoria's Secret Stores, Inc., over the domain name victoriassecretexposed.com, a National Arbitration Forum panel found that the registrant had not acted in bad faith because none of the bad-faith circumstances stated in the UDRP applied and because Victoria's Secret's suggestion that the respondent "might have a planned use other than for commentary about Victoria's Secret's corporate policies [had] not been proven."[15]

As these cases illustrate, proving bad faith in a UDRP proceeding is not necessarily predictable. And while each of the few cases discussed above is different from the others, even cases with similar facts are sometimes decided differently. That's because, unlike in the court system, where precedent—that is, reliance on previous rulings—is key, panelists in UDRP proceedings are not bound by any other decisions. As a result, what constitutes bad faith to one panel may not constitute bad faith to another. This is one of the primary criticisms of the UDRP process.

Despite its flaws, the UDRP is a popular method for resolving domain name disputes. In most cases—about 80 percent—administrative panels have ruled in favor of the party who files the complaint. While some have argued that this shows the process is biased, it more likely shows that the process is working for trademark owners and helping to reduce the prevalence of cybersquatting. And in those cases where one party to a dispute believes that a panel's ruling was truly flawed, the UDRP may not be the final word. Although the UDRP has no process for appealing a decision, the UDRP does not prevent either party from filing a lawsuit after the UDRP's ruling has been issued. (At least one court, the U.S. District Court for the Eastern District of Virginia, in *Parisi* v. *Netlearning*,[16] has said that it is not bound by the outcome of a UDRP proceeding, though it is unclear what deference, if any, a court will give it; and another court, the U.S. Court of Appeals for the First Circuit, in *Sallen* v. *Corinthians*,[17] made clear that federal courts have jurisdiction over domain name disputes under the ACPA even after resolution under the UDRP.) If the suit is filed within ten business days after the ruling and the registrar is properly notified, the registrar will not implement the panel's decision until the lawsuit has been settled, dismissed, or resolved by a court order. (If either party files a lawsuit before or during a UDRP proceeding, the panel has the option to suspend or terminate its proceeding.)

CHAPTER TEN

Other Trademark Issues

It may appear as if domain names are the only trademark-related issue on the Internet, but that's not true. Although domain names clearly represent an extremely important part of Internet trademark law, there are other issues you should know about, too. To avoid legal problems online, you should keep trademarks in mind as you select a company, product, or service name and also as you build your website.

REAL-LIFE EXAMPLES OF TRADEMARK VIOLATIONS AND THE INTERNET

Amazingly, even some of the largest computer and Internet companies in the world have made some pretty poor decisions on trademarks, which often have proved costly. A look at just some of these

issues, drawn from news reports in the past few years, should help
you realize the importance of taking trademarks seriously:

• The Walt Disney Company was sued by GoTo.com, Inc., after
Disney launched its Go Network in December 1998. Disney had
adopted a logo for the site that resembled a traffic light, specifically,
a green circle within a yellow square with the word "GO" in the
middle in a white font. However, GoTo.com previously had begun
using a logo on its site with the words "GO" and "TO" in a white
font stacked vertically within a green circle and often displayed
against a square yellow background. A court ruled that the two
companies' logos were "remarkably similar."[1] As a result, not only
did Disney change its logo, but it paid GoTo.com an astounding
$21.5 million to avoid a judge or jury from awarding damages.[2]

• In an Internet trademark case of similar proportions, a jury
awarded Simon Property Group (the owner and operator of retail shopping malls) $26.8 million in damages after mySimon,
Inc. (an online comparative shopping service), began using the
"Simon" trademark. Although a federal district court rejected
Simon Property Group's claims of trademark dilution (because
its "Simon" trademark did not meet the U.S. Anti-Dilution Act's
requirement of famousness), a jury found that mySimon had
committed trademark infringement. A judge set aside most of
the jury's verdict on damages but entered a permanent injunction against mySimon, preventing it from using the "mySimon"
name, the domain name mysimon.com, and the character named
"Simon."[3]

• In 1998, Microsoft paid $5 million to a defunct Internet
company to settle a trademark infringement lawsuit over rights to
the name "Internet Explorer."[4] SyNet said it started using the
name in 1994, before Microsoft began distributing its identically
named Web browser. "We are confident we would have won this
case on the merits, but we are pleased to put this issue behind us,"
a company spokesman said.

• As if Napster didn't have enough legal problems defending itself against charges of copyright infringement from the music industry, the company sued an online retailer for using its trademark cat design on T-shirts and caps.[5]

• An Internet-based education company named itself "NotHarvard.com" and, after hearing from the obvious university, filed a declaratory judgment suit asking a court to protect its name. However, after Harvard University countersued for trademark infringement, NotHarvard.com quickly changed its name to Powered.[6]

• Cobalt Networks suggested that it might file a trademark suit against Apple after the personal computer company unveiled its "Cube" computer.[7] "In 1998 we brought out the Qube, which measured seven inches by seven inches by eight inches, and guess what? Apple later launched a product called the Cube that just happened to measure seven inches by seven inches by eight inches," a Cobalt official said, although no lawsuit was ever filed.

• Microsoft paid an undisclosed sum to a company called XBOX Technologies to settle a dispute over rights to the "Xbox" trademark.[8] XBOX Technologies had filed federal trademark applications to use the name more than six months before Microsoft.

• Proving that not all trademark disputes involve names, computer maker Gateway—whose advertisements, hardware boxes, and even mouse pads sport a distinctive cow-spot design—sued a company that used a black-and-white cow pattern on a portable compact disc holder. Gateway has a registered trademark for black cow spots on a white background for computer-related items.[9] A settlement prevented the defendant from using the pattern.

META TAGS

Finally, in addition to obvious trademark issues such as company, product, and service names, you need to be aware of subtler trademark traps on the Internet. One particularly important area involves the use of trademarks in "meta tags." As you may know, the HTML code that makes up every page on the Web can contain various elements that have nothing to do with the page's display, including so-called meta tags that include details such as a description of the site and relevant keywords; these are used by some search engines to help index pages, allowing Web surfers who enter search terms to find tagged pages.

However, because the meta tags are entirely within a website designer's control, the tags are not limited to including information solely about the products and services offered on that particular site. The tags can include information about anything, including a competitor's products or services. Some companies have found that doing so is a tricky way to attract visitors looking for a competitor's website. And some companies have found that doing so can constitute a violation of U.S. trademark law.

In more than one case, a defendant has been ordered to alter or delete its meta tags after a plaintiff has filed a trademark lawsuit against it. In one case, a court enjoined the manufacturer of turbine engines from using the word "Seawind" in its meta tags because the plaintiff owned trademark rights to that word, which it used as the name of an amphibious aircraft kit it manufactured. The court said it "agrees that defendants intentionally use plaintiffs' marks in this way to lure internet users to their site instead of [the plaintiffs'] official site. . . . [B]ased on the repetitive usage and the evidence of defendants' general intent to harm plaintiffs, . . . it is a bad faith effort to confuse internet users that is likely to succeed."

And, in another case, an appeals court ruled against West Coast Entertainment, which used the term "MovieBuff" in meta tags on its website, in a trademark lawsuit brought by Brookfield Communications, which apparently began using "MovieBuff" as a trademark first.[10] "Web surfers looking for Brookfield's 'MovieBuff' products who are taken by a search engine to 'westcoastvideo.com' will find a database similar enough to 'MovieBuff' such that a sizeable number of consumers who were originally looking for Brookfield's product will simply decide to utilize West Coast's offerings instead," the court found. The court found that this type of confusion—what it called "initial interest confusion"—is "exactly what the trademark laws are designed to prevent."

However, not all uses of a meta tag containing someone else's trademarks constitute trademark violations, as one well-known and important case involving popular Internet law litigant Playboy indicates. In that case, Terri Welles, a former *Playboy* magazine cover model and "Playmate of the Year" (1981), created a website of her own in 1997 at www.terriwelles.com. The heading of the site said, "Terri Welles—Playmate of the Year 1981," and the title was "Terri Welles—Playboy Playmate of the Year 1981." Each page also used "PMOY '81" as a repeating watermark in the background. In addition, the words "Playboy" and "Playmate" were used as keywords in meta tags on the site. The site also included a disclaimer on most of the pages, which stated: "This site is neither endorsed, nor sponsored by, nor affiliated with Playboy Enterprises, Inc. PLAYBOY, PLAYMATE OF THE YEAR and PLAYMATE OF THE MONTH are registered trademarks of Playboy Enterprises, Inc."

Despite this disclaimer, Playboy Enterprises, Inc. (PEI), which was building its own significant presence on the Internet, was obviously not pleased with Welles's use of its trademarks, and it filed a complaint against her, alleging, among other things, trademark infringement and trademark dilution. Welles's primary defense was that her use of the Playboy trademarks was protected by "fair use" because she used the marks in a factual manner to describe herself. The court agreed, and, on the meta tag issue, said:[11]

> Finding that Ms. Welles' use of PEI's trademarked terms in the metatags of her website is a fair use comports with the fact web users must utilize identifying words to find their intended site.

Not all web searches utilizing the words "Playboy," "Playmate," and "Playboy Playmate of the Year 1981" are intended to find "Playboy" goods or the official "Playboy" site. Plaintiff has not addressed the fact that Ms. Welles' fame and recognition derive from her popularity as a Playboy model and Playmate of the Year. If a consumer cannot remember her name, the logical way to find her site on the web is by using key words that identify her source of recognition to the public: "Playboy Playmate of the Year 1981," "Playboy," and "Playmate." These are the words to which PEI objects. PEI, however, fails to suggest alternative, non-offending words to locate Ms. Welles' website. The World Wide Web is a commercial marketplace and a free speech marketplace. To give consumers access to it, the court must also be careful to give consumers the freedom to locate desired sites while protecting the integrity of trademarks and trade names. The court stresses that the underlying or foundational purpose of trademark protection is *not* to create a property interest in *all* words used in a commercial context, but rather "[t]he policies of free competition and free use of language dictate that trademark law cannot forbid the commercial use of terms in their descriptive sense." . . . As Justice Holmes in [a 1924 case] put more eloquently, "[W]hen the mark is used in a way that does not deceive the public we see no such sanctity in the word as to prevent its being used to tell the truth."

As a result, the court granted Welles's request for a ruling in her favor on the trademark infringement claim related to the meta tags on her site. And the court also found that the meta tags did not constitute trademark dilution.

The truth is, the courts are still learning how to apply traditional trademark law in this area. But a few rules are clear, at least as of now: If you are using someone else's trademarks in your meta tags to divert traffic from the trademark owner's website, you may be violating the trademark owner's legal rights. But if you are using the trademarks in a factual manner to describe content otherwise legally permissible on your site, you may be protected by the "fair use" privilege of trademark law.

Along with cybersquatting, the trademark issues discussed in this chapter represent many of the most common legal problems companies and individuals face on the Internet. Unlike in the "physical world," where bricks and mortar can be as important as a name, on the Internet trademarks are even more important. To protect yourself in cyberspace, you must know how to use trademarks properly to avoid violating someone else's rights. And if your rights are violated, you need to take action, because trademark law requires it. If you fail to "police" your trademark rights on the Internet (or anywhere else), you risk a court finding that you've lost your rights.

PART III

PATENT LAW

CHAPTER ELEVEN

CASE STUDY: AN INTRODUCTION TO PATENTS ON THE INTERNET, *AMAZON.COM* V. *BARNESANDNOBLE.COM*

In the fall of 1999, excitement over the Internet was contagious. Numerous startup companies had raised significant funds to grow their Internet-enabled businesses, and the promise of a "new economy" driven by new communication technologies created a great deal of optimism regarding the potential of the Internet.

Among the companies at the time already benefiting from Internet-enabled communication were Amazon.com and Barnes andNoble.com, which both sold (and continue to sell) books and other products online. By the fall of 1999, Amazon.com, which had opened its online doors in July 1995, had several years under its belt as an online retailer and was quickly becoming a household name in the fast-growing e-commerce space. Likewise, BarnesandNoble.com, which opened online in March 1997, was gaining in popularity, perhaps in part because of its affiliated and well-known Barnes & Noble chain of traditional retail bookstores.

At the time, both Amazon.com and BarnesandNoble.com were building strong followings among customers who were seeking a convenient and powerful tool for researching, sharing information about, and purchasing books. Both Amazon.com and BarnesandNoble.com invested heavily in adding features to their websites that would create a more convenient, powerful, and enjoyable experience for their customers. While Amazon.com and BarnesandNoble.com seemingly were headed down a similar path in building their on-line businesses, there was one major distinction that set them apart: Amazon.com actively sought patent protection for its innovation, and BarnesandNoble.com did not.

At first glance, patents seem a bit out of place in the world of retailing (even online retailing). Traditionally, patents have been associated with more industrial or scientific innovations, such as machinery, manufacturing processes, computer chips, and pharmaceuticals. However, as technology changes, so do the patent laws available to protect it.

On September 12, 1997, Amazon.com filed a patent application with the U.S. Patent and Trademark Office[1] (PTO) for a "Method and System for Placing a Purchase Order via a Communications Network" (see sidebar, "Amazon.com's '1-Click' Patent," on page 109). In its patent application, Amazon.com claimed as its invention a business methodology for placing an order, whereby in response to only a single action performed by a consumer (such as the click of a mouse), a requested item may be ordered. Additional information necessary to complete the order, such as credit card number and shipping address, is obtained from information previously received from the consumer and stored in a database by the vendor. In part due to a federal appeals court ruling in 1998 that business methodologies could be patented, the U.S. Patent Office granted Amazon.com's patent on September 25, 1999. U.S. Patent No. 5,960,411[2] was born—dubbed the "1-click" patent because users of the invention need click only once with the mouse on a hyperlink to complete the purchase of an item.

Amazon.com's "1-Click" Patent

Contrary to what has been reported in the popular press, the invention claimed in Amazon.com's U.S. Patent No. 5,960,411 is actually a bit more specific than simply "1-click." For example, claim 1 (of twenty-five claims) of the patent reads:

A method of placing an order for an item comprising:

- under control of a client system,
  - ○ displaying information identifying the item; and
  - ○ in response to only a single action being performed, sending a request to order the item along with an identifier of a purchaser of the item to a server system;
- under control of a single-action ordering component of the server system,
  - ○ receiving the request;
  - ○ retrieving additional information previously stored for the purchaser identified by the identifier in the received request; and
- generating an order to purchase the requested item for the purchaser identified by the identifier in the received request using the retrieved additional information; and
- fulfilling the generated order to complete purchase of the item
- whereby the item is ordered without using a shopping cart ordering model.

Like any patent claim, in order to infringe claim 1, an alleged infringer (such as BarnesandNoble.com) must practice *all* of the elements in the claim. If even one element of the claim is not being practiced by the alleged infringer, then there is no infringement. Thus, while the popular press sometimes may generalize

> what is covered by a patent, without a detailed analysis of the
> patent claims, it is impossible to truly understand the protection
> that the Patent Office granted.

Under U.S. patent law, a patent grants its owner the right to exclude others from making, using, selling, or offering to sell the patented invention. As the owner of the "1-click" patent, Amazon .com therefore could attempt to stop others from using it by pursuing legal claims for patent infringement, or Amazon.com could seek to license its patent to others in exchange for payment of some type of royalty fee or similar arrangement.

Perhaps not surprisingly, Amazon.com acted quickly after its patent was issued. Knowing that the December 1999 holiday shopping season was soon approaching, and that online sales would be brisk, Amazon.com decided to strike while the iron was hot. Soon after its "1-click" patent was issued, Amazon.com sued Barnesand Noble.com for infringement of the patent, arguing that Barnes andNoble.com incorporated into its website Amazon.com's patented functionality. Rather than just seeking monetary damages, Amazon .com requested that the court grant an injunction against Barnes andNoble.com, so that BarnesandNoble.com would have to remove the patented functionality, at least until the dispute was resolved. Injunctions in patent infringement actions are rare and are granted only in exceptional circumstances where the facts and the law clearly appear to favor the patent holder's position. Nevertheless, on December 1, 1999, the court went ahead and granted the injunction, forcing BarnesandNoble.com to immediately remove the allegedly infringing functionality from its website.[3] With no other option, BarnesandNoble.com complied with the court's order, by adding an additional step to its online ordering system.

The court's decision no doubt stunned BarnesandNoble.com, as it was focusing its efforts on the holiday shopping season. Barnesand-Noble.com's website suddenly became less convenient as compared to Amazon.com's site, given that BarnesandNoble.com's customers could no longer use the time-saving "1-click" feature claimed in Amazon.com's patent. While it is difficult to quantify the resulting effect the injunction had on BarnesandNoble.com's business, it no doubt caused a great deal of embarrassment to BarnesandNoble.com and certainly put it at a disadvantage feature-wise with Amazon.com.

In February 2001, the court lifted the injunction against BarnesandNoble.com, holding that BarnesandNoble.com had mounted a substantial challenge to the validity of the Amazon.com patent, and therefore the injunction should not stand.[4] Amazon.com and BarnesandNoble.com eventually settled the lawsuit in March 2002, although the terms of the settlement were not publicly disclosed.[5]

Some commentators have criticized the "1-click" patent as an example of a patent system gone astray. These critics contend that the patent system has been stretched too far with the allowance of business-method patents, and that even if business methods are worthy of patent protection, the U.S. Patent and Trademark Office is not equipped to handle the examination of patent applications for this type of innovation. At the same time, others herald the patenting of business methods as a natural progression in an ever-changing, technology-driven world. As so often, the truth probably lies somewhere in between.

Regardless, few will dispute that business-method patents, as well as software patents in general, are having a profound impact on how software and Internet companies are conducting business. Technology companies that just a few years ago wouldn't have ever considered the impact of patent protection—either offensively or defensively—are now devoting many resources to ensuring they are protected, and minimizing the possibility of infringing third-party patent rights. Those companies that don't consider these issues do so at their peril.

CHAPTER TWELVE

THE BASICS OF PATENT LAW AND PROTECTION

A U.S. patent is a contract between an inventor and the government. Like all contracts, both parties to a patent (the inventor and the government) agree to certain obligations, and in exchange for this agreement expect certain benefits from the contract.

THE PURPOSE OF PATENT LAW

The purpose behind the patent "contract" is to encourage inventors to disclose inventions to the public. Without some form of patent protection, inventors may be reluctant or unwilling to spend time and money developing inventions, or even if they did develop inventions, they might otherwise keep the inventions secret. Because it is in society's best interest to encourage innovation and to have such innovations made public, the U.S. patent laws[1] were created to provide an incentive to inventors to innovate and to publicly disclose their inventions.

Because the ultimate purpose behind patents is public disclosure of inventions, an inventor's obligations under a patent include disclosing the invention in sufficient detail that a person working in the particular field of technology would be able to take the disclosure and actually make and use the invention. The inventor also has an obligation to disclose the best-known way of implementing the invention.

These obligations of the inventor are quite important, because if the government is to grant patent rights to an inventor, the government needs to ensure that the inventor has upheld his or her side of the bargain. Full disclosure of the invention is therefore an important obligation of the inventor, to ensure the public ultimately benefits from the patent.

COMPARISON WITH OTHER FORMS OF INTELLECTUAL PROPERTY

Unlike other forms of intellectual property protection in the United States, such as trademarks (see Chapter 6) and copyrights (see Chapter 2), patent rights do not automatically arise upon creation of the underlying invention. Whereas trademark rights can exist the moment a mark is first used in commerce, and copyright protection may arise simply by creating a work of expression in a tangible form, patent rights come into being only if a patent application is filed with the U.S. Patent and Trademark Office[2] (PTO) and the application is ultimately granted. (Trademarks and copyrights also can be protected by registering them, but the registrations are not essential.) Moreover, failure to timely file a patent application can result in an effective donation of any available patent rights to the public domain, essentially forfeiting something that might otherwise have been protectable by patent laws.

Another major difference between patents and other forms of intellectual property is the length of protection. While copyright protection can last ninety-five years or longer, and trademark protection can last indefinitely, under current U.S. law patents generally expire twenty years after a patent application is filed (although this term can be extended in certain limited circumstances, such as if the PTO delays in granting the patent, or for pharmaceutical inventions that must go through an approval process with the Food and Drug Administration). While the *term* of a patent can be considerably less than copyright and trademark protection, this distinction quite often can be offset by the *scope* of protection afforded by a patent. Patent protection may provide a much broader level of protection, and can be more difficult to circumvent, than copyright protection (at least for software inventions), so the shorter term of protection matters less than the potentially valuable and broad scope of protection patents offer.

REQUIREMENTS FOR PATENTABILITY

To be patentable, an invention must be useful, novel (new), and nonobvious. If these tests are met, then an inventor is entitled to patent protection and the government is obligated to grant it. A patent entitles the patent owner (the inventor, the inventor's employer, etc.) to exclude others from making, using, selling, or even offering to sell the patented invention.

It is important to understand that patent rights are exclusionary in this manner—the patent owner does not necessarily have the right to make, use, sell, and offer to sell the patented invention, since the patent owner's rights might be subject to the patent rights of others. This distinction can most readily be understood with the classic stool/chair illustration. Suppose a first inventor invents and obtains a patent on a stool, and a second inventor invents and obtains a patent on a chair (which is essentially an improved stool). The first patent owner may be able to exclude the second patent owner from making, using, selling, and offering to sell both a stool and a chair, since both might be covered by the first broad patent. Thus, even though the second patent owner has a patent on a chair, he or she may be unable to make, use, sell, or offer to sell a chair without infringing the first patent. Therefore, to take advantage of his or her patent in the chair, the second patent owner would have to obtain certain rights from the first patent owner. It is for this reason that patent rights are exclusionary in nature, and only govern what rights the patent owner has with respect to others.

THE ADVANTAGES OF PATENT PROTECTION

In certain situations, patents can serve as a valuable, and even critical, asset for a business that has developed innovative technology. Patents by themselves seldom make a company successful; they must be part of an otherwise sound business plan. However, in some cases, failure to secure patent protection can have disastrous results for a company.

Obviously, if a company develops an innovative technology that is at the core of the company's business, then patent protection makes perfect sense in order to provide exclusivity in the relevant market. One or more patents may be obtained on the core technology, as well as related technologies, to maintain the company's market position.

In contrast, when a company begins developing technology that is perhaps not part of its core business but that may somehow support it, then a decision has to be made whether patent protection is worthwhile. Obtaining a patent can be expensive, and a cost-benefit analysis must be performed: Does the benefit of obtaining the patent justify the cost?

However, there may be ancillary reasons, rather than purely offensive, to obtain a patent. For example, if an invention is made at a company, yet the company has no intentions of marketing a product based on the technology, a patent might still have value as a source of licensing revenue, that is, requiring payment from others who want to market products based on the technology. (For more on patent licensing, see Chapter 14.) Or the patent may have value defensively, such as if a competitor has products or services within the patented field. In such a case, the patent owner may have no plans whatsoever to assert the patent against others, but the patent serves as an "insurance policy" to thwart a patent attack by the competitor.

In the end, many companies strike a balance between adequately protecting themselves offensively and defensively, and spending their resources on patent protection. Core technologies and technologies that offer a strategic advantage over competition are protected, while other less relevant technologies are not.

PATENT OWNERSHIP

According to U.S. patent law, an application for a patent must be filed in the name of the inventor or coinventors (in contrast to much of the rest of the world, which allows companies to file patent applications in their own name). Moreover, absent an agreement to the contrary, the inventors are considered to be the initial owners of the patent application and any patent that issues from it. This can be true even for an invention developed by an employee within the scope of the employee's job duties. (This is quite different from copyright ownership, in which employers automatically obtain ownership of copyrighted works created by their employees under the "work made for hire" doctrine, discussed in Chapter 2.) This can also be true for an invention developed by third-party contractors who are paid by a company to invent. By default, the employee or contractor owns the patent, not the company, even if the company paid a salary or other fee to the employee or contractor for the inventive work.

It is therefore imperative for companies to require employees and outside contractors to be subject to a written agreement regarding ownership of inventions and patents. In such an agreement, it must be clear that the employee or contractor is obligated to transfer ownership of inventions and patents to the company, and to cooperate with the company in signing any documents and performing any other steps to ensure that ownership is duly transferred. This latter requirement can be important, because after a patent application is filed, inventors are required to execute a formal assignment document, which preferably should be recorded with the U.S. Patent and Trademark Office, to perfect ownership of the patent application and resulting patent with the company.

Failure to enter into a written agreement with employees and contractors can cause major problems later, in the event that the individual decides not to cooperate with the company (a more common situation than many people would think, especially if the value of the patent causes the inventor to rethink his or her relationship with the company!). With an agreement, the company has a legally binding contract that can be enforced against the inventor. Also, the PTO has provisions for dealing with uncooperative inventors who are otherwise obligated to sign various papers required by this government agency, and a written agreement with the inventor can provide the necessary evidence for the company to proceed without the inventor, if needed.

Thus, as a matter of course, and preferably as a precondition of employment or becoming a contractor with the company, it is to a company's benefit that an individual always should be required to sign an appropriate agreement with the company. Because it can sometimes be difficult to have such an agreement signed after the fact, this step should be taken at an early stage in the relationship.

THE PATENT APPLICATION PROCESS

Prior Art

Patent attorneys often recommend to their clients that a search for "prior art" be performed before a decision is made whether to apply for patent protection. Prior art is essentially those prior published documents and activities that serve as evidence of the state of the art. Since a patentable invention must not only be useful but also new and nonobvious, the U.S. Patent and Trademark Office will compare the patent application to the prior art to determine whether the latter two tests are satisfied. If the invention as claimed in the patent application is deemed to be new and nonobvious over the prior art, then the PTO will grant a patent.

Traditionally, prior art searches have been performed by professional searchers who manually search the records of the Patent Office for prior issued patents and other technical literature. This type of search may be sufficient for simple inventions, but with more complex inventions (such as biotechnology and software) and inventions in fast-moving technologies (such as the Internet), traditional searching techniques are often inadequate. Because prior art may be found in commercially available online databases (such as Lexis and Dialog), on the World Wide Web, as well as in specialized databases, these additional search locations also may be explored for search purposes.

Once the results of the search(es) are in hand, the patent attorney often is asked to render an opinion of patentability—that is, whether the invention is likely patentable over the known prior art, and if so, what aspects of the invention might be patentable. This opinion serves both to aid the inventor in determining whether a patent application is justified and, if so, to help the patent attorney in due course to determine how broadly to claim the invention in the patent application.

Timing of Patent Applications

In the United States, the timing of the filing of a patent application can be critical. If the filing of the patent application is delayed too long, then patent protection may be barred, and the invention effectively donated to the public domain. Specifically, according to U.S. patent law, a patent application must be filed within one year of any one of the following events:

- the description of the invention in a publication;
- the public use of the invention;
- the patenting of the invention by another; or
- an offer to sell the invention (regardless of whether a sale is made).

Therefore, if any one of these events occurs, then a one-year timer begins, and if a patent application is not filed within the one-year period, patent protection is barred. This can be problematic for companies that are trying to market or otherwise publicize their inventions, as it forces a decision to be made soon thereafter whether to pursue patent protection.

It is important to note that the United States has some of the more lenient rules regarding timing, and that most other countries have no such one-year grace period. For example, in Europe, if an invention is described in a publication or is otherwise publicized before a patent application is filed, then patent protection is barred. Thus, for companies interested in patent protection outside the United States, the lowest common denominator requires that a patent application be filed before *any* publication or public disclosure of the invention, to maintain the possibility of patent protection.

The Patent Application

If the inventor (or the inventor's employer) decides to move forward with a patent application, the inventor and the patent attorney begin working together to draft a patent application. A regular utility patent application contains two parts: (1) a detailed specification, describing how to make and use the invention, and (2) one or more patent claims, which define the scope of the invention.

The detailed specification can be thought of as the proof that the inventor actually knows how to make and use the invention. While there is no requirement that the inventor actually build a prototype of the invention, the written specification must be sufficiently detailed that an ordinary designer in the field of the invention (such as an ordinary software programmer or Web designer) would be able to review the specification and actually make and use the invention, without further input from the inventor. The specification need not be a basic tutorial in the relevant technical field; it can assume that the reader has a basic understanding of the technical field and has access to reference material as needed. However, the specification cannot leave out any substantive details of the invention, and the best-known way for implementing the invention also must be included.

The patent claims are sentences that define the scope of the invention, and they are analogous to the "metes and bounds" of a real estate land deed. In the same way that any deed for the sale of land will include a legal description of the land owned, a patent claim comprises a sentence that defines the essential elements of the invention protected by the patent. To infringe a patent, a person or entity must make, use, sell, or offer to sell a product, or use a process, that falls within the scope of at least one claim of the patent. If one or more elements of each claim of a patent is missing, then there is no infringement.

At least some of the patent claims are initially drafted so that they define the invention as broadly as possible, with other claims defining the invention more narrowly. Generally speaking, shorter patent claims are broader, because they have fewer "limitations" in them. To be valid, patent claims must find "support" in the specification— that is, the claimed invention must be described in detail in the specification.

Once the patent application is drafted, it is filed with the PTO. Ultimately, a patent examiner is assigned to review the patent application, and the examiner initially reviews the application and performs a search for prior art related to the claimed invention. The patent examiner thereafter compares the patent claims to the prior art and makes an initial determination whether the claimed invention satisfies the tests for patentability—useful, new, and nonobvious. If the invention is deemed useful, and it is new and nonobvious over the prior art, then the patent application is allowed to issue as a patent.

More often than not, the patent examiner will reject the patent claims as being too broad, or having some syntactical problems. Similar to the process for registering a trademark, a written "office action" is mailed from the PTO to the patent attorney, outlining the rejections and inviting the patent attorney to respond. The patent attorney and the inventor may thereafter review the office action, as well as the cited prior art, and respond by amending the patent claims and/or presenting an argument that the patent claims are in fact patentable. This process is repeated, until (hopefully) the patent examiner allows the patent application to issue.

In the United States, while the patent application is pending (before issuance as a patent), it is generally maintained in secrecy by the PTO. The only exception to this rule is if the patent application is also filed in foreign countries or jurisdictions. If so, then the patent application is published eighteen months after the original filing date. If the patent application is filed just in the United States, then only after the patent actually issues are all the details of the patent application published—including the detailed description of the invention, the patent claims, and all correspondence between the patent examiner and the inventor.

Issuance of the Patent

Once a patent issues, it is made public and is enforceable by its owner against others (except in certain cases when a patent application is published before issuance of a patent, there is no enforceable protection while the patent application is pending). The patent owner may use the patent to extract a royalty or other compensation from an infringer or even attempt to force an infringer to stop infringing altogether. If the patent owner can't persuade an accused infringer to pay or to stop infringing, a lawsuit may be filed in federal court to enforce the patent rights, to recover monetary compensation, or to pursue an injunction or temporary restraining order against the infringer. (Patent infringement is discussed in further detail in Chapter 14.)

Because a patent application is examined by a patent examiner, it is presumed to be valid by the courts. While patents can be invalidated for a variety of reasons, it is an accused infringer's burden to prove that a patent is invalid and should not have been granted. Some of the reasons that a patent may be invalidated include prior art not previously considered by the patent examiner, insufficient disclosure of the invention, or fraud perpetrated on the Patent Office by the inventor.

Finally, after issuance of a patent, the Patent Office requires periodic maintenance fees to be paid, to keep the patent active. Specifically, within four, eight, and twelve years after issuance of a patent, escalating fees must be paid to the Patent Office; otherwise the patent becomes abandoned and unenforceable.

PATENT PROTECTION IN OTHER COUNTRIES AND JURISDICTIONS

Because each country or region has its own patent laws, patents are territorial by definition. A U.S. patent is enforceable only in the United States and its territories; thus, if an inventor wishes to obtain patent protection elsewhere, patent applications must be filed in other jurisdictions. While most countries have their own patent laws, certain regional patent systems have been created in recent years, including in Europe,[3] the former Soviet Union,[4] and Africa, which maintains one office for many French-speaking countries[5] and another for many English-speaking countries.[6]

While a separate patent system exists in most countries and jurisdictions outside the United States, certain treaties have been developed to help coordinate the pursuit of patents around the world. Both the Paris Convention[7] and the Patent Cooperation Treaty[8] have been signed by many countries and jurisdictions, and they help streamline the patent process. The Paris Convention allows an inventor to file a patent application in a first country, and then to file a patent application in a second country within a year of the first filing, while obtaining for priority purposes the benefit of the first filing date. The Patent Cooperation Treaty allows an inventor to file an "international application," which delays the time by which patent applications must be filed in other countries or jurisdictions by up to thirty months.

In the United States, if two inventors are independently developing similar inventions, a patent will be awarded to the first to invent, with certain restrictions. This differs from almost all other countries and jurisdictions, which instead of a "first to invent" system have a "first to file" system. Thus, in most countries outside the United States, the first to file a patent application will be awarded the patent, without regard to who invented first.

The U.S. patent system also differs from most of the rest of the world in that in the United States an inventor has up to a year to file a patent application after the invention has first been publicly disclosed, published, or offered for sale, as discussed above. Most other countries and jurisdictions follow an "absolute novelty" rule, which provides no such one-year grace period. In those countries and jurisdictions, if the invention has been publicly disclosed before a patent application is filed, then the inventor is barred from obtaining a patent on this invention.

CHAPTER THIRTEEN

Patents for Software and Internet Business Methods

Although patent law is not new, it has taken on new significance in recent years because of the rise of the high-tech economy. Software and "business methods"—two mainstays of many Internet companies—are each protectable by patents in the United States (and software is also protectable by copyright law, as discussed below and in Chapter 2), though the scope of protection is still emerging and often controversial. While the courts and Congress debate the future of patent protection for high-tech inventions, any company that creates software or invents new methods of doing business on the Internet must consider the tremendous benefits available under the patent laws.

THE RISE AND LIMITS OF COPYRIGHT PROTECTION
FOR SOFTWARE

Computer programs, either in their original "source code" format (readable by human beings) or in their "object code" format (readable only by computers), are generally deemed to fall within the definition of a "writing" for copyright purposes. In fact, in 1980, the U.S. copyright laws were amended to make explicit that computer programs, to the extent they embody an author's original creation, are a proper subject matter of copyright. However, this has not always been clear, and even today the scope of copyright protection for software is sometimes unclear, despite—or perhaps because of—varying interpretations by the courts. As a result, patent protection for software has taken on a greater importance as it has become recognized by the courts.

Perhaps the most notable software copyright case in the mid-1980s was *Whelan Associates, Inc.* v. *Jaslow Dental Laboratory, Inc.,*[1] a 1986 case from the U.S. Court of Appeals for the Third Circuit. In *Whelan,* the defendant obtained an unauthorized copy of the plaintiff's source code for its software and developed its own competing version of the plaintiff's software application. In finding for the plaintiff, the court ruled that "copyright protection of computer programs may extend beyond the programs' literal code to their *structure, sequence* and *organization.*" In reaching this decision, the court noted that the majority of the creative effort in developing a computer program involves the design rather than the mere coding of the program. The court in *Whelan* therefore created a relatively broad definition for copyrightable subject matter of software—everything that is not necessary to the computer program's purpose or function, including its "structure, sequence and organization."

After the *Whelan* case was decided, a number of later cases cited *Whelan* for support, including some cases that purportedly upheld copyright protection for the "look and feel" of software. While many of these cases utilized the very general and broad test outlined in *Whelan,* a number of the cases took different approaches, resulting in much confusion as to the appropriate scope of copyright protection for software. And in one case, *Computer Associates International* v. *Altai, Inc.,*[2] a court specifically rejected the simplistic test regarding the scope of copyright protection formulated in *Whelan.*

In *Computer Associates,* the U.S. Court of Appeals for the Second Circuit in 1992 developed a three-part test for determining whether software is infringed under the copyright laws. The test, which has become known as the "abstraction/filtration/comparison" test, is based upon a similar copyright infringement test enunciated by Judge Learned Hand in 1930, many years before the introduction of computer software. In the first step of the revised *Computer Associates* test, the computer program is divided into its various levels of abstraction. The second test, the "filtration step," entails examining the structural components of the software at each level of abstraction to determine (1) whether their particular inclusion at that level was an "idea" or was dictated by considerations of efficiency, (2) whether their inclusion was required by factors external to the program itself, such as a required data input or output protocol, or (3) whether the structural components were taken from the public domain. If a particular structural component at each level of abstraction satisfies any of the three criteria, then it is an expression not protectable by copyright law, and it is not considered in the final step of the test, described next. The third and final step, the "comparison" step, involves comparing the expression left after the filtration step at each level of abstraction to the accused software to determine whether there is substantial similarity between the two. If there is substantial similarity, and it can be shown that the developer of the accused software had access to the original software, then copyright infringement may be found.

While the *Computer Associates* test may be confusing, the important point is this: It has been adopted fairly uniformly in court decisions around the country and is likely to result in a lesser scope of copyright protection for computer software than the old *Whelan* test. The *Whelan* test gave a more expansive view of protectable copyright expression, while the *Computer Associates* test provides a more detailed approach whereby great care is taken to examine the software code on many levels and to remove nonprotectable expression before an infringement comparison is made. Regardless of which test is more appropriate, it is clear that the *Computer Associates* test represents a general narrowing of protection afforded to software under the copyright laws.

Also, under either test, the scope of copyright protection for software in general can be somewhat limited. As discussed in Chapter 2, the copyright laws serve to protect the "writings" of "authors" against unauthorized copying. Only those works that are "original" are protected; therefore, independent creation by another without access to the copyrighted work would not be copyright infringement, and would, in fact, entitle the second work to copyright protection in its own right.

THE RISE AND ADVANTAGES OF PATENT PROTECTION FOR SOFTWARE

Consequently, during the past several years, many high-tech and Internet companies increasingly have begun to use patents for legally protecting their computer software and other innovative techniques from misappropriation by others. At the same time, many software companies have grown to rely less on copyright protection to protect their innovations. This divergent, but possibly related, trend has caused a dramatic shift in thinking in the high-tech and Internet industries—a change destined to have a major impact on the continued advancement of these technologies.

As discussed in Chapters 2 and 12, copyright law requires that the protected subject matter be original, while patent law requires that it be novel (new) and nonobvious. To be novel and nonobvious, the invention must not have been a part of the "prior art," and must not have been an obvious variation of the prior art, regardless of whether the invention was created independently of the prior art. This is markedly different from copyright law, where independent creation of even an identical work results in copyright protection in the second created work. An issued patent allows the patent owner to exclude others from making, using, selling, or offering to sell the patented invention. Such a right operates regardless of whether another copied the invention from the inventor of the patented subject matter. In this manner, patent protection can be significantly stronger than copyright protection.

Like copyright protection, the allowable scope of patent protection for software-related inventions has changed considerably. However, unlike copyright protection, the allowable scope for software-related patents has enlarged in recent years. Prior to the early 1980s, conventional wisdom held that software was not patentable. This view was furthered by two notable U.S. Supreme Court cases, *Gottschalk v. Benson*[3] (1972) and *Parker* v. *Flook*[4] (1978), in which software-implemented inventions were held to be not patentable.

Although Congress has never passed a patent statute expressly providing for federal patent protection of computer software, in 1981 the U.S. Supreme Court decided *Diamond* v. *Diehr,*[5] which expressly held for the first time that computer software was patentable (or put another way, that an invention was not necessarily unpatentable simply because it utilized software). In *Diehr,* the Supreme Court found that computer software was patentable provided that any claims to the computer software were not merely a procedure for solving a mathematical formula. Though the significance of this case was not immediately appreciated by most computer software companies, certain companies recognized that the Supreme Court had provided a road map for patenting computer software. In addition to the Supreme Court's opening of the door for protecting computer software with patents, the Court of Appeals for the Federal Circuit[6] was established in 1982 as the sole appellate court authorized to hear all patent cases. The Federal Circuit promptly made it clear that patent protection for software would assume greater prominence in the future.

During the mid and late 1980s, the preferred means of protecting computer software began to shift from copyrights to patents. Specifically, more companies began to file patent applications for their computer software inventions as the U.S. Patent and Trademark Office began to relax its standards somewhat for issuing computer software patents and the federal courts upheld the majority of patents issued.

However, it was not until the early 1990s that software vendors clearly favored patents for computer software. The reason for the change stemmed in part from a series of federal court decisions, led by *Computer Associates* v. *Altai*[7] as well as *Lotus* v. *Borland,*[8] which ruled that copyright protection for computer software should be applied narrowly to essentially protect little more than the exact copying of software code. These courts sent the message that broad protection for the functionality of computer software should be sought under patent laws. Many legal scholars agree with this view. The trend toward broader patents directed to software inventions was arguably furthered in cases such as *In re Alappat,* decided by the Court of Appeals for the Federal Circuit in 1994. In *Alappat* the Federal Circuit judges decided that the patent application presented proper "useful" statutory subject matter, even though the patent claims merely presented the software process in terms of different physical "elements" within a machine to perform the functions.

CHOOSING BETWEEN COPYRIGHT AND PATENT PROTECTION FOR SOFTWARE

Protecting software legally can thus be accomplished by either copyright or patent laws, or both. Deciding which course to pursue requires an understanding of the reasons for obtaining protection in the first place. When developing computer software, the creator of the software usually wishes to ensure that the time and effort expended are somehow protected against misappropriation by, for example, a competitor. By the same token, the software developer wants to prevent others not only from making verbatim copies of the software, but also from copying as much of the innovation that went into the software as possible.

Software operating on a computer causes the computer to perform a process, and the process can usually be represented by any one of a multitude of different (even if functionally equivalent) sequences of software code. Thus, a software developer does not merely wish to rely on the prevention of verbatim copying of the software, since a competitor may observe the functions performed by the software and, without knowing the details of the software code underlying the functions, write equivalent code.

Thus, given the choice, most software developers want to be able to (1) prevent others from making, using, or selling verbatim copies of the software, and (2) prevent others from utilizing the functionality by which the software operates. From the software developer's point of view, the broader such protection, the better.

Just as the software developer wants to protect its software from being copied, either exactly or functionally, society (you, me, and everybody other than the software developer) wants to have broad and inexpensive access to software that performs useful functions in new and innovative ways. It would benefit society the greatest if it could (1) have access to a wide variety of innovative and useful software products, and (2) pay little for such software.

Because software lends itself well to being easily copied and distributed, it would be possible for the laws to allow for society to pay little for software—by simply allowing for any and all copying and distribution of software by third parties. Of course, such a law would provide little incentive for software development, as few companies or individuals would be willing to go to the trouble to develop software knowing that it could be easily copied without recourse (although the recent prevalence of open-source "freeware"—software written by programmers who seek fame over fortune—means that this is not always the case).

Thus, assuming that society wants to have wide access to innovative software, it is safe to say that society is willing to pay for this access, such as by allowing software developers to have proprietary rights in their creations. However, unlike the software developer, who wishes to have broad rights that allow him or her to reap a maximum return on investment, society likely is only willing to grant the software developer enough of an incentive so as to create a minimum threshold of innovation—or usefulness—in the developed software. In the end, society wishes to reward the software developer, but not to the extent that the developer would optimally desire.

Obviously, a gap exists between the level of legal protection afforded software that the developer ideally wants and that which society is willing to grant. However, as with any other difficult legal determination, a line, albeit not always a *bright* line, can be created that is equally fair to both the creator of software and society. When creating the ideal level of protection for software, a number of factors can be taken into account, including:

- At what minimum level of protection will a software developer be willing to develop a particular piece of software?
- What is the maximum price society is willing to pay for such a piece of software?
- How can the level of protection be created so that the maximum amount of innovation in software is generated, at a price suitable for the maximum number of members of society?

Regardless of these policy issues, though, what practical advice should an Internet or high-tech company follow to obtain the highest level of protection for its software? Because software can be protected by both copyright and patent law, the ideal approach is to pursue both. While patents are generally viewed as providing broader legal protection than copyrights, patents almost always cost much more to procure than copyrights. Obtaining copyright protection is simple, because no formal application process is required, although filing with the U.S. Copyright Office[9] is a wise and easy step that, if taken quickly enough, can allow the software's owner to obtain the often important "statutory" damages in case of an infringement. (For further details, see Chapter 2.) However, although you may be able to easily claim and register the copyright in your software, the real strength of the protection will only be tested in court in the event of a lawsuit, because the Copyright Office does not scrutinize applications except for formalities. And, as discussed earlier, any claims for copyright infringement are limited to those who had access to the software; anyone who created similar software independently has not violated copyright law.

Patent protection for software, on the other hand, can provide a significantly greater level of protection, because software protected by a patent prohibits anyone else from making, using, or selling it, even someone who may have developed a program independently. And because patents are subject to a rigorous examination process by the U.S. Patent and Trademark Office, software protected by patents is often taken more seriously by would-be infringers than software that its owner claims is protected by copyright. Of course, the patent protection comes at a much higher price, literally, because obtaining the patent can be a time-consuming and expensive process, given the slow pace of the Patent Office, the application fees, and the legal fees involved. A patent application may not result in the issuance of a patent for many years, during which time the applicant cannot enforce any patent rights. Finally, despite the heightened protection patents offer for software (and other inventions), the protection lasts for a much shorter period of time (20 years from the date the application was filed) than copyright protection (95 years from the year of first publication or 120 years from the year of creation—whichever occurs first—for software that qualifies as a "work made for hire").

Ultimately, therefore, whether to seek patent and/or copyright protection for your software is a complicated decision that involves an evaluation of the makeup of the software itself, the importance of the software to your company, your goals in obtaining legal protection, and your resources for seeking it. Ideally, all of these factors and more should be discussed with a patent attorney with experience in software issues.

BUSINESS-METHOD PATENTS

In addition to software, many companies, including high-tech and Internet companies, have learned in recent years that patent law offers them an incredible opportunity to gain legal protection for another intangible asset—methods of doing business. Business-method patents are not unique to the Internet, but they have received significant attention because of a number of controversial patents.

In addition to the Amazon.com "1-click" patent discussed in Chapter 11, here are a couple of other business-method patents:

• Priceline "reverse auction" patent (U.S. Patent No. 5,794,207).[10] This patent, which issued in August 1998, is directed to a "reverse auction" methodology, whereby a buyer enters via a computer an offer to purchase an item at a specified price as well as credit card account information, and thereafter a seller may accept the purchase offer. Once a seller accepts the purchase offer, the transaction is consummated with the credit card information. Priceline.com exploits this patent at its travel site, and in 1999 filed suit against Microsoft for infringing this patent. The parties ultimately settled.

• E-Data patent (U.S. Patent 4,528,643).[11] In 1983, long before the Internet entered the vocabulary of most people, Charles Freeney, Jr., filed a patent application titled "System for Reproducing Information in Material Objects at a Point of Sale Location." Freeney's system was directed to a methodology for transmitting and copying such things as music, movies, and video games from one location to an object such as paper, recording tape, or video disc to be purchased at another location. While Freeney's invention was conceived long before the Internet e-commerce revolution, E-Data, the current owner of the patent, believes that it covers the distribution of software and other content via the Web. Beginning in 1995, E-Data began filing various lawsuits against online and media companies. E-Data was dealt a blow in 1998 by a federal district court judge who ruled that the Freeney patent should be read very narrowly, and that the defendants likely did not infringe.[12] However, an appeals court in November 2000 disagreed, greatly expanding the scope of protection that should be afforded the Freeney patent, resulting in the likelihood that the defendants are infringing.[13] The case was returned to the district court for further proceedings, and as of this writing was still pending. However, since the November 2000 ruling, five of the original ten defendants in the patent lawsuit settled with E-Data, and the details of the terms of the settlements have been kept confidential. Obviously, this case is being watched very closely by those in the downloadable content field.

As the E-Data patent illustrates, business-method patents are not new. But their history is relatively recent. One of the most important cases on business-method patents was only decided in 1998, in *State Street Bank* v. *Signature Financial Group*.[14] In that case, the U.S. Court of Appeals for the Federal Circuit in 1998 ruled that a patent directed to a "hub and spoke" data-processing system that allows mutual funds (spokes) to pool their assets into an investment portfolio (hub) organized as a partnership was valid. The claimed invention made several calculations on a daily basis related to the financial configuration of the mutual funds, including each fund's percentage share of the investment's assets and expenses. In ruling that the subject patent was valid, the court held that a long-standing doctrine known as the "business method exception" was ill-conceived and not appropriate. The business-method exception to patentability has traditionally been used to strike down patents directed to methods of doing business.

As a result, the courts and the U.S. Patent and Trademark Office have now made it abundantly clear that virtually any kind of software or other computer-implemented invention is subject to patent protection so long as the standard tests for patentability (useful, new, and not obvious) are met. While many software companies in a variety of fields already have begun to file for patent protection in increasing volume, the *State Street Bank* case will undoubtedly further this trend among companies developing all types of software.

THE CONTROVERSIAL ROLE OF THE U.S. PATENT OFFICE IN SOFTWARE AND BUSINESS-METHOD PATENTS

The rise in the number of business-method patents being issued by the U.S. Patent and Trademark Office, along with the number of software patents, has created a very controversial system. The office reportedly has tens of thousands of software patent applications pending, and in response to public pressure, in 1996 prepared a manual titled "Examination Guidelines for Computer-Implemented Inventions"[15] to assist its patent examiners and the public in prosecuting software patent applications.

Whenever the laws change dramatically, there is typically a reaction from the public, often negative. In the patent context, this occurred in the early 1980s when the courts began allowing patents to issue on living organisms (bacteria, genetically engineered organisms, etc.) and the PTO began issuing these types of patents. Naysayers immediately began protesting, stating that patenting life-forms would open a floodgate that may not easily be closed, and that it is immoral to take ownership in, for example, a genetically engineered organism. In the end, such patents have been deemed to be instrumental in the expansion of the biotech industry, and many useful inventions have resulted. The protests have died out, and most people now see the benefits of this expansion of patent law.

Likewise, in the early 1980s and early 1990s, when courts declared that software inventions could be patented and the Patent Office obliged, programmers and others in the software industry were alarmed. To these people, patents represented just the opposite of how the software industry needed to operate. To many programmers, sharing experiences and techniques was a hallmark of a fast- and ever-changing industry, and patents impeded such progress.

More recently, with the courts and the Patent Office now allowing patents to issue on business-method inventions (after a long-held precedent forbidding such patents), many have declared that patent law has entered territory that it neither was intended to nor should cover. With the explosion of the Internet, business-method patents are viewed by many as unnecessary and unwanted.

Critics of business-method patents (and software patents) have a point, but perhaps only to a degree. The courts have mandated that the Patent Office grant patents on business methods that satisfy the three-pronged test for patentability—stated repeatedly throughout this part of the book—that the invention must be useful, new, and nonobvious. However, in the past, the Patent Office hasn't had the expertise or the tools to make this determination, and so patents of undue scope have issued. Such overly broad patents are commonly used as examples of bad patents and have led to the broad-brush condemnation of software and business methods as a whole.

While there's no doubt that the Patent Office has made and continues to make mistakes, it might be foolish to abolish software and business-method patents in concept merely because the procedure is flawed. If patent examiners at the Patent Office were given the tools and training to do their jobs properly, then we'd likely see patents issuing only on truly innovative concepts that deserve patent protection.

To determine whether the patentability criteria are met, a patent examiner, and ultimately a court, must have a point of reference. After a patent application is filed, a patent examiner reviews the application, including the invention defined by the patent claims, which are sentences prepared by the applicant (or his or her attorney) that define the scope of the invention. Based upon the claims, the examiner performs a search for the closest "prior art" (publications, previously issued patents, etc.) that the examiner can find. The examiner then compares the claimed invention to the prior art found in the search and determines whether the defined invention is new and nonobvious.

Under U.S. patent law, prior art can include publicly available documents from anywhere in the world and previously issued patents from any country, as well as prior uses, sales, and even offers for sale that occurred in the United States. Even assuming the patent examiner performs competently in applying the rules associated with the new and nonobvious determinations, for the examination to be meaningful, the prior art search must be meaningful. The most competent patent examiner will fail if the most relevant prior art is not discovered.

It's a big world we live in, and there are a huge number of sources of publications and other prior art. The Patent Office maintains a collection of all issued U.S. patents, dating back to 1790, as well as databases of certain technical literature and foreign patents. As a government agency with a limited budget, the office is unable to subscribe to or maintain access to databases for most types of literature, even though they all qualify as prior art. Patent examiners are therefore forced to rely primarily on prior issued patents as prior art. Because patent applications can take two to three years to issue—during which time they are maintained in secrecy and are therefore not yet considered public prior art—by default patent examiners therefore primarily rely on prior art that is two to three years old when they make the patentability determination. For some types of inventions, two to three years might not matter much, but for software and Internet-related inventions, this amount of time is an eternity! Innovations in e-commerce and automated business methodologies are simply progressing too quickly for the prior art available to patent examiners to keep pace.

Because of its limited resources, many people feel that the Patent Office is not doing an adequate job examining patent applications for business-method and e-commerce inventions, resulting in the issuance of overly broad or otherwise defective patents. As evidence of this problem, many have cited specific patents that have issued over the course of the past couple of years and argued that these patents should never have issued. While such anecdotal evidence is suspect, it does raise an important question. Of course, it's difficult to quantify the scope of the problem, since the issue of patent validity can be so complex.

Regardless of the scope of the problem, the Patent Office, perhaps in response to public pressure, appears to be taking more seriously the question of business-method patent quality. In March 2000, the then undersecretary of commerce for intellectual property and director of the U.S. Patent and Trademark Office, Q. Todd Dickinson, announced a new initiative that would be undertaken by the PTO to improve the patent process for business-method inventions.[16] Under this initiative, the PTO issued a plan for implementation with respect to business-method patents, which includes (among many other things) improving prior-art searches and the quality of patent examinations by enhancing technical training for patent examiners and expanding search activities to provide for mandatory searching in certain databases, and to provide a second level of review by senior patent examiners for patent applications relating to business methods.[17]

Much debate regarding software patents continues within the PTO, within the federal government in general, and among the public at large. While many may question the appropriateness of patent protection for software, in terms of the appropriateness of the incentives it provides to software developers, few question the impact that software patents are having on the software marketplace.

For software patent owners, software patents represent a worthwhile way in which to protect the fruits of their labors. For would-be infringers, software patents represent a nuisance at best, and at least an impediment to the expansion into new or existing marketplaces. For everyone, software patents represent powerful legal rights that cannot be ignored. Those who fail to recognize the importance of software patents—either as protection of their proprietary knowledge or as a barrier to their use of the proprietary knowledge of others—undoubtedly do so at their own peril.

CHAPTER FOURTEEN

Exploiting and Enforcing Patents

Because a patent only gives its owner the right to exclude others from making, using, or selling the covered invention, owning a patent is not valuable in and of itself. Instead, a patent owner can benefit from the significant protection afforded under the law either by licensing the patent to others for a fee or enforcing the patent against others by suing them for patent infringement. Each of these options has advantages and disadvantages, and the path a patent owner chooses will depend on a number of factors, including the nature of the patent owner's business and the conduct of its competitors.

LICENSING

While on its face a patent appears rigid—third parties are prohibited from infringing the patent—the exclusionary nature of patents can be modified by an agreement between the patent holder and another party. For example, it may be in a patent owner's best interest to grant to someone else the ability to make, use, or sell the patented invention, in exchange for some benefit to the patent owner (such as a monetary payment). The ownership of the patent would remain with the original patent owner, but rights under a contractual agreement would be extended to others.

Such an agreement is referred to as a "license," sometimes as a "covenant not to sue." That is, in exchange for certain obligations being met by the licensee (the party paying for rights to the patent), the licensor (the party that owns the patent) agrees not to sue the licensee for patent infringement. Licensing agreements for patents and other types of intellectual property are analogous in some ways to lease or rental agreements for real estate.

Over the years, the owners of Internet and computer technology patents have used licenses quite effectively to exploit the patented technology through others while creating a real revenue stream to the licensor. Most notably, companies such as IBM and Texas Instruments have pioneered the aggressive protection and exploitation of their innovation through patents and licensing programs. For example, it has been reported that in 1990 IBM received about $30 million in revenue from patent licensing, but that amount has swelled to well over $1 billion in each of the last few years![1] Likewise, during the 1980s, Texas Instruments, a leading computer chip company, saw its profits declining, but it suddenly realized that it had a portfolio of patents that was not being fully exploited. After instituting an aggressive licensing and enforcement campaign, TI's annual licensing revenue has been reported at more than half of its $2 billion total annual revenue.[2]

Large institutional companies such as IBM and Texas Instruments are not the only ones who are effectively licensing their patented technology. After Priceline.com sued Microsoft in 1999 for infringement of Priceline.com's reverse-auction patent, based on Microsoft's operation of its Expedia.com travel website, the two parties eventually settled in January 2001. As part of the settlement, it was reported that Expedia.com would pay royalties to Priceline.com, to compensate for use of the patented technology.[3] Without this patent, Priceline.com would not have been able to extract such royalties, and anyone would have been able to use the technology in any way, without recourse.

A patent licensing agreement can take many forms and can be crafted to meet the specific business needs of the patent owner and the licensed party. For example, a license can be exclusive (only one licensee) or nonexclusive (more than one licensee). Obviously, an exclusive license is usually more valuable to a licensee, since no other parties are licensed under the patent, but such an arrangement may not be advantageous to the patent owner, at least not without higher monetary or other compensation from the licensee. Likewise, a nonexclusive license may be more valuable to the licensor/patent owner, possibly allowing for more sources of revenue from multiple licensees.

In addition to limits on patent licenses based on the number of licensees, patent licenses may be limited by geography. For example, a patent licensor may grant a license to a company to make, use, or sell a patented invention, but only within certain states or regions. Thus, the entire country could be carved up into pieces, whereby different sets of parties may be licensed in each region. Within each region, a licensee may be exclusive or nonexclusive, depending upon the business needs and negotiations between the parties. Of course, with Internet-based technology, geography often either is blurred or has no real meaning. Since the physical location of Web servers may matter little given the ubiquitous nature of the Internet, where a patented technology is "made," "used," or "sold" can become difficult to quantify. Nevertheless, in some cases, geographical limitations can be useful when licensing Internet technology patents.

Field of use limitations in license agreements are perhaps better suited than geographical limitations for Internet technology patents. With field of use limitations, the patent owner grants a licensee the right to use the patented technology in a defined field of use. For example, while the Priceline.com reverse-auction patent (discussed in Chapter 13) has become best known in the field of airline ticket purchases, it's possible that the invention claimed in the patent has other uses, such as purchasing other travel-related tickets (train, bus, boat, etc.), or purchasing goods (groceries, automobiles, etc.). Thus, the owner of this patent could license one company the right to the patented technology for airline ticket purchases and a second company the right to use the patented technology for grocery purchases, thus generating licensing revenue from multiple markets and industries.

As with the rental or lease of real property, patent licenses are granted at a price that's negotiated between the parties. Depending upon what makes sense under the circumstances, and what is negotiated between the parties, a patent licensee may be obligated under the license agreement to pay the licensor an ongoing royalty, a paid-up license fee, or fees based upon other milestones. For example, a royalty may be calculated based upon the value of a transaction, or it can be a flat amount triggered by a certain event. There are countless ways in which compensation to the patent owner may be calculated, limited only by the business needs of both the licensor and licensee.

If a patent owner is making, using, or selling the patented invention itself, then it may be quite content to simply exclude others from making, using, or selling the patented invention. By retaining exclusivity for itself, the patent owner in this case is perhaps able to increase demand for its patented invention and charge a higher price for it.

However, patent owners are under no obligation to make, use, or sell the patented invention themselves. In this case, licenses can be especially useful to patent owners, in order to obtain a benefit from the patent. Without a license, such a patent owner would derive little benefit from the patent, since the exclusion of others would not drive increased sales to the patent owner. Rather, the ability to encourage others to become licensees of an otherwise dormant patent can result in the only direct benefit to the patent owner, in the form of royalty revenue or other compensation.

ENFORCEMENT

For various reasons, sometimes patent licensing is not a viable option, perhaps because a would-be licensee believes it has the right to make, use, or sell the patent without the patent owner's permission or because the patent owner does not have sufficient leverage to demand a license. Of course, making, using, or selling someone else's patented technology without a license is a risky proposition, because the patent owner may seek to enforce its rights by filing a patent infringement lawsuit.

While almost always a last resort, filing a patent infringement lawsuit against an infringer may in some situations be necessary, especially when the stakes are high. In recent years, there have been a number of patent lawsuits involving software technology, in which either the court awarded a significant amount in damages to the patent owner or the parties settled for a large sum. For example:

- In June 2001, Pitney Bowes settled a patent infringement lawsuit that it had brought against Hewlett-Packard six years earlier, relating to software technology for printing characters more clearly on computer printers.[4] As part of the settlement, Hewlett-Packard agreed to pay Pitney Bowes more than $400 million, and Hewlett-Packard agreed to cross-license certain of its patents to Pitney Bowes, royalty-free.
- In late 1999, Internet Pictures Corporation (IPIX) was awarded more than $1 million from two competitors that were found to be infringing IPIX's patent on 360-degree interactive photograph technology for use on the Internet.[5]
- In December 2001, a federal court held[6] that Palm, Inc., the manufacturer of personal digital assistants (PDAs), infringed a patent[7] owned by Xerox covering a "unistroke" handwriting-recognition system. The system allows users to input letters, numbers, and other characters into the device using a handheld stylus and a special "unistroke" notation. Xerox sought monetary damages from Palm for past infringement of the patent, as well as a

royalty for continued use of the technology in the Palm devices. Given the immense popularity of PDAs utilizing the Palm platform and its Graffiti input system, the potential damages at stake are believed to be quite large. As of this writing, Palm is appealing the court's ruling.[8]

Numerous patent lawsuits relating to software and Internet-related technologies are currently pending, and the results of these cases remain to be seen. One lawsuit that has attracted a lot of attention involves British Telecom's attempt to enforce a patent it claims applies broadly to the common World Wide Web technology known as hyperlinking (see sidebar, "Patenting the World Wide Web?" on next page).

While a patent grants certain exclusionary rights to its owner, like any property right, the value of a patent is sometimes only as good as the owner's ability and interest in enforcing it. Just as a trespasser on your land may continue to trespass until you object and take legal action if necessary, patent rights can in some cases require legal action to enforce.

In the United States, because patents are granted by the federal government, federal courts (and not state or local courts) have jurisdiction to resolve patent disputes. Because of the complexity of the underlying technology, as well as the complex nature of patent law, patent litigation can be expensive to both the patent owner and the alleged infringer. Many factors can affect the scope of protection and the validity of the patent, and the ability to prove a case of infringement, and so patent litigation can require extensive time by the litigating attorneys to pursue and defend, thus the high cost. Of course, if the stakes are high to either side, the cost may be minimal compared to the cost of defeat.

Nevertheless, the courts are equipped ultimately to decide the questions of patent validity, infringement, and amount of damages to be awarded to the prevailing party. A patent lawsuit is filed in one of the numerous federal district courts around the country, which serve as the trial court for the dispute. However, all appeals in patent

Patenting the World Wide Web?

In July 1976, British Telecom filed a patent application titled "Information Handling System and Terminal Apparatus Therefore," directed to an information storage, retrieval, and display system. British Telecom had developed this system for the British Post Office and had sought patent protection for its invention. The claims in the resulting patent that eventually issued in October 1989 (U.S. Patent No. 4,873,662) recite, *in part,* "a system in which blocks of information are stored along with associated addresses, whereby using a telephone modem a user of the system can retrieve and display the blocks of information using the addresses associated with each block."[9]

Several years ago, British Telecom decided to review its patent portfolio in an effort to assess its value and stumbled across Patent No. 4,873,662. The lawyers working for British Telecom read the claims of the patent as potentially covering the broad concept of hyperlinking as found on the World Wide Web. Hyperlinking, of course, allows a user of the Internet to "click" (with a pointing device, such as a computer mouse) on a visual link found on a page of one website, resulting in another page of the same or a different website being retrieved and displayed to the user. While the World Wide Web did not exist when British Telecom filed its original patent application in 1976, British Telecom decided that the patent covered the use of hyperlinking as it had evolved on the Web.

In December 2000, British Telecom decided to make its move, and it sued Prodigy, the eighth-largest Internet service provider in the United States, for infringing its patent by providing Internet and Web access services to the public.[10] As of this writing, the case is pending, and it may be some time before it is resolved.

In the wake of this lawsuit, critics have argued that British Telecom is attempting to greatly expand its patent rights to cover a technology that was never even contemplated when the original patent application was filed in 1976. Moreover, many feel that hyperlinking technology was actually developed in the late 1960s by other companies, and Prodigy undoubtedly will attempt to invalidate British Telecom's patent claims by trying to dig up prior art. In contrast, British Telecom obviously feels that it has contributed to the knowledgebase of society with its patent, and that the World Wide Web is a logical extension of its early development efforts for which it should be entitled to fair compensation.

Many Internet-related companies, patent attorneys, and other observers are on the sidelines, watching the *British Telecom* v. *Prodigy* lawsuit closely. Whether British Telecom ultimately prevails remains to be seen, but lawsuits like this one further illustrate the potential power and value of patents.

cases are taken to the U.S. Court of Appeals for the Federal Circuit (CAFC) in Washington, D.C. Established in 1982, the CAFC hears and decides all appeals in patent cases, and as a result the application of patent law has become much more consistent, resulting in a higher degree of certainty for both patent owners and alleged infringers. Thus, while it can be complex and costly, litigation is sometimes a necessary evil to resolve patent-related disputes.

PART IV

PRIVACY

CHAPTER FIFTEEN

CASE STUDY: AN INTRODUCTION TO PRIVACY ON THE

INTERNET, *FEDERAL TRADE COMMISSION* V. *GEOCITIES*

In the mid-1990s, as the World Wide Web began catching on as a popular medium for the general public, the whole idea of creating a personal website was something altogether new. Not too many people knew how to do it. HTML was a foreign language, Web servers were difficult to access, and there were no home software applications that made Web publishing easy. In the early days of the Web, most people who published personal sites were able to do so because they had received a small allotment of Web space from their Internet service provider as a part of their monthly Internet access service. But for those people who did not have an ISP account or had one with a company that did not provide Web space, creating a site was not an easy thing to do.

One company helped change all of that. GeoCities, a California corporation founded in 1994, reintroduced the term "homesteader" into the English language, a word that in the 1870s described a person who acquired and settled on U.S. public land. But in the Geo-

Cities world, homesteaders acquired space on the World Wide Web, where they began to develop their own virtual communities.

The concept was essentially this: GeoCities offered anyone who asked a designated amount of space on its own Web servers where people could build their own sites. GeoCities also offered a number of easy-to-use tools that allowed people to create sites without learning HTML and without mastering file-transfer applications such as WS_FTP. The idea, which seems so simple and commonplace today, was revolutionary at the time. By January 1999, GeoCities had attracted more than 3.5 million homesteaders who authored and hosted sites with the company, making it one of the Web's largest online communities. GeoCities became one of the top three individual sites on the Web, and although its success sparked competitors to offer similar services, the granddaddy of homesteading reached 74 percent more people than its closest competitor.

Of course, GeoCities was not in business simply to dole out cyberspace for free. GeoCities, like every good Internet company of the mid to late 1990s, hoped to make a lot of money. And at a time when the number of "eyeballs" a website attracted was the magical figure by which success was being measured, GeoCities obviously wanted to do everything possible to lure the maximum number of customers. One means by which GeoCities intended to leverage its ubiquity into revenue was obvious on its customers' websites, which were required to display advertising sold by GeoCities, for which GeoCities kept the profit. And while this sort of forced advertising made many websites appear unprofessional, obviously millions of consumers thought this price was one worth paying; in exchange for free Web space and Web-authoring tools, plenty of people did not mind that their personal websites displayed someone else's advertising.

But apparently GeoCities had other plans for making money, too, some of which were not nearly so obvious as the advertisements that couldn't be overlooked. Before anyone could become a homesteader, GeoCities required applicants to fill out a registration form. The form collected some information that was mandatory, such as first and last name, zip code, e-mail address, gender, date of birth, and member name. The form also collected some information that was optional, such as education level, income, marital status, occupation, and interests. The form also asked applicants whether they wanted to receive "special offers" from advertisers, and if so, they could select from a list of special offer topics and designate specific products and services from individual companies.

Having millions of customers provide this type of information could prove highly lucrative. Marketers always are looking to target groups of people they know may be especially interested in their products, and the personal information GeoCities collected certainly could have been highly desirable. Perhaps a luxury car company wanted a mailing list composed only of women over fifty with college degrees earning more than $100,000 a year. Or a toy retailer wanted to reach children between the ages of ten and fifteen who live in New York. Or a computer manufacturer wanted to target single men between twenty-two and thirty-five who work as high school teachers. The value of lists that could identify these people is enormous.

Some people may be naturally reluctant to provide personal information about themselves to others. So, apparently to encourage people to complete the GeoCities application, the company included privacy statements on the forms. For example, one privacy statement said:

> When homesteaders apply to GeoCities we ask if they would like to receive information on a variety of topics. We present this option because our staff keeps an eye out for value-added opportunities that our homesteaders might enjoy.
>
> Before we send anything out, we deliver an orientation e-mail to explain the program, to ensure that only those people who requested topically-oriented mail receive it and to protect your privacy.
>
> We assure you this is a free service provided only to GeoCitizens who request this information, and we will NEVER give your information to anyone without your permission.

However, apparently GeoCities did not keep its promise, and in 1998, the U.S. Federal Trade Commission[1] (FTC) filed a complaint against the company, alleging that GeoCities "sold, rented, or otherwise marketed or disclosed [members' personal information], including information collected from children, to third parties who have used this information for purposes other than those for which members have given permission."[2] This practice, and several others outlined in the twenty-paragraph complaint filed by the FTC, amounted to unfair or deceptive acts in violation of the Federal Trade Commission Act,[3] according to the complaint.

Suddenly, GeoCities, which had gathered its share of favorable press for its groundbreaking services and phenomenal success, became the poster child for privacy on the Internet. If an Internet company could collect personal information about its users, promise to use that information only for certain purposes, but then turn around and sell the information to the highest bidder, how could the system be trusted? Many people found this practice not just immoral (and, ultimately, a horrible business practice because of the adverse public reaction it generates) but probably illegal, too. The FTC has broad powers to prevent "unfair methods of competition in or affecting commerce and unfair or deceptive acts or practices in or affecting commerce,"[4] and it acted under those powers to stop GeoCities from violating its members' privacy.

Ultimately, GeoCities settled the FTC's charges, entering into a consent order in August 1998 in which the company admitted no wrongdoing but agreed to take certain steps demanded by the FTC.[5] Among other things, GeoCities agreed:

- not to misrepresent in the future how it would use personal information collected from its members;
- not to collect any personal information from children without their parents' permission;
- to provide a "clear and prominent notice" about its privacy practices on its home page and at each location where information is collected;

• to include a link from its privacy statement, for five years, to information about "safe surfing" on the FTC's website; and

• to establish an "information practices training program" for its employees.

Although these obligations may not seem too burdensome—and, after all, GeoCities escaped without having to pay a fine—they go far beyond what the law requires. But, perhaps just as bad, GeoCities became the subject of a lot of adverse publicity. Because the dispute represented the first case for the FTC involving Internet privacy, the government commission was eager to use it as a lesson for other Internet companies. "GeoCities misled its customers, both children and adults, by not telling the truth about how it was using their personal information," an FTC official said in a press release about the matter.[6] "This case is a message to all Internet marketers that statements about their information collection practices must be accurate and complete."

Despite the adverse publicity, GeoCities continued to grow, and just five months after the settlement and at the peak of the Internet boom, Yahoo agreed to buy the company in a stock deal reported to be worth $3.6 billion![7] The deal was completed in May 1999, and today GeoCities is a fully integrated part of Yahoo's diverse offering of Web services.[8]

While GeoCities always will be remembered as a pioneer in the world of personal Web publishing and as a mind-boggling success that typified the irrational exuberance of the new economy, Geo-Cities also will be remembered by technology lawyers as the company that helped make privacy one of the most debated legal issues in cyberspace. In light of GeoCities' missteps, consumer groups and some lawmakers suddenly awoke to the fact that the United States has few laws governing privacy, particularly what uses a company can make of information gathered on the Internet. And the GeoCities privacy affair made one thing suddenly clear: If making promises about privacy and then breaking them can lead to legal troubles, perhaps the safest approach for any company with a website is to

avoid making any promises at all! Though perhaps a predictable result of the FTC's complaint, some lawyers began telling their clients
that they might be better off simply by not having a privacy policy,
because then they couldn't violate anything. As a result, Congress
quickly took up the crusade and began offering many bills that
would require companies to follow certain privacy practices, but
then the new chairman of the FTC under President George W. Bush,
Timothy J. Muris, announced in October 2001 that the commission
would not seek to pass broad-based privacy legislation, reversing the
FTC's previous position.[9] In April 2002, Muris reiterated this position, calling a proposed federal privacy bill "premature."[10] Consequently, the debate still has not been resolved.

CHAPTER SIXTEEN

INTERNET PRIVACY LAWS AND PRIVACY POLICIES

You may be surprised to learn that, despite highly publicized cases such as the one involving GeoCities, the United States—unlike some other countries, including those in the European Union (Chapter 19) and Canada (Chapter 20)—has very few laws that directly affect privacy on the Internet. In fact, while some existing laws, such as the Federal Trade Commission Act[1] in the GeoCities case, can be applied to online privacy issues, the United States has no general Internet privacy law at the federal level. In response to concerns about breaches of privacy on the Internet, the U.S. Congress has responded by passing only one Internet-specific law, the Children's Online Privacy Protection Act[2] (COPPA). Although COPPA is very important (it is discussed in detail in Chapter 18), the law applies only to the collection of personal information from children under thirteen. Adults must rely on other laws, very few of which affect the way companies conduct e-commerce.

Similarly, a number of states have debated whether they should pass Internet privacy legislation, particularly because the federal government had failed to do so. However, few state legislatures have acted, and some lawmakers and others believe a variety of state laws inevitably would cause conflicts and create obstacles to online commerce. Still, in May 2002, Minnesota Governor Jesse Ventura signed a bill that prohibits Internet service providers from disclosing certain personally identifiable information about its users.[3] Because the law was not scheduled to become effective until March 2003, it was unclear as of this writing what effect it would have, but the scope of the law may be broad: It applies to every ISP that provides services to consumers in Minnesota, regardless of where the ISP itself is located. Particularly if other states follow suit, Congress may decide to pass a comprehensive Internet privacy law after all, simply to bring uniformity to this area of the law.

One significant law passed by the U.S. Congress in recent years, the USA PATRIOT Act, also addresses privacy and the Internet, although the law—overwhelmingly approved in the wake of the September 11, 2001, terrorist attacks—is far too sprawling (it affects fifteen different statutes) to be considered simply an online privacy law.[4] Still, the act (an acronym for the lengthy "Uniting and Strengthening America by Providing Appropriate Tools Required to Intercept and Obstruct Terrorism") is particularly important to Internet service providers, since it addresses the circumstances under which they must respond to requests from law enforcement officials to reveal information about their users. Civil libertarians such as those at the Electronic Frontier Foundation have criticized the USA PATRIOT Act as unnecessarily overreaching, ineffective in truly fighting terrorism, and a violation of civil rights.[5] Regardless of what one thinks of the USA PATRIOT Act, it is primarily criminal legislation that, although tremendously important to those affected by it, has little impact on the daily activities of most companies that conduct business online. This chapter, and the following chapters on privacy in this book, focus instead on civil laws and how they affect common daily business practices as they relate to privacy.

read. But occasionally, if you do collect personal information from visitors to your website, you may hear from someone who says: "I cannot locate your privacy policy, and I will not sign up for such-and-such or order products from your website without knowing what you plan to do with my personal information." And as a result, you will either have lost a customer or be encouraged to adopt a privacy policy after all.

As privacy grows in importance to Internet users, more and more people may demand to see a website privacy policy before they'll do business with you or access your site (although, ironically, it's impossible to know whether a website has a privacy policy, and, if so, what the policy actually says, without first actually accessing the website on which it appears). And eventually, Congress may indeed pass a comprehensive Internet privacy law that would require all commercial websites to have a privacy policy. Also, adopting a privacy policy for your website may help you comply with existing state laws on privacy or the laws of other countries. For these reasons, you should seriously consider drafting (or, better yet, having your attorney draft) a privacy policy to post on your website.

But keep in mind that if you do so, you are essentially creating your own law. In other words, as soon as you tell people what your website's privacy practices are, you must follow them. Or, like Geo-Cities, you could face a legal complaint from the FTC or visitors to your site. This lesson cannot be emphasized strongly enough: If you promise not to share any of your users' names and e-mail addresses with anyone else, and then you're approached by a marketer who wants to buy your list of customers for a handsome fee, you will not be able to do so. If you promise to take certain technological steps to protect your customers' credit cards during e-commerce transactions, you must continue to do so even if you find that the steps are very burdensome. And if you promise to allow your users to access the personal information that you maintain on them, you cannot deny a request to do so simply because you thought nobody would bother to ask.

HISTORICAL RECOGNITION OF PRIVACY

But before going any further, it will be helpful now to discuss what is really meant by "privacy." As lawyers are quick to point out, the U.S. Constitution[6] does not include the word "privacy," although through the years a long line of court cases have made clear that Americans are entitled to some degree of privacy. For example, the police cannot under many circumstances randomly search your home without first obtaining a warrant based on probable cause, because your home is private. A famous legal article titled "The Right to Privacy,"[7] written by Samuel Warren and Louis Brandeis and published by the *Harvard Law Review* in 1890, is largely credited as one of the first recognitions of the right to privacy in the United States. Interestingly, the authors were concerned more than a century ago about how new technology could affect privacy. They wrote:

> Recent inventions and business methods call attention to the next step which must be taken for the protection of the person, and for securing to the individual what Judge Cooley calls the right "to be let alone." Instantaneous photographs and newspaper enterprise have invaded the sacred precincts of private and domestic life; and numerous mechanical devices threaten to make good the prediction that "what is whispered in the closet shall be proclaimed from the house-tops." For years there has been a feeling that the law must afford some remedy for the unauthorized circulation of portraits of private persons; and the evil of the invasion of privacy by the newspapers, long keenly felt, has been but recently discussed by an able writer. The alleged facts of a somewhat notorious case brought before an inferior tribunal in New York a few months ago, directly involved the consideration of the right of circulating portraits; and the question whether our law will recognize and protect the right to privacy in this and in other respects must soon come before our courts for consideration.

Technology has come a long way since the 1890s, but we're still struggling with the right to privacy. Warren and Brandeis wrote that "the existing law affords a principle which may be invoked to protect the privacy of the individual from invasion either by the too enterprising press, the photographer, or the possessor of any other modern device for recording or reproducing scenes or sounds." Today's "modern device," the Internet, has created a new host of legal issues relating to privacy.

PRIVACY AND TECHNOLOGY

The issue typically boils down to this: What type of information may a company collect about individuals online, and what may the company do with that information?

As discussed in Chapter 15, personally identifiable information—such as name, address, date of birth, occupation, income, and hobbies—is highly valued by marketers because having it enables them to reach highly targeted audiences. However, not all information that a company gathers online is always directly submitted by a user. For example, any well-run e-commerce site keeps a record of every item ever ordered by a particular customer, and some may even keep a record of items viewed but not ordered by a customer. That's how Amazon.com offers its users "personalized recommendations"; when a user accesses the Amazon.com website, the retailer can "recognize" the user either when he or she logs in or by reading a "cookie" (a unique identifier placed by the website on the user's hard drive). While some people may find this type of personalization useful, others find it invasive and disturbing.

Regardless of what users may think of this type of information collecting, no U.S. law outright forbids it. And no U.S. law—with a few exceptions, such as those relating to medical and financial information—prevents what a company may do with it. One interesting exception applies to videotape rentals, and here's the quick

story behind it. In 1987, President Reagan nominated Robert Bork to fill a vacancy as a justice of the U.S. Supreme Court. In the course of Bork's nomination process, a reporter obtained a list from a video rental store of the movies Bork had rented; according to some accounts, the reporter had hoped to learn that Bork had rented pornographic videos, but as it turned out the list was innocuous. Still, so many people were disturbed by the fact that records of this type could be obtained that Congress passed the Video Privacy Protection Act of 1988, also known as the "Bork bill," which made it illegal under many circumstances for any video company to disclose what videos someone has requested or obtained.[8] So if you're in the business of renting or selling videotapes (online or off), the Bork bill would restrict your ability to use some personal information about your customers.

THE ROLE OF WEBSITE PRIVACY POLICIES

The greatest restriction on your ability to collect and use customer information will be outlined in your website's privacy policy. So, what must a privacy policy state? Surprisingly, nothing. That's right—you do not need to have a privacy policy on your website. So why do so many websites have them? The answer is simple: "Because everybody does it," in theory, because creating and disseminating a privacy policy makes a website trustworthy and, as a result, visitors will be more likely to use the site and reveal personal information about themselves.

As you no doubt know, privacy policies are very common. Seemingly every well-known and large company with a website has one. Should you, too, have a privacy policy? Chances are that if you do not, few will notice. After all, when was the last time you read any other site's privacy policy? Although the policies are typically easy to find—simply scroll to the bottom of any popular website and look for the link labeled, appropriately, "Privacy Policy"—they're rarely

THE PROBLEMS OF CHANGING A WEBSITE PRIVACY POLICY

Granted, websites change their privacy policies from time to time. But doing so can be very tricky—from both a legal and a public relations perspective. For example, in 2000, Amazon.com changed its privacy policy and caused a little storm. Under the previous version of Amazon.com's privacy policy, the retailer said:

> Amazon.com does not sell, trade, or rent your personal information to others. We may choose to do so in the future with trustworthy third parties, but you can tell us not to by sending a blank e-mail message to never@amazon.com

Later, Amazon.com notified its customers that it was changing its privacy policy, in part to:

> As we continue to develop our business, we might sell or buy stores or assets. In such transactions, customer information generally is one of the transferred business assets. Also, in the unlikely event that Amazon.com, Inc., or substantially all of its assets are acquired, customer information will of course be one of the transferred assets.

In light of this change, two privacy groups, the Electronic Privacy Information Center (EPIC) and Junkbusters, wrote to the Federal Trade Commission, asking it to "investigate whether Amazon has deceived consumers in its representations about privacy, particularly regarding the circumstances under which information about customers and their purchases might be sold or otherwise disclosed."[9] Ultimately, in May 2001, the FTC reported: "Based upon information we received from Amazon concerning its actual information disclosure practices . . . [FTC] staff believes that Amazon's revised privacy policy does not materially conflict with representations Amazon made in its previous privacy policy and that it likely has not violated Section 5 of the FTC Act."[10]

While Amazon was vindicated by the FTC staff, the company surely was required to expend time and effort responding to this issue, which could have been avoided altogether if Amazon had not changed its privacy policy—that is, if Amazon had decided earlier what it really wanted to say. And (perhaps because Amazon is always held out as an example of any Internet trend), the company endured a number of unfavorable news articles sparked by its decision to change its privacy policy and by the FTC's investigation.

Amazon.com is not the only well-known Internet company that has encountered these types of problems. In February 2002, Junkbusters also criticized eBay when the online auctioneer proposed adding the following language to its privacy policy: "Please note that this privacy policy alone governs our privacy practices. If there is a conflict between the terms and conditions in this privacy policy and other privacy representations that may appear on our site (e.g., privacy tools, easy to read summaries, charts and P3P statements), you agree that the terms and conditions of this privacy policy shall control." In an open letter to the FTC asking it to investigate the proposed changes, Junkbusters president Jason Catlett wrote, "I believe such an attempt to repudiate explicit representations is as a principle and on its face deceptive. . . ."[11] Ultimately, eBay backed away from its proposed change.[12] And, in March 2002, as it was searching for ways to generate revenue amid an ongoing lack of online advertising, Yahoo updated its privacy policy. Among other things, the company reset some of its users' "marketing preferences," giving them sixty days to opt out of receiving marketing messages—even if the users had opted out previously.[13] The move sparked strong criticism and adverse publicity.[14]

The lesson from these cases is clear: If you're going to adopt a privacy policy, think it through up front.

THE ELEMENTS OF A WEBSITE PRIVACY POLICY

The best way to understand what a typical privacy policy contains is to review the policies on websites you frequently visit. You'll probably notice that the policies have many things in common, but you'll also notice—if you read carefully—that they contain subtle differences, too. Interestingly, many policies may at first appear to be very protective but ultimately allow the company to do just about anything with its visitors' personal information.

Here are the most common issues covered in a privacy policy:

• what personally identifiable information is collected from visitors to the website;
• who collects the information;
• how the information is used;
• with whom the information may be shared;
• what choices visitors have about collection, use, and distribution of the information;
• the kind of security procedures that are in place to protect the loss, misuse, or alteration of information; and
• how visitors can access and correct any inaccuracies in the information collected.

Most policies also will contain contact information so visitors can ask questions about the policy or voice complaints about it.

Probably the most important item in this list is with whom you intend to share your visitors' personal information. Because the information you collect can be very valuable, you surely will be tempted at one time or another to sell, or, as it's called in the world of marketing, "rent," your customer information to someone else. Certainly, a statement in your privacy policy such as "We may share personal information collected from visitors with other parties from time to time" is very broad and could allow you to rent your lists to just about anyone. Also, if you fail to say anything in your privacy policy about with whom you will share personal information, you also will have no self-imposed restrictions. But the most difficult issues arise when you decide whether to limit the other companies with which you will share your visitors' personal information. That's what got GeoCities into trouble. Examples of these limiting statements are:

- "We will not release personal information about you as an individual to third parties."
- "As a matter of policy, we do not sell or rent any personally identifiable information about you to any third party."
- "We will share your e-mail address with pre-screened third parties ONLY if you request to receive offers of interest from these companies when you register as a new user."

Drafting a good privacy statement—one that reassures your customers yet leaves you with the flexibility you need to make money—is no easy task and should be handled by a lawyer. However, a number of online tools can help you create a privacy policy for your website. One of them is available from the OECD, the Organization for Economic Cooperation and Development, established by a group of thirty countries to provide governments with a setting in which to discuss, develop, and perfect economic and social policy. The OECD offers a "privacy statement generator" that allows users to respond to a questionnaire to create a privacy policy.[15] But you should be very careful about using any automatically created policies or form policies available on the Web, because your needs may be very different from someone else's.

THE PLATFORM FOR PRIVACY PREFERENCE (P3P)

Predictably, many people complain that websites' privacy policies are difficult to understand, sometimes because they're vague and other times because they're full of legalese. Partially as a result of this complaint, the World Wide Web Consortium (W3C) has developed something called the Platform for Privacy Preference, commonly known as P3P, a technological approach to interpreting and applying privacy policies. As stated by the W3C:

> At its most basic level, P3P is a standardized set of multiple-choice questions, covering all the major aspects of a Web site's privacy policies. Taken together, they present a clear snapshot of how a site handles personal information about its users. P3P-enabled Web sites make this information available in a standard, machine-readable format. P3P-enabled browsers can "read" this snapshot automatically and compare it to the consumer's own set of privacy preferences. P3P enhances user control by putting privacy policies where users can find them, in a form users can understand, and, most importantly, enables users to act on what they see.[16]

Any website may choose to implement P3P, but no law requires any site to do so.

In theory, P3P should help consumers protect their privacy online. In practice, however, the impact of P3P is unclear. Although, by early 2002, six of the top ten websites had adopted P3P, and the other four sites were considering it,[17] the technology has not yet been widely implemented and it is not certain that consumers really understand it. In one article criticizing Microsoft's adoption of P3P in version 6 of its Internet browser, two lawyers said that the technology is expensive to implement and maintain; lacks enforcement and security; confuses consumers; and could create unclear legal consequences, such as if the P3P technology cannot accurately convey a subtle legal distinction in a site's privacy policy.[18]

Ultimately, until the acceptability of P3P becomes better known, consumers and businesses should not ignore it. In particular, consumers should understand the limits of P3P, how their Web browsers interpret it, and how to respond to the messages P3P can provide. And businesses should pay particular attention to whether consumers are demanding that the sites they visit implement P3P; if this privacy technology takes off, drafting a P3P-complaint privacy policy could become very important for a website's success.

BANKRUPTCY AND PRIVACY POLICIES

Although you may intend not to disclose your visitors' personal information to anyone else, you should plan for unlikely events, such as bankruptcy. In one case that received quite a bit of attention, the Federal Trade Commission in July 2000 filed a complaint against Toysmart.com after the online retailer filed bankruptcy and attempted to sell its customer information as an asset.[19] The Toysmart privacy policy said, "Personal information, voluntarily submitted by visitors to our site, such as name, address, billing information and shopping preferences, is never shared with a third party" and "When you register with toysmart.com, you can rest assured that your information will never be shared with a third party." As a result, Toysmart's attempted sale of its customers' personal information violated Section 5 of the FTC Act, according to the complaint filed against it. "Even failing dot-coms must abide by their promise to protect the privacy rights of their customers," FTC chairman Robert Pitofsky said in a press release about the case.[20] Ultimately, the FTC and Toysmart settled the case, and the personal information was not sold.

In a similar case, when eTour, a failed dot-com, announced in May 2001 that it was selling its assets, including its customers' personal information, to Ask Jeeves, EPIC wrote a letter to the FTC and the National Association of Attorneys General to block the sale as an unfair and deceptive trade practice because eTour's privacy statement said: "eTour will not give out your name, residence address, or e-mail address to any third parties without your permission, for any reason, at any time, ever."[21]

"OPT-OUT" VERSUS "OPT-IN"

You may have heard something about the debate over "opt-out" versus "opt-in"—and you may have found this a little confusing. That's understandable. For one thing, the concept itself can be difficult to grasp. For another thing, it's mostly an academic debate at this point in time, since the United States has no general Internet privacy law. Here's the issue: What should a company be able to do with a user's personal information *by default,* that is, if the user does not communicate any restrictions on the use of his or her personal information? Under the framework known as "opt-out," a company can do whatever it wants with that information (subject to any applicable laws), unless the user has opted out by informing the company of some restrictions. So, for example, if a user registers at a website, the website operator can send e-mail advertisements to the user unless, during the registration process or elsewhere, the user has somehow indicated (such as by checking an appropriately labeled box) that he or she *does not* want to receive e-mail advertisements. On the other hand, under the framework known as "opt-in," the company could not send any advertisements unless the user had specifically indicated that he or she *did* want to receive them. While some lawmakers want to change the system, for the most part the United States subscribes to the "opt-out" system for Internet privacy issues. Of course, it may be good business practice to let customers affirmatively decide how their personal information will be used, but in many instances U.S. law does not require it.

PRIVACY SEAL PROGRAMS

If you want to be very serious about privacy, you may want to consider joining one of the privacy seal programs. Doing so is usually a time-consuming, costly, and rigorous process, but for some companies the reward of being able to display the seal of a respected privacy watchdog is very high. The two best-known privacy seal programs are offered by TRUSTe[22] and BBBOnline[23] (a wholly owned subsidiary of the Council of Better Business Bureaus). Typically, the companies that participate in these programs are very large and collect or have access to lots of sensitive personal information from their customers. Among TRUSTe's customers are America Online and Microsoft; among BBBOnline's are The New York Times and Procter & Gamble. Generally, participation in a privacy seal program requires a company to adopt certain privacy practices and submit to regular examinations to ensure compliance with its practices.

CHAPTER SEVENTEEN

GENERAL PRIVACY LAWS

Although no U.S. law other than the Children's Online Privacy Protection Act (see Chapter 18) directly addresses privacy issues on the Internet, you should be aware of a number of laws that could affect how you conduct business online. Some of these laws have been around for a long time—some more than twenty-five years, obviously enacted long before the World Wide Web even existed. Although they do not apply specifically to e-commerce, they could have a role in cyberspace. And two relatively new laws, the Gramm-Leach-Bliley Act of 1999 (also known as the Financial Modernization Services Act), applicable to financial records, and the Health Insurance Portability and Accountability Act of 1996 (HIPAA), applicable to health records, have specific application to companies that conduct business online.

Also, you always should check to see whether any state in which you conduct business has enacted additional privacy laws that may affect how your website operates or how you can otherwise collect or use personal information. Because Congress has not passed a general Internet privacy law, a number of state legislatures have discussed whether to pass privacy laws of their own. Although this patchwork system could create a difficult legal landscape to navigate and could raise questions about the role of the states versus the role of the federal government, you should never assume that only federal laws affect your work. (Plus, as Chapters 19 and 20 illustrate, you need to be concerned about laws from other countries, too, making privacy—like all aspects of Internet law—a very complicated and ever-evolving topic.)

Here are very brief summaries of some of the relevant federal privacy laws you should consult:

FAIR CREDIT REPORTING ACT (FCRA) (1970)[1]

This act places limits on the use of "consumer reports," that is, "information by a consumer reporting agency bearing on a consumer's credit worthiness, credit standing, credit capacity, character, general reputation, personal characteristics, or mode of living" where the information is for, among other things, credit, insurance, or employment purposes. If you are engaged in the business of creating, distributing, or using consumer reports on the Internet, you will certainly want to see whether the FCRA permits your activity.

ELECTRONIC COMMUNICATIONS PRIVACY ACT (ECPA) (1986)[2]

The ECPA has been used, with varying success, in a number of Internet-related cases. The law became effective many years before the rise of the Internet as a popular communications medium, but it is probably the one preexisting law that has the greatest applicability to online privacy today. In general, the ECPA governs the interception of "wire, oral or electronic communications." Although the

ECPA does not refer to the Internet, a number of lawyers believe the act's reference to "electronic communications" applies to certain on-line activities. The ECPA defines "electronic communications" as "any transfer of signs, signals, writing, images, sounds, data, or intelligence of any nature transmitted in whole or in part by a wire, radio, electromagnetic, photoelectronic or photooptical system that affects interstate or foreign commerce." This act has been cited in the following cases, among others:

- In a lawsuit against Amazon.com, a plaintiff alleged that software known as Alexa and distributed by the online retailer enabled Alexa and Amazon.com to intercept and access users' personal information in violation of their rights to privacy as prohibited by the ECPA. The case was settled for $1.9 million.[3]
- America Online alleged in a lawsuit against a company called Cyber Promotions that the company violated the ECPA by sending millions of e-mail messages each day to AOL's servers free of charge and resulting in the overload of the e-mail servers.[4]
- A group of college athletes cited the ECPA in a lawsuit involving allegations that they were videotaped "in various states of undress by hidden cameras in rest rooms, locker rooms, or showers" and that the videotapes were sold on websites.[5]
- In a class-action lawsuit against DoubleClick, a number of plaintiffs said the Internet advertising company's use of "cookies" to track Web surfers violated the ECPA.[6]

Although these and other cases have met with varying success, it's clear that, at the least, the Electronic Communications Privacy Act can be used to allege a variety of privacy-related claims online.

HEALTH INSURANCE PORTABILITY AND
ACCOUNTABILITY ACT (HIPAA) (1996)[7]

Along with financial information, health care information is probably the most strongly protected and personal data that exists. Therefore, it's no surprise that the U.S. Congress has passed laws that specifically protect certain health-related information, and HIPAA is one of the newest. HIPAA was passed in 1996, but full compliance is not required until April 14, 2003. According to the U.S. Department of Health and Human Services, the agency responsible for proposing regulations to provide the privacy protections required by HIPAA, this act requires, among other things, health providers to give clear written explanations of their privacy practices; limits the disclosure of health information for non-health-related purposes; compels the appointment of a privacy officer; and sets civil and criminal penalties for violating patient privacy.[8] HIPAA is particularly important to those companies doing business online that have access to health-related information. For example, certain health or fitness websites—as well as, of course, websites for doctors' offices—may be subjected to HIPAA's requirements. So if you publish one of these websites or if you do business (such as Web design or back-end technical work) for a company that has a health site, you should consult with an attorney who knows this complicated law well.

GRAMM-LEACH-BLILEY ACT (1999)[9]

If you recall receiving a steady stream of notices in the mail starting during the spring of 2001 regarding the privacy practices at your bank, your brokerage house, your credit companies, and other financial institutions, you already know something about the Gramm-Leach-Bliley Act ("G-L-B"). This law limits the instances in which financial institutions may disclose nonpublic personal information about a consumer to nonaffiliated third parties and requires them to disclose certain privacy policies and practices to all of its customers. G-L-B was signed by President Clinton in November 1999, became effective a year later, and required full compliance by July 1, 2001. The act's requirements could fill a book unto themselves, but the important thing for you to keep in mind is that if your company is a financial institution—or if you do business with a financial institution—you may need to satisfy certain legal requirements relating to privacy.

CHAPTER EIGHTEEN

The Children's Online Privacy Protection Act

If you collect, or want to collect, information from children under thirteen on your website, you must be aware of the Children's Online Privacy Protection Act[1] (COPPA). This is a 1998 law passed by the U.S. Congress that controls how website operators can collect or maintain personal information about children. It is the only Internet-specific federal privacy law in the United States, it is very controversial, and it can be very complicated. But ignoring COPPA can be painful and costly.

CHILDREN AND THE INTERNET

Although privacy on the Internet is a "hot-button" topic in general, children's privacy is certainly the hottest. While Congress and the state legislatures continue to debate whether new privacy laws are needed to protect personal information in cyberspace, federal lawmakers acted relatively quickly to protect children online. This is somewhat understandable. After all, children are less able to appreciate the ramifications of disclosing personal information to others, or perhaps they don't even know what "personal information" really is. And although some news reports painting the Internet as just one big stomping ground for child predators and molesters are obvious exaggerations, the truth is that some criminals and other devious people have gone online to lure unsuspecting children into horrible positions. The U.S. Federal Trade Commission has reported, "[A]n investigation by the FBI and the Justice Department revealed that [chat rooms and bulletin boards] are quickly becoming the most common resources used by predators for identifying and contacting children."[2]

In addition to criminal predators, marketers are equally interested in reaching children on the Internet, because they—and their parents—are an obviously attractive audience for many products. Think about it. If an online retailer could persuade a child to submit his name and e-mail address along with a list of his favorite TV shows and toys and, perhaps, his parents' car type, that would be a real goldmine. As a result, the retailer could send targeted promotions to the child's e-mail address specifically identifying products that would interest the child and possibly be in line with his parents' spending habits or financial means. While there's nothing inherently criminal about this, it's easy to understand how many people could find it unsettling. We like to think of children as somewhat immune from this type of high-tech, highly targeted, persistent marketing.

Interestingly, the United States has never had a law that prevented marketing to children before COPPA. For example, plenty of children have magazine subscriptions in their own names, and many magazine companies for years have been free to aggregate those names and addresses and sell them to advertisers or use them to pitch other magazines. But, as with many other aspects of our lives, the Internet seems to have changed everything. And, as a result, Congress stepped in.

COPPA'S REQUIREMENTS

To understand COPPA, it's important to understand a little bit about the lawmaking process. First, although it's easy to do, try not to confuse COPPA (the Children's Online Privacy Protection Act) with COPA (the Child Online Protection Act). Admittedly, the two laws have very similar names and are known by very similar acronyms, but there are huge differences between the two. COPPA, the subject of this chapter, was passed by the U.S. Congress in 1998 to govern how companies can collect personal information from children on the Internet. Although controversial, the law is valid and being enforced by the FTC. The other law, COPA, is discussed in Chapter 22. It was also passed by Congress in 1998, but it has nothing to do with privacy. Instead, COPA makes it a federal crime to use the World Wide Web to communicate "for commercial purposes" material considered "harmful to minors." COPA was immediately challenged by a number of civil liberties and other groups and has never been enforced because a federal district court and the U.S. Court of Appeals for the Third Circuit found that it violated the First Amendment; the U.S. Supreme Court in May 2002 expressed doubts about the Third Circuit's opinion but still blocked the law from being applied.

Also, although you hear a lot about the Children's Online Privacy Protection Act,[3] you also may hear a lot about the Children's Online Privacy Protection *Rule*.[4] They're certainly related, but they're not the same thing. The act is the law that was actually passed by Congress. In the act, Congress authorized the Federal Trade Commission to create regulations—ultimately, the rule—to carry out the purposes of the act itself. After the act became law, the FTC in April 1999 published a Notice of Proposed Rulemaking and Request for Public Comment in the *Federal Register,* a government publication, seeking comments on its draft of the rule. The FTC received comments from 132 interested parties about its proposal. Also, the FTC conducted a public workshop on its proposal in July 1999, attended by thirty-two panelists—from the high-tech industry, as well as privacy advocates, consumer groups, and representatives of other government agencies—and approximately one hundred other people.[5] After considering all of this input, the FTC in November 1999 issued the Children's Online Privacy Protection Rule, which became effective on April 21, 2000.

So, what does COPPA actually do? In general, it requires that operators of websites directed to children and operators who knowingly collect personal information from children do the following:

- provide parents notice of their information practices;
- obtain prior verifiable parental consent for the collection, use, and/or disclosure of personal information from children (with certain limited exceptions for the collection of "online contact information," such as an e-mail address);
- provide a parent, upon request, with the means to review the personal information collected from his/her child;
- provide a parent with the opportunity to prevent the further use of personal information that has already been collected, or the future collection of personal information from that child;
- limit collection of personal information for a child's online participation in a game, prize offer, or other activity to information that is reasonably necessary for the activity; and
- establish and maintain reasonable procedures to protect the confidentiality, security, and integrity of the personal information collected.

As you can imagine, accomplishing these goals is not an easy task. Indeed, after the FTC issued the Children's Online Privacy Protection Rule, many websites that had collected information from children simply decided that the law was either too complicated or too costly and they simply stopped collecting personal information from children altogether. Surf Monkey, a community site for children, reportedly spent $50,000 to $100,000 to comply with the law's numerous legal requirements.[6]

For a while after the Children's Online Privacy Protection Rule became effective, the FTC seemed reluctant to enforce the law. Though many websites clearly violated the rule shortly after it became law, the FTC did not publicly report that it had taken any legal actions against the sites. According to one lawyer who attended an FTC briefing on the law in August 2000, about half of all websites actually surveyed by the FTC failed to comply with COPPA.[7] The FTC seemed content to work with website operators to correct their legal shortcomings. But then, in April 2001, following the first anniversary of the rule's effective date, the FTC announced the first civil penalty cases it had brought under the COPPA rule, reaching settlements with three Web operators: Monarch Services, Inc., and Girls' Life, Inc., operators of the Girls' Life website; BigMailBox.com, Inc., and Nolan Quan, operators of BigMailBox.com; and Looksmart Ltd., operator of InsideTheWeb.[8] The FTC charged those three operators with illegally collecting personally identifying information from children under thirteen years of age without parental consent, in violation of the COPPA rule. To settle the FTC charges, the companies together agreed to pay a total of $100,000 in civil penalties for their COPPA violations. In addition, the companies agreed to comply with COPPA in connection with any future online collection of personally identifying information from children under thirteen and to delete all personally identifying information collected from children online at any time since the rule's effective date.

A year later, on the second anniversary of the COPPA rule's effective date, the FTC announced another enforcement case, this one against the Ohio Art Company, operators of the Etch A Sketch website.[9] The FTC alleged that Ohio Art collected personal information from children who registered for "Etchy's Birthday Club" on the site without first obtaining their parents' consent. According to the FTC, the company merely directed children to "get your parent or guardian's permission first" and then collected the information regardless. In addition, the FTC alleged that Ohio Art collected more information from children than was reasonably necessary to participate in the "birthday club" activity, and that the site's privacy policy did not clearly or completely disclose all of its information collection practices or make certain disclosures required by COPPA. The site also failed to provide parents the opportunity to review the personal information collected from their children and to inform them of their ability to prevent the further collection and use of this information, the FTC alleged.[10] To settle the charges, Ohio Art paid a $35,000 civil penalty.[11]

So, as should be obvious, you must take COPPA very seriously. If you collect any information from children under thirteen, the first thing you should do is determine whether this law applies to you. COPPA does not apply to every website, but it does apply to the operators of any "website or online service directed to children, or any operator that has actual knowledge that it is collecting or maintaining personal information from a child." A "child" is defined as an individual under the age of thirteen. In determining whether a website is "directed to children," the FTC will consider such things as the site's subject matter, its visual or audio content, age of models, language or other characteristics, and whether advertising on the site is directed to children. The FTC also will consider evidence about a site's actual or intended audience and whether a site uses animated characters and/or child-oriented activities and incentives. Some sites clearly fall within this category. The Girls' Life website targeted by the FTC in April 2001, for example, uses colorful navigation buttons, teenage models, and cartoon characters. The site also offers content that obviously appeals to young girls. If a website is not directed to children, the operator need not comply with the COPPA rule unless the operator actually knows that it is collecting information from children. "Actual knowledge will be present, for example, where an operator learns of a child's age or grade from the child's registration at the site or from a concerned parent who has learned that his child is participating at the site," the FTC has said.

You also need to determine whether the type of information you collect is within the FTC's definition of "personal information." The COPPA rule defines this as "individually identifiable information about an individual collected online." This definition includes the following:

- a first and last name;
- a home or other physical address including street name and name of a city or town;
- an e-mail address or other online contact information, including but not limited to an instant messaging user identifier, or a screen name that reveals an individual's e-mail address;
- a telephone number;
- a Social Security number;
- a persistent identifier, such as a customer number held in a cookie or a processor serial number, where such identifier is associated with individually identifiable information; or a combination of a last name or photograph of the individual with other information such that the combination permits physical or online contacting; or
- information concerning the child or the parents of that child that the operator collects online from the child and combines with an identifier described in this definition.

Once you determine whether your site is covered by the COPPA rule, you must provide notice about your information-collection practices. The notice must be posted from a link on the site's home page as well as from each area of the site where information is collected from children. The notice must be clearly labeled and placed in a clear and prominent place. In other words, you can't hide the notice! The FTC suggests that a larger font size or a different color on a contrasting background would be acceptable; a link in small print at the bottom of the page, or a link that is indistinguishable from other nearby links, would not.

What about the privacy notice itself? According to the COPPA rule, here's what it must contain:

- the name, address, telephone number, and e-mail address of all operators collecting or maintaining personal information from children through the website or online service (the operators of a website or online service may list the name, address, phone num-

for data protection. To protect U.S. businesses against the possible interruptions in data transfer concerning their business dealings with European companies and the potential prosecutions by European authorities under European privacy laws, the United States negotiated with the European Commission for a "safe harbor" framework, which allows U.S. companies to satisfy the European "adequacy" standard while maintaining their traditional self-regulatory approach to data protection.

In July 2000, the European Commission approved the safe harbor framework and issued a decision that the framework meets the European "adequacy" standard. To allow companies to decide whether they would participate in the safe harbor and to implement information practices that will be needed to comply with the framework, the European Union granted U.S. companies a one-year moratorium, which ended on July 1, 2001.

WHAT THE EU DIRECTIVE REQUIRES

Under the EU Directive, every business is required to ensure that the personal information collected from its customers is:

- processed fairly and lawfully;
- collected and processed for specified, explicit, and legitimate purposes;
- adequate, relevant, and not excessive in relation to the purposes for which the data are collected or processed;
- accurate and updated as necessary; and
- kept in a form that permits identification of individuals for no longer than is necessary.

In addition, the business must tell its customers who the controller (the person in charge of the data) is and whether the customers are obligated to provide their personal information, and provide customers with the right to access such information, and the right to correct any inaccuracies in the data.

Once collected, these data may not be processed unless the customer has unambiguously given his or her consent or unless processing is necessary for any of the following:

- the performance of a contract involving the customer or the implementation of precontractual measures at the customer's request;
- compliance with the controller's legal obligation;
- protection of the customer's vital interests;
- the public interest or the exercise of official authority vested in the controller or a third party to whom the data are disclosed; or
- legitimate interests pursued by the controller or a third party, except where the customer has greater privacy interests.

In the event personal data are mishandled, the EU Directive grants an individual a right of redress. Remedies will be determined by national law and may vary from one member state to another.

In addition, the EU Directive requires all member states to establish an independent supervisory authority to oversee the regulation of personal data. This supervisory body possesses independent power to investigate and ban data-processing activities, to order the destruction of personal data, to block data transfer to third parties, to hear complaints from data subjects, and to issue regular public reports. Unless statutory exemptions apply, the controller must notify this supervisory body before carrying out any automated processing operation.

THE EU "ADEQUACY" STANDARD

To prevent circumvention of the EU Directive and the creation of "data havens" outside the European Union, the EU Directive prohibits the transfer of personal data to non-EU countries that do not meet the European "adequacy" standard for privacy protection.

Whether a country will meet this adequacy standard depends on all the circumstances surrounding the data transfer operation. Particular consideration will be given to the nature of the data, the purposes and duration of the processing operation, the country of origin and country of final destination, the rules of law in force in the country in question, and the procedural rules and security measures that are compiled in that country.

This provision is particularly alarming to U.S. businesses, for it can cut off all personal data flows from the European Union. Such disruption would affect a large variety of transatlantic business activities, including personal banking and brokerage transactions, airline and hotel reservations, Internet sales, credit checks, credit card purchases, and interoffice communication between EU and non-EU branches of a multinational corporation.

Notwithstanding this harsh provision, the EU Directive offers some exceptions if:

• the data subject has unambiguously given his or her consent to the data transfer;

• the transfer is necessary for the performance of a contract between the data subject and the controller or the implementation of precontractual measures at the data subject's request;

• the transfer is necessary for the conclusion or performance of a contract in the interest of the data subject between the controller and a third party;

• the transfer is necessary or legally required in the public interest or for legal claims;

• the transfer is necessary to protect the vital interests of the data subject;

• the transfer is made from a register that is intended to provide information to the public and that is open to the public or any person having a legitimate interest; or

• the controller is able to demonstrate the existence and applicability of safeguards sufficient to protect the privacy of the data subject.

DIFFERENCES BETWEEN THE EU AND U.S. PRIVACY APPROACHES

As discussed in previous chapters, the United States traditionally has adopted a different approach to data protection.

First, the European Union embraces privacy as a fundamental human right and thus considers comprehensive legislation to be the most appropriate means to protect personal information. Such an approach requires the creation of government data protection agencies, registration of databases with those agencies, and approval before the processing of personal data. By contrast, many Americans believe in the free market and are constantly suspicious of government intrusions. Thus, as discussed in Chapter 16, prevailing U.S. opinion prefers a sectoral approach that relies on a mix of legislation, administrative regulation, and industry self-regulation (through codes of conduct developed by industries as an alternative to government regulation).

Second, the First Amendment[2] to the U.S. Constitution imposes limits on the government's ability to regulate the flow of information, including personal data. Comprehensive legislation like the EU Directive would undermine significant interests protected by the First Amendment. Thus, U.S. privacy laws tend to be carefully drafted so that they are narrowly tailored to the information (such as video rental records), victims (such as children), and businesses (such as credit reporting agencies, financial institutions, and health care organizations) the laws are designed to regulate.

Third, the United States does not have a specific government data protection agency. Instead, data privacy is supervised by a large and diverse array of government agencies, including the Department of Commerce, the Department of Health and Human Services, the Department of Transportation, the Federal Reserve Board, the Federal Trade Commission, the Internal Revenue Service, the National Telecommunications and Information Administration, the Office of the Comptroller of the Currency, the Office of Management and Budget, and the Social Security Administration.

THE "SAFE HARBOR"

To reconcile these differences, the U.S. Department of Commerce reached an agreement with the European Commission on a "safe harbor" framework.[3] This framework provides predictability and continuity for U.S. companies transmitting personal information from Europe. It also eliminates the need for prior approval of data transfers and benefits small and medium enterprises by offering a simpler and cheaper means of complying with the EU Directive. Consistent with the U.S. self-regulatory approach, the safe harbor framework allows companies to decide whether they want to participate in the framework. To qualify for the safe harbor, a business must notify the Department of Commerce in writing annually and declare publicly in its published privacy statements that it adheres to the safe harbor principles,[4] which will be summarized shortly.

The Department of Commerce will maintain and make publicly available a list of all organizations that have self-certified. If a business that has self-certified persistently fails to comply with the safe harbor principles, the Department of Commerce will indicate in the list the business's noncompliance and thus ineligibility for the safe harbor benefits. Such noncompliance may lead to sanctions under Section 5 of the Federal Trade Commission Act, which prohibits unfair and deceptive trade practices.[5]

There are two ways to adhere to the safe harbor principles. First, a business can develop its own self-regulatory privacy program that conforms to the principles. Alternatively, it can participate in a self-regulatory privacy program that adheres to the principles. The seven safe harbor principles are summarized as follows:

- Notice. The business must clearly tell its customers why it collects their personal information, how it plans to use such information, whom they can contact with inquiries and complaints, the types of third parties to which the business intends to disclose their personal information, and the choices and means through which they can restrict the use and disclosure of such information.

- Choice. If the business wants to disclose to a third party the personal information of its customers or to use such information in a way that has not been previously authorized, the business must give the customers an opportunity to opt out of such disclosure or use. For sensitive information—such as data revealing racial or ethnic origin, political opinions, religious or philosophical beliefs, and trade union membership, and information concerning health or sex life—the business also must provide an affirmative or explicit opt-in procedure.

- Onward transfer. To disclose personal information to a third party, the business must comply with the notice and choice principles. In addition, the business must limit its disclosure to third parties that subscribe to the safe harbor principles or that are subject to the EU Directive or an "adequacy" finding. Contracts ensuring that the third party will offer the same level of protection as required under the safe harbor principles will satisfy this principle.

- Security. The business must take reasonable precautions to protect personal information from loss, misuse, and unauthorized access, disclosure, alteration, and destruction.

- Data integrity. All personal information must be relevant for the purposes for which it is to be used. The business must not process any personal information in a way that has not been previously authorized and should take reasonable precautions to ensure that data are reliable for their intended use, accurate, complete, and current.

- Access. Each customer should have reasonable access to the stored information about him or her and an opportunity to correct, amend, or delete any inaccuracies, except where the burden or expense of providing access would be disproportionate to the risks to the customer's privacy or where the rights of other persons would be violated.

- Enforcement. The business must provide an independent, readily available, and affordable dispute resolution mechanism for investigating and resolving customers' complaints and disputes. It also must institute a procedure for independently verifying its compliance with the safe harbor principles. In addition, the business must be committed to remedy problems arising out of its failure to comply with the principles. To ensure compliance, the dispute resolution body must be able to impose sanctions that are sufficiently rigorous. Examples of such sanctions include publicity for findings of noncompliance, deletion of data, suspension from membership in the privacy program, injunctive orders, and damages. A privacy seal program that incorporates and satisfies the safe harbor principles will satisfy this principle.

Like the EU Directive, the safe harbor principles allow for several exceptions. These exceptions include national security; public interest; law enforcement; conflicting obligations created by, or explicit authorizations stipulated in, statutes, regulations, or case law; and exceptions and derogations provided by the EU Directive or adopted by the member state from which the personal data originate.

THE EFFECT AND FUTURE OF THE EU DIRECTIVE

Since the passage of the EU Directive, commentators have noted how the European Union has shaped the global privacy protection debate and how the EU Directive would impose on the United States a protective scheme that is inconsistent with the U.S. tradition. However, as indicated by the European Commission's approval of the safe harbor framework, the European Union is hesitant to insist on its legislative approach if such insistence would jeopardize its economy and e-commerce development. After all, the United States provides a very lucrative market for the European Internet industries. Sanctions on U.S. companies would hurt the European Union as much as they would hurt the United States.

When evaluating the EU legislative approach, one must not forget that the EU Directive was enacted in 1995 and drafted even earlier. To some extent, the directive was outdated even before it entered into force. Using terms such as "controller" and "data subject," the EU Directive assumes a top-down architecture that is more applicable to big corporations and mainframe computers than to individuals, small and medium enterprises, and a network of personal computers. Thus, it will be interesting to see how the EU Directive evolves in light of the challenges posed by the Internet, the e-commerce explosion, and the proliferation of automated data-transfer devices such as cookies and Web "bots."

In stark contrast to the rigid EU legislative approach, the U.S. self-regulatory approach is more adaptable to new communications technologies. Such an approach also may promote the development of technical standards and default settings, which supplement nicely the existing privacy legislation and self-regulatory mechanism. The United States may have started in a defensive position. Yet it may very well have the final say over how the global community should protect data privacy.

CHAPTER TWENTY

The Canadian Privacy Act

On January 1, 2001, a new national privacy law for Canada, the Personal Information Protection and Electronic Documents Act[1] (the Canadian Privacy Act), came into effect. The Canadian Privacy Act for the first time established rules to govern the collection, use, and disclosure of personal information by the private sector in Canada. Although it is obviously a Canadian law, the act can affect U.S companies that conduct business on the Internet.

Through 2004, the Canadian Privacy Act's application in general is limited to private-sector entities that are federally regulated within Canada, including the financial services, telecommunications, broadcast media, and air and water transportation industries (other industries will be phased in after 2004). However, since January 1, 2001, the Canadian Privacy Act also applies to disclosures, for a fee, of personal information across national borders by businesses located in Canada. Examples of U.S. companies that could be affected by this application of the Canadian Privacy Act are list brokers, credit bureaus, and any other U.S. entity that would purchase personal information from a business located in Canada. Since January 1, 2002, the act also has applied to uses and disclosures of health care information within or from Canada. Since that date, the act generally has applied to personal health information, including all such information that crosses Canada's borders to the United States or any other country electronically or by other means.

CANADA'S FAIR INFORMATION PRINCIPLES

The Canadian Privacy Act requires Canadian companies providing personal information to entities in the United States for a fee to make sure that any such data they transfer remains subject to the Canadian Privacy Act's ten principles of Fair Information Practices after it leaves Canada.[2] Significantly, not only must they follow these ten principles, but they also must ensure that those to whom they transfer personal information abide by the principles. The ten principles are:

• Accountability. Every Canadian commercial entity must appoint a privacy officer responsible for compliance with the Canadian Privacy Act, whose job includes protecting all personal information held by the organization or transferred to a third party for processing.

• Identifying purposes. Covered entities must identify the reasons for collecting personal information before or at the time of collection, document why the information is collected, inform the individual from whom the information is collected why it is needed, and ensure that the purposes are limited to what a reasonable person would expect under the circumstances.

• Consent. Individual consent must be obtained before or at the time of collection and whenever a new use for the personal information is identified. Consent may not be made a condition for the supply of a product or service, unless the information is required to provide the product or service. Express consent is usually required, though in the case of nonsensitive data, the reasonable expectations of the data subject may be used in determining whether the consent of the data subject may be implied.

• Limiting collection. Personal information must only be collected to the extent necessary for the purposes identified.

• Limiting use, disclosure, and retention. Covered entities must put guidelines and procedures into place for retaining personal information. These include instituting maximum and minimum retention periods that take into account legal requirements or restrictions and redress mechanisms, and destroying information that is no longer required in a way that prevents improper access (such as shredding and electronic erasures).

• Accuracy. Covered entities are responsible for minimizing the possibility of using incorrect personal information through adopting such techniques as checklists that list specific items of personal information required to provide a service; list the location where all related personal information can be retrieved; record the data when the personal information was obtained or updated; and record the steps taken to verify the accuracy, completeness, and timeliness of the information.

• Safeguards. Personal information must be protected against loss or theft and unauthorized access, disclosure, copying, use, or modification through a company security policy that includes, as appropriate, physical and technological protections, as well as organizational controls.

• Openness. Covered entities must make their privacy policies and practices understandable and easily available, including advising the public of the identity of their privacy officer and how to get in touch with that person.

• Access. In general, individuals are to have access to all information held by an organization about them at no or minimal cost within thirty days, unless the information comes under one of the Canadian Privacy Act's statutory exceptions, such as information disclosed to law enforcement, information covered by the attorney-client privilege, cases where disclosure could harm an individual's life or security, and (under certain circumstances) confidential commercial information.

• Challenges to compliance. Covered entities must develop simple, easily accessible complaint procedures, investigate all complaints received, and take appropriate measures to correct information handling practices and policies in light of complaints.

WHAT THE LAW REQUIRES

Canada's law comes into effect in three stages. Initially, it covered only two categories of personal data: (1) that processed by federally regulated industries such as financial services, telecommunications, broadcast media, and air transportation; and (2) that which crosses Canadian provincial or international borders. Since January 1, 2002, it also has applied to health information. As of January 1, 2004, it will apply to all commercial transactions in Canada involving personal information.

In general, entities covered by the Canadian Privacy Act must obtain an individual's consent when they collect, use, or disclose the individual's personal information. They must provide the individual the right to access personal information they hold and to challenge its accuracy. They may only use personal information for the purposes for which it was collected and for which consent was given. And they must obtain further consent from the data subject to use it for any other purposes.

Guidance to the Canadian Privacy Act defines personal information in the broadest possible terms, as "any factual or subjective information, recorded or not, about an identifiable individual." It includes personal information in any form, including age, name, any ID number, income information, ethnic origin, blood type, employee file, credit record, loan record, medical record, and consumer disputes, and includes any personal information contained in any evaluation, comment, opinion, disciplinary action, or dispute. Commercial activity covered by the Canadian Privacy Act includes any transaction or conduct of a commercial character, including the selling, bartering, or leasing of donor, membership, or other fundraising lists.

The Canadian Privacy Act exempts from its coverage the collection, use, or disclosure of personal information by the Canadian government; the name, title, business address, and business telephone number of a company's employee; personal information strictly for noncommercial personal purposes, such as a personal greeting card; and personal information by an organization solely for journalistic, artistic, or literary purposes. In addition, the privacy commissioner's staff has provided informal guidance that Canadian companies that limit their activities to data processing for non-Canadian companies (rather than selling the personal data and treating the data as a commodity) will not be covered by the Canadian Privacy Act until January 1, 2004.

The Canadian Privacy Act permits companies to retain personal data collected prior to its effective date. However, companies are prohibited from using such data without obtaining consent. Therefore, no Canadian commercial entity covered by the act may continue to use or disclose this information without having the consent of the data subject for the particular use.

EFFECT ON U.S. COMPANIES

The Canadian Privacy Act already has an impact on two categories of companies. Since January 1, 2001, federally regulated Canadian companies and all Canadian companies transferring personal information for a fee must take steps to ensure that U.S. entities to which they transfer personal information take the following steps, among other obligations:

• obtain the consent of the data subject prior to using or disclosing the data;

• limit the uses of the data to the purpose agreed to by the data subject;

• provide data subjects access to all of the personal information held about them that has been transferred from Canada; and

• provide data subjects the ability to correct any such information that they view to be inaccurate or incomplete.

Thus, commercial entities in Canada are not supposed to sell personal data for a fee to anyone in the United States without ensuring that the recipient is obligated to protect and treat the data just as the firm operating in Canada would have to do under the Canadian Privacy Act. Under new guidelines issued in connection with the Canadian Privacy Act, Canadian entities to which the act is applicable must include privacy protection clauses in contracts to guarantee that third parties to whom personal information is transferred across provincial or national borders provide the same level of protection as the Canadian entity. Therefore, U.S. companies doing business with Canadian commercial entities that provide them personal data for a fee could find themselves facing a choice of either (1) being required by contract to live up to the obligations of the Canadian Privacy Act in their handling of that data, or (2) halting business with Canadian entities and instead obtaining the information from firms outside Canadian jurisdiction.

U.S. companies receiving personal data from federally regulated Canadian companies, whether or not received for a fee, face similar challenges. As mentioned above, federally regulated firms include those in the financial services, telecommunications, broadcast media, and air and water transportation industries. For these entities, the protections of the Canadian Privacy Act extend to personal data regarding employees of the Canadian firm as well as the personal data collected in the course of the Canadian firm's commercial activities. This may present particular difficulties for U.S. companies receiving employee data from their Canadian affiliates as part of company-wide employee plans or similar arrangements. In such cases, the Canadian affiliate remains responsible for ensuring that the U.S. affiliate adheres to the Canadian Privacy Act's ten principles of Fair Information Practices in its treatment of the personal data.

ENFORCEMENT OF THE ACT

The privacy commissioner of Canada[3] is charged with enforcing the Canadian Privacy Act. Counsel for the privacy commissioner have stated informally that the transnational provisions of the Canadian Privacy Act do not currently reach cases in which the Canadian entity is engaged only in processing the personal data, rather than selling the data for a consideration. However, pure processing activities will be covered as well by the Canadian Privacy Act as of January 1, 2004.

Generally, the privacy commissioner has characterized his initial enforcement efforts as "giving help to businesses searching for better ways to protect privacy," through a "vigorous, respectful relationship with business as we move into this new era of privacy protection." Nevertheless, while initial Canadian enforcement efforts may not be punitive, the commissioner's powers are broad, mirroring and in some areas going well beyond comparable Federal Trade Commission (FTC) jurisdiction over unfair trade and business practices in the United States.

Under the Canadian Privacy Act, a data subject who believes his or her personal information has been treated improperly may complain to the privacy commissioner. The privacy commissioner is then required to investigate, and if possible mediate, the complaint and issue a report. The aggrieved data subject may then go to court in a private right of action seeking damages, which are not limited in amount by statute. Interestingly, the Canadian law explicitly permits damages to be awarded to the data subject for "humiliation" if a firm has not lived up to its obligations to protect the data properly.

The Canadian privacy commissioner is an independent office, separate from the executive branch and appointed by the Canadian Parliament. The commissioner when the law came into effect, George Radwanski, a former journalist, promised to resolve issues that arise with Canadian businesses under the Canadian Privacy Act through "whenever possible . . . voluntary compliance, rather than heavy-handed enforcement." However, he also has broad enforcement powers, including the right to audit the personal information management practices of any organization in Canada, to investigate complaints, to report publicly matters he considers to be abuses, and to bring complaints against companies in Canada's federal courts. The privacy commissioner has made clear his intention to work with Canadian businesses to secure full compliance over the next several years.

PART V

FREE SPEECH AND
THE FIRST AMENDMENT

CHAPTER TWENTY-ONE

CASE STUDY: AN INTRODUCTION TO FREE SPEECH
ON THE INTERNET, *ZERAN* V. *AMERICA ONLINE*

Sometimes, as First Amendment and free-speech advocates know all too well, the most distasteful cases help create some of the most important law. On the Internet—where sex, crime, and hate have found a home—this is quite true.

One case that helps illustrate the difficult relationship of free speech in cyberspace involves an incredibly insensitive act—a malicious hoax celebrating the 1995 bombing of the Alfred P. Murrah Federal Building in Oklahoma City. The facts that follow are based on those contained in two 1997 U.S. federal court opinions, one from the U.S. District Court for the Eastern District of Virginia[1] and the other from the U.S. Court of Appeals for the Fourth Circuit.[2]

The Oklahoma City federal building was bombed on April 19, 1995, killing 168 people, a crime for which Timothy McVeigh was executed in 2001. Six days after the bombing, a notice appeared on an America Online (AOL) bulletin board, written by an unknown person identified only as "Ken ZZ03." The notice's subject was "Naughty Oklahoma T-Shirts," and the notice itself advertised

T-shirts containing what would later be described by a court as "vulgar and offensive slogans." The slogans included "Visit Oklahoma . . . It's a Blast!!!"; "Putting the Kids to Bed . . . Oklahoma 1995"; and "McVeigh for President 1996." The notice asked readers to call "Ken" to purchase the T-shirts, and it listed a telephone number for a man named Ken Zeran, a Seattle publisher of apartment listings who had nothing to do with the advertisement, had never been an AOL subscriber, and was not selling the offensive shirts.

Whoever posted the notice—and his or her identity is still not publicly known—apparently achieved the desired result. On the same day the notice first appeared, Zeran began receiving phone calls from angry people, some of whom threatened his life over the bogus notice. Quickly, Zeran's phone was inundated, and because he used the advertised phone number to conduct an apartment-listing service out of his home, he could not change the number to stop the harassing calls. Zeran also received a phone call from a reporter investigating the sale of the T-shirts. Later that day, Zeran called AOL and told a company representative what had happened. The AOL employee told Zeran the posting would be removed (which it was) but that, as a matter of policy, AOL would not post a retraction.

Despite AOL's deletion of the notice, a second notice was published on its bulletin board the following day, this time from someone identified as "Ken ZZ033." This notice stated that some T-shirts advertised in the previous notice had been sold out and that several new slogans—at least as vulgar and offensive as those previously advertised—were now available: "Forget the rescue, let the maggots take over—Oklahoma 1995" and "Finally a day care center that keeps the kids quiet—Oklahoma 1995." Like the first notice, this one asked readers to call "Ken," and it again listed Zeran's phone number. The notice also told interested buyers to "please call back if busy" because of high demand for the T-shirts. Zeran contacted AOL again, demanding that the notice be deleted and that steps be taken to prevent further notices from being posted. AOL said it would delete the message and terminate the account from which it was posted. AOL also suggested to Zeran that he contact the police, so he called the FBI to file a report.

Despite AOL's assurances, however, messages continued to be posted on its bulletin board over the following four days, advertising additional items for sale with offensive slogans, including bumper stickers and key chains. Zeran continued to complain to AOL, which continued to provide him with reassurances that it would take action to delete and prevent the postings. By April 30, Zeran was receiving an angry phone call in response to the notices about once every two minutes. As if the notices themselves weren't problematic enough, a radio announcer in Oklahoma City who had received a copy of the first notice did not realize it was a cruel hoax and discussed it on-air, encouraging listeners to call Zeran, after which Zeran received death threats and other violent calls from Oklahoma City residents. As a result, local police ultimately had to provide Zeran with protection at his home.

Finally, after an Oklahoma City newspaper reported that the notices on AOL were a hoax and the radio station issued an on-air apology, the calls subsided. By May 14, the number of calls had dropped to about one every fifteen minutes.

Because "Ken ZZ03" or "Ken ZZ033" remained anonymous, and because AOL's record-keeping practices apparently made it impossible to identify the malicious poster, Zeran was unable to file a lawsuit against the person ultimately responsible for this malicious hoax. If he had been able to do so, surely Zeran would have filed a defamation suit based on the publication of false information that damaged his name or reputation. However, because of the poster's anonymity and AOL's practices, this option was not available to Zeran. So instead he sued AOL, alleging that the online service provider was negligent in failing to respond adequately to his complaints about the malicious notices even after it had been notified.

Although Zeran was what lawyers sometimes call a "sympathetic plaintiff"—that is, someone who has been obviously wronged and for whom a judge or jury would want to provide relief—his claim against AOL was rejected by the courts because of a 1996 law Congress had passed to protect Internet service providers from lawsuits based on content published by others. (Note that this law, which largely applies in the context of defamation-based suits, is distinct from the protection provided to ISPs for copyright infringement committed by its users under the Digital Millennium Copyright Act,[3] discussed in Chapter 4.) The law, part of the Communications Decency Act (CDA), states: "No provider or user of an interactive computer service shall be treated as the publisher or speaker of any information provided by another information content provider." These few words, contained in Section 230[4] of the CDA, have formed one of the most important legal protections for Internet service providers and others who publish content on the Web.

To understand the importance of Section 230, you must first understand its origin. The law is a direct response to a 1995 case involving another online service provider, Prodigy, which once created a bulletin board called "Money Talk" on which an anonymous poster made statements that a securities investment firm and its president committed criminal and fraudulent acts in connection with a particular initial public offering. The firm and its president sued Prodigy for defamation, based on Prodigy's claim that it was a family-oriented computer network that exercised editorial control over the content of messages posted on its computer bulletin boards, thereby differentiating itself from the competition and expressly likening itself to a newspaper. The plaintiffs' lawsuit depended upon their ability to cast Prodigy as a publisher (such as a newspaper publisher) rather than as a distributor (such as a newsstand), because only the former traditionally has been responsible for defamation claims based upon content in its products. The Supreme Court of New York ruled that, based on Prodigy's exercise of editorial control, it indeed was a publisher and could be held legally responsible for the anonymous postings made on its service:

> By actively utilizing technology and the man power to delete notes from its computer bulletin boards on the basis of offensive-

ness and "bad taste," for example, Prodigy is clearly making decisions as to content, . . . and such decisions constitute editorial
control. . . . That such control is not complete and is enforced
both as early as the notes arrive and as late as a complaint is made,
does not minimize or eviscerate the simple fact that Prodigy has
uniquely arrogated to itself the role of determining what is proper
for its members to post and read on its bulletin boards. Based on
the forgoing, this Court is compelled to conclude that for the purposes of plaintiffs' claims in this action, Prodigy is a publisher
rather than a distributor.[5]

This ruling created a great deal of alarm among ISPs and other
Internet publishers, who suddenly feared that they could be held
liable for content created by their users. And the court's ruling in the
Prodigy case actually created a *disincentive* for publishers to take any
action to control their users' content, because by doing so they could
create legal responsibility for themselves that otherwise might not
exist. In other words, in at least one court's reasoning, the law would
actually reward those who did nothing to delete offensive postings.

As a result of this twisted outcome, the U.S. Congress passed Section 230 of the CDA. "Section 230 was enacted, in part, to maintain
the robust nature of Internet communication and, accordingly, to
keep government interference in the medium to a minimum," the
appeals court would later write in the Zeran case.

The appeals court found that AOL was acting as a publisher in the
Zeran case and that Section 230 of the CDA prevented it from being
held legally responsible for the malicious hoax perpetrated by one of
its subscribers against Ken Zeran. This unique legal protection afforded to Internet publishers, unlike traditional publishers, is necessary because of the unique nature of the Internet, the court said.
Holding Internet publishers liable for defamatory content created by
others once they've received notice of it "would require a careful yet
rapid investigation of the circumstances surrounding the posted information, a legal judgment concerning the information's defamatory character, and an on-the-spot editorial decision whether to risk

liability by allowing the continued publication of that information," the court said. "Although this might be feasible for the traditional print publisher, the sheer number of postings on interactive computer services would create an impossible burden in the Internet context."

Thanks to Section 230, Zeran's claims against AOL were rejected by the trial court, a decision affirmed by the appeals court. The U.S. Supreme Court ultimately refused to hear the case. Therefore, the bottom line in this case is that Zeran, the subject of a cruel online hoax, was forced to endure harassment, death threats, and significant disruptions to his personal and professional life without the ability to hold anyone legally responsible for anything. This result is not very satisfying, because we typically like to think that our legal system has the ability to right wrongs. (Of course, as the appeals court noted, "None of this means . . . that the original culpable party who posts defamatory messages would escape accountability," but the trick is unmasking an anonymous online poster—something the courts will sometimes do, but something made impossible in the Zeran case because of AOL's record-keeping practices. The issue of whether ISPs have a legal obligation to disclose the identity of anonymous posters when they are able to do so is discussed in Chapter 23.)

While Section 230 may seem to have created an undesirable result in the Zeran case, leaving a poor Seattle businessman without a legal remedy for the wrong inflicted on him, First Amendment and free-speech advocates are quick to argue that this law helps ensure that the Internet remains useful as a communications medium for everyone (not just those who perpetrate cruel hoaxes). Indeed, Congress agreed with this argument in passing Section 230, which includes a number of "findings" set forth in this law:

• The rapidly developing array of Internet and other interactive computer services available to individual Americans represents an extraordinary advance in the availability of educational and informational resources to our citizens.

• These services offer users a great degree of control over the information that they receive, as well as the potential for even greater control in the future as technology develops.

• The Internet and other interactive computer services offer a forum for a true diversity of political discourse, unique opportunities for cultural development, and myriad avenues for intellectual activity.

• The Internet and other interactive computer services have flourished, to the benefit of all Americans, with a minimum of government regulation.

• Increasingly Americans are relying on interactive media for a variety of political, educational, cultural, and entertainment services.

Further, Section 230 contains a number of policy positions the United States adopted along with this law:

• to promote the continued development of the Internet and other interactive computer services and other interactive media;

• to preserve the vibrant and competitive free market that presently exists for the Internet and other interactive computer services, unfettered by federal or state regulation;

• to encourage the development of technologies which maximize user control over what information is received by individuals, families, and schools that use the Internet and other interactive computer services;

• to remove disincentives for the development and utilization of blocking and filtering technologies that empower parents to restrict their children's access to objectionable or inappropriate online material; and

• to ensure vigorous enforcement of federal criminal laws to deter and punish trafficking in obscenity, stalking, and harassment by means of computer.

Of course, as the Zeran case makes clear, sometimes these policy positions are incompatible or impossible (such as using criminal laws to deter computer-related harassment when the criminal is anonymous). But if you're a website publisher, you'll probably grow to appreciate the protections Congress has granted. If you or your company meets Section 230's requirements, the law will protect you from being held liable for some content created by your subscribers or users. Still, simply because the law no longer provides a disincentive for you to police the content on your site for potential defamatory postings, you may have a strong incentive to do so. Acting quickly to remove offensive content—particularly if you've forewarned users that you'll do so, such as through a sign-up agreement—is usually the "right" thing to do and could help you avoid negative publicity and backlash from your customers, even if the law does not require it. Had AOL been more responsive to Ken Zeran, perhaps it could have avoided the expense and aggravation of fighting a lawsuit in the first place.

CHAPTER TWENTY-TWO

SEX, THE FIRST AMENDMENT, AND THE INTERNET

While the purpose of this book is not to teach anyone how to create an online sex business, no discussion of the First Amendment and the Internet would be complete without an examination of two laws about sex in cyberspace and their greater effect on online communications. Though each of the two laws—the Communications Decency Act (CDA) and the Child Online Protection Act (COPA)—was enacted by Congress to limit sexually oriented material on the Internet, the courts have found them to be unconstitutional violations of the First Amendment. As a result, at least with respect to U.S. law, Web publishers and surfers have a well-established, wide scope of protection for many forms of communication on the Internet.

THE COMMUNICATIONS DECENCY ACT

The CDA[1] was passed by Congress in 1996 as part of the 103-page Telecommunications Act. The primary purpose of the Telecommunications Act was to reduce regulations and encourage new telecommunications technologies, including competition for local telephone service. Most of the Telecom Act had nothing to do with the Internet. However, one of the act's seven titles, the Communications Decency Act, addresses a number of legal issues relating to the Internet, which, in 1996, was bursting onto the scene as an incredible new communications technology. As the previous chapter shows, the CDA contained some provisions that helped encourage the Internet's growth, such as the protection provided to ISPs under Section 230.

However, not all provisions in the CDA were equally friendly to the First Amendment and free speech in cyberspace. In particular, two provisions were added to the CDA very late in the lawmaking process and without the benefit of congressional hearings such as those that preceded other portions of the Telecom Act. These two provisions, informally described as the "indecent transmission" and "patently offensive display" provisions, would spark an explosive battle over civil rights on the Internet that ultimately would be settled by the U.S. Supreme Court.

The "indecent transmission" provision of the CDA stated:

> Whoever . . . in interstate or foreign communications . . . by means of a telecommunications device knowingly . . . makes, creates, or solicits, and . . . initiates the transmission of, any comment, request, suggestion, proposal, image, or other communication which is obscene or indecent, knowing that the recipient of the communication is under 18 years of age, regardless of whether the maker of such communication placed the call or initiated the communication . . . or . . . knowingly permits any telecommunications facility under his control to be used for any [of this type of] activity . . . with the intent that it be used for such activity,

shall be fined under [federal criminal laws] or imprisoned not more than two years, or both.[2]

And the "patently offensive display" provision of the CDA stated:

> Whoever . . . in interstate or foreign communications knowingly . . . uses an interactive computer service to send to a specific person or persons under 18 years of age, or . . . uses any interactive computer service to display in a manner available to a person under 18 years of age, any comment, request, suggestion, proposal, image, or other communication that, in context, depicts or describes, in terms patently offensive as measured by contemporary community standards, sexual or excretory activities or organs, regardless of whether the user of such service placed the call or initiated the communication; or . . . knowingly permits any telecommunications facility under such person's control to be used for an activity [of this type] with the intent that it be used for such activity, shall be fined under [federal criminal laws] or imprisoned not more than two years, or both.[3]

In other words, very generally speaking, these two provisions from the CDA made it illegal to transmit indecent material or display patently offensive material on the Internet.

Congress's motive in passing these provisions was understandable. As a new medium, the Internet was proving itself to be capable of conveying not only news and financial information, for example, but also sexually explicit images. Though it was later discredited by some,[4] a report in the *Georgetown Law Journal* provided the basis for a *Time* magazine cover story on "cyberporn" in November 1994 that found pornography to be widespread on the Internet. "Sex" was reported to be one of the most common terms used on emerging search engines. And relatively respected "soft-core" publications such as *Playboy* were playing catch-up to create a Web presence where hard-core sites already were proving to be popular.

But Congress's action proved to be too swift. According to a congressional hearing on the "indecent transmission" and "patently offensive display" provisions, held *after* they had been adopted by the Senate, Senator Patrick Leahy (D, Vt.) said: "It really struck me in your opening statement when you mentioned, Mr. Chairman, that it is the first ever hearing, and you are absolutely right. And yet we had a major debate on the floor, passed legislation overwhelmingly on a subject involving the Internet, legislation that could dramatically change—some would say even wreak havoc—on the Internet. The Senate went in willy-nilly, passed legislation, and never once had a hearing, never once had a discussion other than an hour or so on the floor."[5] This lack of debate in passing these well-intended provisions of the CDA would later prove to be a costly mistake for those who wanted to rein in the dissemination of objectionable content on the Internet—and a tremendous benefit for those who wanted to ensure freedom of speech in cyberspace.

Immediately after President Clinton signed into law the Telecommunications Act of 1996, containing the controversial provisions in the Communications Decency Act, twenty plaintiffs filed a lawsuit against the attorney general of the United States and the Department of Justice on February 8, 1996.[6] Their lawsuit charged that those portions of the CDA were unconstitutional because they violated the First Amendment's free-speech protections: "Congress shall make no law . . . abridging the freedom of speech. . . ." A second suit was later filed by twenty-seven additional plaintiffs. Interestingly, though the forty-seven plaintiffs were led by the American Civil Liberties Union (ACLU)—an organization known for advocating what some characterize as excessively liberal causes—they also included some of the country's most respected publications (represented by the National Writers Union, the American Society of Newspaper Editors, the Society of Professional Journalists, and others) and leading technology companies (including Apple, AOL, CompuServe, Microsoft, and Prodigy). All of these plaintiffs were concerned that the CDA would trample their rights to freedom of speech—even though they were not engaged in any sex-related businesses on the Internet.

Following the lawsuit, a three-judge district court entered a temporary restraining order that prohibited the U.S. government from enforcing the "indecent transmission" and "patently offensive display" provisions, and a three-judge panel later unanimously entered a preliminary injunction against the provisions.[7] The government then appealed the case to the U.S. Supreme Court under a special review provision, presenting the highest court in the land with its first case on this new thing called the Internet. On June 26, 1997, an important date for Internet lawyers and free-speech advocates, the U.S. Supreme Court, in a 9–0 opinion, found the CDA's restrictions on Internet communications to be contrary to the First Amendment, permanently striking down the enforceability of this new law.[8]

"The breadth of the CDA's coverage is wholly unprecedented," the Supreme Court wrote in the case, *Reno* v. *ACLU*. "The general, undefined terms 'indecent' and 'patently offensive' cover large amounts of nonpornographic material with serious educational or other value." In other words, while the CDA provisions were intended to combat only certain material online, they could be applied to restrict a whole lot of content—including, as the Court noted, a parent sending information via e-mail about birth control to his or her seventeen-year-old child at college, if the college town's community found such information indecent or patently offensive. Similar activities also could fall into the restrictions of the CDA provisions: photos on a website about breast cancer, a digital video on childbirth, or even news articles simply reporting on topics such as prison rape or homosexuality.

Interestingly, the CDA provisions were not even needed to prohibit much of the activity its supporters wanted to target, because obscenity and child pornography have been illegal in the United States since long before the World Wide Web even existed. The CDA provisions, though, encompassed potentially much more—much more than the First Amendment would allow it to prohibit. (The "indecent transmission" provision's reference to "obscene" communications was not at issue.) As the Court wrote: "We are persuaded that the CDA lacks the precision that the First Amendment requires when a statute regulates the content of speech. In order to deny minors access to potentially harmful speech, the CDA effectively suppresses a large amount of speech that adults have a constitutional right to receive and to address to one another. That burden on adult speech is unacceptable if less restrictive alternatives would be at least as effective in achieving the legitimate purpose that the statute was enacted to serve." As a result, the law would have what First Amendment lawyers refer to as a "chilling effect" on free speech; that is, it would discourage people from communicating certain things simply because people would be afraid of violating the law, even if their communications were not necessarily illegal.

Of course, the First Amendment is not absolute; some U.S. laws restricting communication have been upheld. For example, laws regulating content broadcast on radio stations are legal. And "fighting words," that is, language that is likely to incite someone to action, are restricted despite the First Amendment because of the obvious consequences they evoke. However, the CDA restrictions, unlike other limits placed on speech, were overly broad and vague.

The Supreme Court acknowledged that the legislative intent behind the CDA provisions may have been good: "It is true that we have repeatedly recognized the governmental interest in protecting children from harmful materials. . . . But that interest does not justify an unnecessarily broad suppression of speech addressed to adults." The Court concluded by saying, "The interest in encouraging freedom of expression in a democratic society outweighs any theoretical but unproven benefit of censorship."

THE CHILD ONLINE PROTECTION ACT

Following the Supreme Court's decision striking down the "indecent transmission" and "patently offensive display" provisions, self-described "Netizens"—advocates of free speech online—celebrated, while those concerned about finding a way to protect children against offensive content went back to the drawing board. Surely, the latter group believed, there must be a way to outlaw certain content on the Internet without violating the First Amendment. Before long, they had drafted a new law, the Child Online Protection Act,[9] enacted just sixteen months after the Supreme Court's ruling against the CDA, on October 21, 1998. (As noted, the Child Online Protection Act, known as COPA, is not the same thing as the Children's Online Privacy Protection Act, known as COPPA. COPPA, the subject of Chapter 18, is an unchallenged law that addresses only privacy issues on the Internet, not sexual content.)

COPA, sometimes dubbed "CDA2," was Congress's attempt to draft a law regulating Internet content that would survive the First Amendment challenges that killed the CDA's "indecent transmission" and "patently offensive display" provisions. The law was intentionally written in a way that, its drafters hoped, responded to the Supreme Court's problems with the CDA. The heart of COPA said:

> Whoever knowingly and with knowledge of the character of the material, in interstate or foreign commerce by means of the World Wide Web, makes any communication for commercial purposes that is available to any minor and that includes any material that is harmful to minors shall be fined not more than $50,000, imprisoned not more than 6 months, or both.

To avoid the vagueness issue of the CDA, COPA included a specific definition of what constitutes "material that is harmful to minors," drawing on established legal precedent outlawing obscenity. Specifically, COPA defined "material that is harmful to minors" as any communication that

> • the average person, applying contemporary community standards, would find, taking the material as a whole and with respect to minors, is designed to appeal to, or is designed to pander to, the prurient interest;
> • depicts, describes, or represents, in a manner patently offensive with respect to minors, an actual or simulated sexual act or

sexual contact, an actual or simulated normal or perverted sexual act, or a lewd exhibition of the genitals or post-pubescent female breast; and

• taken as a whole, lacks serious literary, artistic, political, or scientific value for minors.

This three-part test attempted to conform to the U.S. Supreme Court's accepted test for determining whether material is obscene (and therefore illegal and unprotected by the First Amendment), first set forth in a 1968 opinion and later modified in a 1973 opinion.

However, as with the CDA, the ACLU immediately filed a lawsuit challenging this new law that placed limits on online communications, alleging that it violated the First Amendment and asking the court to prevent the government from enforcing it. The U.S. District Court granted a temporary restraining order against the law,[10] then held a hearing on it and entered a preliminary injunction against it.[11] The government appealed and, in June 2000, the U.S. Court of Appeals for the Third Circuit affirmed the district court's judgment, continuing to prevent COPA from being enforced.[12] In May 2001, the U.S. Supreme Court agreed to hear the case, and, one year later, the Court let the injunction against COPA stand, although it cast doubt on the appeals court's reasoning and sent the case back down the judicial ladder for further review.[13]

In granting the initial temporary restraining order, the district court was the first judicial body to express doubts about COPA's constitutionality. "While the public certainly has an interest in protecting its minors, the public interest is not served by the enforcement of an unconstitutional law," the district court wrote. "Indeed, to the extent that other members of the public who are not parties to this lawsuit may be [a]ffected by this statute, the interest of the public is served by preservation of the status quo until such time that this Court, with the benefit of a fuller factual record and thorough advocacy from the parties, may more closely examine the constitutionality of this statute."

Later, after hearing five days of testimony and one day of argument on the law, the district court granted a preliminary injunction against COPA. The plaintiffs argued that COPA, like the CDA, is overbroad and vague, characteristics that the First Amendment forbids in any law. The government, on the other hand, argued that COPA passed constitutional muster because it is narrowly tailored to its compelling interest in protecting minors from harmful materials. Ultimately, the court concluded that COPA would impose economic costs on websites to comply with the law, forcing some content providers to self-censor their sites, leading to a burden on speech that is protected for adults. Further, the court found that COPA was not the least restrictive means nor was it narrowly tailored to meet the government's goal in protecting children, because children still would be able to access harmful material on foreign and noncommercial websites and via Internet protocols other than the Web, none of which was covered by COPA. Accordingly, the district court concluded: "This Court and many parents and grandparents would like to see the efforts of Congress to protect children from harmful materials on the Internet to ultimately succeed and the will of the majority of citizens in this country to be realized through the enforcement of an act of Congress. However, the Court is acutely cognizant of its charge under the law of this country not to protect the majoritarian will at the expense of stifling the rights embodied in the Constitution."

On appeal, the Third Circuit took an entirely different approach to reviewing the constitutionality of COPA, focusing solely on the first of the three-part test in COPA, which required that "the average person, applying contemporary community standards, would find, taking the material as a whole and with respect to minors, is designed to appeal to, or is designed to pander to, the prurient interest." Traditionally, this reference to "contemporary community standards" provided a useful way for courts to pass judgment on whether laws regulating sexually oriented material could be upheld. Because, for example, residents of New York City might be less offended by certain content than residents of Monroe, North Carolina, a law regulating that content might be upheld in Monroe and struck down in

New York. This system had worked well in a number of previous cases, including those relating to the mailing of unsolicited sexually explicit material and companies engaged in the "dial-a-porn" business. However, the Internet presents new challenges to the ability to apply "contemporary community standards," the Third Circuit said.

"In each of those [earlier] cases, the defendants had the ability to control the distribution of controversial material with respect to the geographic communities into which they released it," the appeals court examining COPA said. "Therefore, the defendants could limit their exposure to liability by avoiding those communities with particularly restrictive standards, while continuing to provide the controversial material in more liberal-minded communities. For example, the pornographer in [the mailing case] could have chosen not to mail unsolicited sexually explicit material to certain communities while continuing to mail them to others. Similarly, the telephone pornographers ('dial-a-porn') . . . could have screened their incoming calls and then only accepted a call if its point of origination was from a community with standards of decency that were not offended by the content of their pornographic telephone messages. . . .

"By contrast," the court continued, "Web publishers have no such comparable control. Web publishers cannot restrict access to their site based on the geographic locale of the Internet user visiting their site."

Indeed, this borderless nature of the Internet meant that applying "contemporary community standards" was an impossible act, the Third Circuit said. Or, rather, because the Internet reached every community, the only standards that could be applied to them all would be the so-called lowest common denominator—that is, the standards of the most conservative community anywhere. "Because no technology *currently* exists by which Web publishers may avoid liability, . . . publishers would necessarily be compelled to abide by the 'standards of the community most likely to be offended by the message' . . . even if the same material would not have been deemed harmful to minors in all other communities," the court said. "Moreover, by restricting their publications to meet the more stringent standards of less liberal communities, adults whose constitutional rights permit them to view such materials would be unconstitutionally deprived of those rights. Thus, this result imposes an overreaching burden and restriction on constitutionally protected speech."

The U.S. Supreme Court did not necessarily agree. In its opinion, the nation's highest judicial body held that "COPA's reliance on community standards to identify 'material that is harmful to minors' does not *by itself* render the statute substantially overbroad for purposes of the First Amendment." The Court said that "community standards need not be defined by reference to a precise geographic area." And, it added: "If a publisher chooses to send its material into a particular community, this Court's jurisprudence teaches that it is the publisher's responsibility to abide by that community's standards. The publisher's burden does not change simply because it decides to distribute its material to every community in the Nation." (In a dissenting opinion, Justice Anthony Kennedy said this reasoning "forecloses an entire medium of expression"—the World Wide Web—to some publishers.) Despite its doubts about the Third Circuit's application of the "community standards" definition, the Supreme Court did not lift the injunction against COPA; instead, it directed the appeals court to examine the law on other grounds, including whether it is unconstitutionally overbroad or vague. Ultimately, therefore, the Supreme Court could revisit COPA.

THE CHILD PORNOGRAPHY PREVENTION ACT AND THE CHILDREN'S INTERNET PROTECTION ACT

In two other opinions relating to sex and the Internet, courts also have struck down laws that regulated content. One of the cases, *Ashcroft* v. *Free Speech Coalition,* was decided by the U.S. Supreme Court in April 2002.[14] In that case, the Court ruled that the Child Pornography Prevention Act of 1996—which banned "virtual" child pornography, including images created solely by using computerized technology to simulate children engaging in sexual conduct—violated the First Amendment. "Protected speech does not become unprotected merely because it resembles the latter," the Court wrote, noting that performances of some literary works—including Shakespeare's *Romeo and Juliet* and the modern films *Traffic* and *American Beauty*—use adult actors to depict children in sexual roles, something that is protected by the First Amendment.

And in May 2002, a special three-judge court struck down as unconstitutional the Children's Internet Protection Act (CIPA), a law that denied certain federal funding to public libraries that refused to implement "filtering" software on Internet-connected computers available to patrons.[15] In that case, *American Library Association* v. *United States,* the court said filtering software suffered from both extensive over- and underblocking and therefore CIPA violated the First Amendment. "We are sympathetic to the position of the government, believing that it would be desirable if there were a means to ensure that public library patrons could share in the informational bonanza of the Internet while being insulated from materials that meet CIPA's definitions, that is, visual depictions that are obscene, child pornography, or in the case of minors, harmful to minors," the court wrote. "Unfortunately this outcome, devoutly to be wished, is not available in this less than best of all possible worlds."

THE IMPLICATIONS OF THE COURTS' RULINGS ON SEX AND THE INTERNET

What do the courts' rulings in these cases mean to you? The most cynical view is that the rulings have allowed sexually oriented material to thrive on the Internet, supporting the online sex industry and creating an environment where children face exposure to content no right-minded parent would ever want them to see. However, these are really only unfortunate side effects of the courts' decisions, the primary purpose of which is to ensure freedom of speech on the Internet.

The courts' rulings indeed guarantee that as a Web surfer, you'll be able to find sexual images, stories, and chat, but they also guarantee that you'll be able to find photos of testicular cancer if you're faced with that ailment; read stories from couples facing infertility treatment if you're coping with that difficult situation; and chat with rape and incest survivors if you need to know about either of those horrific acts. As a Web publisher, the courts' rulings ensure that you can provide websites and Internet services to fulfill these needs.

But it must be remembered that none of these judicial rulings on content in cyberspace mean that "anything goes." As mentioned earlier, even before Congress passed the CDA, the United States had (and still has) laws outlawing child pornography. In August 2001, U.S. Attorney General John Ashcroft announced an undercover sting investigation, "Operation Avalanche," into the largest-known international commercial child pornography business ever uncovered; at the center of the investigation was a company that distributed lewd pictures of children having sex to subscribers over the Internet.[16] The company's owners earlier had been convicted after a trial on charges of conspiracy to distribute and possession of child pornography. According to the U.S. Postal Inspection Service, Operation Avalanche led to the arrest of more than one hundred people for trafficking in child pornography through the mail and via the Internet.[17] Seven months later, in March 2002, the FBI announced "Operation Candyman," a nationwide enforcement action in which eighty-six people in twenty-six states were charged with posting, exchanging, and transmitting child pornography through three Yahoo "egroups."[18] Also, in March 2002, the U.S. Customs Service announced the execution of seven search warrants on eight people in the United States and as many as thirty simultaneous warrants in ten other countries on members of a private Internet group it said was exchanging and downloading child pornography.[19]

As stated at the outset, this chapter is not intended to provide anyone with a road map for how to run an online sex business, nor is it intended to espouse one point of view or another. Rather, the primary lessons to be learned are these: Congress has repeatedly tried to regulate content on the Internet, but the courts thus far have found that the regulations violate the First Amendment, because they are vague (by not defining what's off-limits) or overly broad (by restricting more content than is necessary). As a result, no enforceable U.S. law exists that specifically prohibits online communications; but existing laws—such as those against child pornography—apply in cyberspace just as they do in other media.

Laws alone cannot protect children from pornography online, the National Academies' National Research Council concluded in a report released in May 2002, "Youth, Pornography, and the Internet."[20] "No single approach can provide a solution, since any one approach alone can be circumvented with enough effort," said Dick Thornburgh, the former U.S. attorney general who chaired the committee that wrote the report.[21] Instead, a combination of technical, legal, economic, and educational approaches are needed, says the report, which provides a thorough overview of the Communications Decency Act, the Child Online Protection Act, and other relevant legal issues.

CHAPTER TWENTY-THREE

MESSAGE BOARD MISCONDUCT AND ONLINE ANONYMITY

With the explosion of Internet message boards and chat rooms has come an avalanche of what many consider to be defamatory statements, as well as postings that wrongfully disseminate confidential, false, or misleading information about businesses and financial securities issues. Not only are these statements potentially damaging to a company's or person's reputation, but—especially in the case of public companies—they may cause real financial damage as well. Given the way the Internet operates, these messages can come from anywhere and be posted by people using aliases that make it very difficult to identify them. Worse, once picked up by search engines, these statements can hang around seemingly forever.

How, then, do companies affected by such statements deal with them? How do they track down the creators of these messages and stop them? At the same time, how do ISPs protect themselves and the privacy rights of their subscribers from an avalanche of bad-faith lawsuits and subpoenas by plaintiffs seeking to chill legitimate criticism that should be protected as free speech? How do the message posters protect themselves from having their ISPs give away their anonymity, possibly exposing them to substantial financial loss and even repercussions in their careers? And, finally, how do the courts protect what they have found under some circumstances to be a First Amendment right to speak anonymously while still holding these anonymous individuals appropriately liable for wrongful speech?

The answers to all these questions involve a combination of technology, contract provisions, and litigation, all occurring against a backdrop of evolving court decisions that make predictions difficult and constant attention to the shifting legal landscape mandatory.

It is vital to remember that court cases on this subject have been issued frequently and have changed the legal landscape significantly. So, before applying the principles written about in this chapter, make sure to check the most current cases available.

THE LEGAL CAUSES OF ACTION

Depending on the exact nature of the statements involved, the legal theories underlying these cases vary. One of the more common legal theories is defamation, that is, a published intentional false communication that injures a person's or company's reputation or good name. If the message posters are employees of a company named in a message and have signed confidentiality agreements, another popular legal theory arises out of a claimed breach of fiduciary duty owed to the company by the employee. Typically, in these cases, the allegations concern breach of an employment agreement containing confidentiality clauses, preventing employees from wrongfully disseminating private information about the company in public. Similarly, if the offender is not necessarily an employee but instead, perhaps, a competitor, other available theories include interference with business relations. And at least one case (discussed in this chapter) has even been brought against someone who never uttered a wrongful word but who, instead, republished it on the Internet, theoretically extending its reach. In a more limited number of cases, where the wrongful posts involve attempts to manipulate securities prices, securities-fraud-related federal and state laws have become involved.

Whatever the legal theory, it's obvious that an individual or corporate plaintiff will not get very far if the message poster or the origin of the offending message cannot be identified, an all-too-common difficulty. Because individuals or groups posting such messages rarely do so in their own names—rather, they use aliases and try to hide their true whereabouts—finding them requires a combination of technological detective work and swift but careful court action.

THE TECHNOLOGY ASPECT

Message boards are usually hosted through the aid of ISPs or other popular Internet companies, including America Online and Yahoo, though many smaller websites offer message boards, too. Subscribers to these message boards typically have self-styled e-mail addresses or user names and, like all Internet users, are assigned an Internet Protocol or "IP" address when they connect to the Internet, which is really how computers identify themselves to other computers on the Internet. Most people don't have a fixed IP address that follows them wherever they go but, instead, are randomly given a new address every time they connect to their ISP. So, behind the scenes of all Internet communications, what's really going on is that computers identified on the Internet by a certain IP address are used to send messages using an e-mail or message board name to message boards located at a different IP address.

Unfortunately, because IP addresses are assigned dynamically, and last only the length of the session, most ISPs don't keep records of them for long. What's more, because IP addresses are randomly assigned, a malicious poster who logs onto the Internet several times will have done so through several different IP addresses, even through the same ISP.

This is where the lawyers step in. Their challenge is to follow the trail backward from the message board, traveling to the IP address from which the message was sent, to the ISP whose server was used to send it, to the actual sender. How do they do it? The simple answer, so far, has been litigation.

EARLY LAWSUITS AND LEGAL LESSONS

When companies first began to seriously pursue these kinds of cases, here's how it worked. As the first salvo, even before a formal complaint was filed, lawyers for a plaintiff sent what is known as a "cease and desist" letter to the message board host to "stop the bleeding" by removing the offensive post from its server. Typically, lawyers also requested that the ISP or host retain whatever evidence it had on the message's origin, taking it out of its ordinary record disposal procedure and thereby avoiding destruction of evidence.

Confronted with this type of dispute, plaintiffs' lawyers typically tried to have the ISPs or hosts give them the IP address and originating computer server of the post, something most would not do voluntarily. As a result, some lawyers swiftly filed a lawsuit and sought quick discovery—that is, production of evidence as required by law—from the host to identify the actual offending party before the trail went cold. At this point, lawyers had to think fast and hard, because they were forced to commence a lawsuit without the benefit of a lot of the standard information normally required by the law.

Obviously, before filing any lawsuit, lawyers needed to know who they were suing. Thanks to a provision of the Communications Decency Act—as discussed in Chapter 21—they generally were not able to sue the message board host because the CDA immunizes them from lawsuits based upon offensive materials originating from someone else. Since lawyers couldn't sue the message board host and didn't know the real identity of the poster, many of them sued one or more "John Does," essentially a placeholder defendant meant to represent the person being sued, until such time as the defendant's real identity was discovered.

Then there was the question of where to bring suit. All lawsuits require a plaintiff to establish that the court has jurisdiction—that is, controlling power and authority—over both the dispute and the defendant. Without knowledge of the identity and location of a defendant, it was unclear where to sue him or her. Here, attorneys got around the problem based upon a concept available in every state known as "long-arm jurisdiction." In simple terms, this means that a state court can exercise its jurisdiction, even over an out-of-state defendant, if that defendant has caused harm within the complaining party's state and that harm is the specific basis of the lawsuit. Additional solutions to the problem of where to sue existed if the lawsuit raised a federal question, that is, a question arising out of the U.S. Constitution or a federal statute, because in such cases a federal court would be a proper place to go, the only question being which state's federal court should be used.

As much as anything else, the paramount concern in matters such as these has always been speed. Particularly, if the message board host refused either to turn over any information or even to isolate it, a lawyer's only immediately meaningful way to identify the mystery poster was to obtain a speedy subpoena from a court ordering the host to reveal the requested information.

When these lawsuits were first brought, plaintiffs' lawyers were understandably assertive in the hopes of getting information when it was still available to help protect their clients from continued damage from harmful anonymous posts. And they were often successful. For a while, if someone anonymously posted a defamatory statement about a company on an Internet newsgroup, the company could run to the courthouse and ask a judge to make the host identify the anonymous poster and then sue the person for libel. In some states, this could be done by a special petition for discovery before a lawsuit was even filed or any proof of the viability of the case needed to be shown.

However, in many cases the message board hosts served with these subpoenas resisted them. In fact, subpoenas directed toward ISPs, seeking to unmask the identities of these anonymous posters, fostered a litany of litigation because of the conflicting interests of the players involved. Why the resistance to these subpoenas? Some groups have claimed that this subpoena procedure of unmasking anonymous posters has been used primarily by corporations as a tool to silence the alleged offender and deter other "wannabe" posters from publicizing critical or unfair statements and opinions to a global audience. In fact, in many cases, unmasking the poster was often the end of the litigation. When the anonymous critics were discovered to be a company's own employees, they were simply fired and the suit was dropped. After all, the employees rarely had sufficient assets to make pursuing them worthwhile and, in some instances, pursuing them for money was often secondary to the goal of stopping the anonymous criticism. As employees increasingly were perceived as having been fired for their opinions and sometimes lost valuable benefits such as bonuses and stock options in the process, public interest groups—including Public Citizen, the Electronic Frontier Foundation, and the ACLU—took notice of this trend and began raising First Amendment free-speech concerns on behalf of these defendants. They argued in cases brought around the country that people should be able to participate online without fear that someone who wishes to harass or embarrass them into silence can file a frivolous lawsuit to reveal their identity without just cause.

These arguments essentially sought to extend the reach of certain U.S. Supreme Court decisions that have applied First Amendment protections to speech on the Internet and to anonymous speech in other areas. The U.S. Supreme Court addressed the issue of First Amendment protection for anonymous speech in 1995 in *McIntyre* v. *Ohio Elections Commission,*[1] protecting the right of an anonymous author of handbills distributed in connection with a local tax referendum. The Court explained that the motives people have for choosing anonymity include fear of economic or official retaliation, concern about social ostracism, and a desire to preserve as much of one's privacy as possible. As the Court noted, "Whatever the motivation may be, . . . the interest in having anonymous works enter the marketplace of ideas unquestionably outweighs any public interest in requiring disclosure as a condition of entry. Accordingly, an author's decision to remain anonymous, like other decisions concerning omissions or additions to the content of a publication, is an aspect of the freedom of speech protected by the First Amendment."

Two years later, the high court implicitly recognized that the Internet functions in the global world as a kind of speakers' corner in England's Hyde Park, a public place where ordinary people may voice their opinions to anyone willing to listen. In its 1997 decision on the Communications Decency Act, *Reno* v. *ACLU*[2] (discussed in detail in Chapter 22), the Court extended First Amendment protection to speech on the Internet, acknowledging that the Internet "constitutes a vast platform from which to address and hear from a worldwide audience of millions of readers, viewers, researchers, and buyers. . . . Through the use of chat rooms, any person with a phone line can become a town crier with a voice that resonates farther than it could from any soapbox."

As public interest groups seized on these concepts and continued with a direct assault on what had been a very successful and relatively quick method of silencing online critics, judges in different states slowly but increasingly shifted their thinking and have responded more favorably to arguments that online anonymous speech deserves constitutional protection. As a result, in a number of cases, a noticeable trend emerged, making it more difficult for plaintiffs to unmask anonymous posters on the Internet without showing their case has merit and without following procedural guidelines created by individual judges in an effort to give posters an opportunity to fight back under pseudonyms before losing their anonymity. Some state courts across the country have handed down even more wide-reaching protections against involuntary identity unmasking of individuals with information useful to cases where they are not parties and against liability for posting alleged defamatory statements made by others.

COURTS CREATE RULES TO PROTECT ANONYMOUS MESSAGE POSTERS

In 2001, a trend began to emerge from several cases that courts will give more weight to arguments that the First Amendment protects the right to speak anonymously on the Internet.

In one case, for example, a New Jersey appellate court in July 2001 upheld a lower court ruling denying a subpoena directed to Yahoo to identify an online poster on one of its message boards. In that case, *Dendrite International, Inc. v. John Doe No.3, et al.,*[3] Dendrite claimed that it was defamed by postings made by John Doe No. 3 under the pseudonym "xxpllr" claiming that the company changed its revenue recognition accounting practices to improve its bottom line and that the company had secret plans for the sale of the company that were unsuccessful. The appellate court, affirming the lower court's conclusion that Dendrite had failed to show any harm from these statements, took advantage of the opportunity to establish a four-pronged test that plaintiffs must meet to outweigh an anonymous defendant's constitutional privilege of anonymity. Applying standards previously laid down in a similar case decided in California, the New Jersey court held that parties seeking discovery to unmask an anonymous poster must

- identify the unknown party with sufficient specificity to allow the court to decide if it has jurisdiction over the party;
- identify all previous steps taken to locate the missing party and notify it of the lawsuit and the opportunity to object;
- establish by proof to the court's satisfaction that the plaintiff's suit could withstand a motion to dismiss, meaning that there must be a viable claim; and

• make a showing justifying why the specific discovery requested is needed, and that the proposed recipients of the subpoena (such as ISPs) are both limited in number and reasonably calculated to produce the identities and whereabouts of the unknown defendants so legal process can be served on them.

In similar fashion, in *Pre-Paid Legal Services* v. *Sturtz,*[4] decided in August 2001, a superior court judge in Santa Clara County, California, quashed a subpoena issued to Yahoo by an Oklahoma-based legal services company that requested identities of anonymous posters after they had posted negative remarks about the company on a Yahoo message board devoted to discussions about the company; the company suspected the posters of being former company employees, now working for a competitor. Even though the company claimed that it needed the posters' identities to determine whether they were subject to a voluntary injunction preventing former sales associates who work for a competitor from revealing the plaintiff's trade secrets, the court declined the requested relief. Similar to the standards reiterated in the *Dendrite* case, the judge in *Pre-Paid Legal* concluded that the posters' anonymity could not be breached by a subpoena absent a clear showing that specifically identified that

• relevant information about the anonymous poster is central to the claims of the party seeking the information;
• those claims are viable; and
• the party cannot acquire the information in another way.

Not only have courts proved increasingly unwilling to unmask anonymous defendants, they have also sometimes imposed an even higher standard when it comes to unmasking nonparties who may have information material to existing lawsuits.

For instance, in *Doe* v. *2TheMart.com, Inc.,*[5] shareholders of the defendant corporation sued in Seattle on various grounds complaining that the corporation had committed a fraud on the securities market, causing damages due to a drop in the price of the company's stock. Among twenty-seven different defenses, the corporation claimed that the stock price dropped because of illegal statements posted on a message board hosted by Silicon Investor, an investment website owned by InfoSpace. As a result, a subpoena was issued to InfoSpace to provide a wide range of information about the posts, including the identities of the anonymous posters. Holding that the balancing test between needs of a plaintiff and the First Amendment protections afforded anonymous posters should be tilted even more in favor of free-speech protections when nonparties were concerned, the court announced its own four-part test to justify unmasking anonymous nonparty posters, requiring that

- the subpoena must be shown not to have been issued in bad faith or for an improper purpose;
- the information sought must relate to a core claim or defense in the case;
- the information sought must be directly material or relevant to such a core claim or defense; and
- the information sought cannot be obtained any other way.

Applying these standards, the Seattle court quashed the subpoenas.

And in *Barrett* v. *Clark*,[6] a California case that made national headlines in July 2001, an Alameda County Superior Court judge's groundbreaking ruling gave sweeping libel protection to Internet users in California who repost arguably libelous material others have written and who express themselves on matters of public concern. The case was commenced by doctors who maintained a group of websites dedicated to exposing those practicing "quack medicine." Ilena Rosenthal, one of the defendants and the director of a San Diego–based international support group for women harmed by breast implants, was sued not only for making allegedly defamatory statements herself but also for reposting an allegedly libelous article that accused one of the doctors of stalking a Canadian journalist. In dismissing the reposting claim, the court applied a key section of the CDA to Rosenthal, saying, "[A]s a user of an interactive computer service, that is, a newsgroup, [the defendant] is not the publisher or speaker of [the] piece. Thus, she cannot be civilly liable for posting it on the Internet. She is immune."

What is especially significant about this case is that in dismissing the remaining defamation claims against Rosenthal, the court for the first time also relied upon a state statute designed to counter lawsuits brought primarily to chill the valid exercise of the constitutional rights of freedom of speech and petition for redress of grievances about matters of public concern. These suits are known as strategic lawsuits against public participation, or SLAPP, suits, and anti-SLAPP statutes like the one in California allow the dismissal of suits complaining of speech regarding matters of public concern unless some showing of a meritorious case can be made at the outset. Finding that the plaintiff doctors were public figures involved in an issue of public concern and that Rosenthal was merely expressing herself, according to her free-speech rights, on an issue of interest to the public, the court broke new ground in the online anonymity area by using California's SLAPP law to dismiss a claim of cyber-libel against someone who reposted allegedly defamatory material.

THE COURTS' EFFECT ON ANONYMITY ONLINE

As a result of these and other cases, it is clear that efforts to compel the unmasking of anonymous Internet posters has risen to an issue of constitutional proportion, where subpoenas in civil suits are being quashed on First Amendment, free-speech grounds and where efforts to unmask Internet posters, whether they be parties to a lawsuit or not, are being balanced against the right to remain anonymous. More important, new law is being made on this issue all the time in different states, so that drawing a conclusion on when anonymous posters can be unmasked and when they can't is becoming harder every day. Still, there are some standards that are emerging as guidelines for would-be plaintiffs and posters alike.

Plaintiffs can't use the court's subpoena powers to go on a fishing expedition or as a technique to silence opposition by launching frivolous lawsuits they have no chance of winning. If a plaintiff cannot show it is likely to win its case based upon the alleged defamatory statements, whether it be on grounds of libel or other business wrong, it isn't likely to be successful in discovering the identities of anonymous online posters either.

If the state in which a suit is brought has an anti-SLAPP law, it's a further consideration before bringing an action for cyber-libel. Aside from the public relations nightmare that could result if the judge rules in favor of the defendant, a plaintiff, depending on the anti-SLAPP law in the state, also could be held liable for the defendant's legal expenses.

What's more, even if it can be shown that there is a good case, before a subpoena will be issued a plaintiff should expect to demonstrate that the requested discovery is necessary to prove its case and that the request is sufficiently tailored to avoid unnecessary infringement of free-speech rights.

These emerging standards make the commencement of litigation and subpoena practice even more of a deliberate and calculating decision than ever before. Potential plaintiffs would be wise to provide enough specificity to convince a judge that measurable harm has been done, that they have a viable claim that will likely prevail if provided the identities of the anonymous attackers, that obtaining the names is vital to their claim, that they have already taken all other steps in their power to obtain the names but have not succeeded, and that they have tried to put the anonymous posters on notice of their claim.

While the general rule in most litigation is that discovery comes first and proof comes later, this particular subset of litigation has now turned that rule upside down.

Does that mean that anyone can say whatever he or she pleases and nothing can be done about it? Hardly. There is no First Amendment right to libel. Where plaintiffs have failed, it has often been because of not meeting all the elements articulated by courts squarely, or not meeting the newly imposed standards for these cases, not because it is impossible to succeed. As these new standards gain traction in cases around the country, the rules will be known and plaintiffs with good-faith, meritorious cases will be better able to frame their claims and discovery requests in a manner calculated to increase their chances of success.

Moreover, when it comes to taking steps to offset the claimed damaging effects of Internet postings, potential plaintiffs can take heart in knowing that the same medium that makes it easy for negative statements to be made makes it equally easy to rebut them. So, as lawyers often advise their clients, being alert to the possibility of these postings in advance can be a huge advantage to a company looking to prevent or minimize damage flowing from mystery posters. To the extent of their resources, companies should seek out message boards likely to elicit posts involving their industry, or even their company, monitor them regularly, and take appropriate action at the first sign of trouble. If any of these types of posts are caught quickly, a company may even be in a position to respond on the same message board, or issue a press release to defray the damage. As was argued by the defendant's attorneys from EFF and the ACLU in the *2TheMart.com* case, one remedy for undesirable speech on the Internet can be "more speech" instead of "enforced silence."

In fact, it may very well turn out that future court decisions will hinge on whether plaintiffs took steps on the same public message boards where they were allegedly damaged to minimize their claimed damages by making efforts to dispel false statements online. To the benefit of posters and hosts alike, the ability of a company to do this will also demonstrate its ability to give anonymous posters notice of its intention to take legal action, giving the posters an opportunity to take action to prevent a host from being compelled to reveal their identities before a subpoena takes effect.

How will posters prevent disclosure of the information? They may continue to use the typical method of making what's known as a motion to quash the subpoena, that is, a request to have the subpoena invalidated in whole or in part. Because of successes in cases such as those profiled above, the most common bases for these motions will revolve around freedom of speech, privacy interests, and even relevance and materiality of the requested information to the allegations contained in the original complaint. As this happens, anonymous posters will also have to honor the developing standards and will have to continue to take the initiative to quash subpoenas that may more closely comply with judicial guidelines. And once the guidelines are more widely accepted, these same posters will have to wonder if their legal costs will continue to be subsidized by public interest groups.

ISPs themselves will have to be ready to modify their privacy policies to stay in line with fast-changing court decisions that will mark the boundaries of when their subscribers' personal identity information may be disclosed in private suits.

If a plaintiff is successful in flushing out the true identity of an offending poster, experience suggests that the worst is over. Once the posters can no longer maintain their anonymity, they know that they will remain potentially liable for the consequences of their statements and that the complaining party now "knows where they live," as the saying goes.

How these disputes will be brought to their conclusions depends on how strong the claims for damages are in the first place and how likely it is that the identified poster has the resources to pay any damages recovered. Many times, an agreed-upon injunction or a public retraction resolves the matter, especially if the identified wrongdoer does not have significant financial resources to pay a large damages award.

Whether you are a potential plaintiff (that is, someone who has been defamed) or a potential defendant (that is, an anonymous online poster), familiarity with the new standards courts are requiring can help you and your attorney craft a strategy that has a better chance of being successful. If you take careful steps to strengthen your legal position, it is still possible for accountability for defamation online, even when it is posted anonymously, while ensuring that free-speech protections derail bad-faith suits.

CHAPTER TWENTY-FOUR

Critical Websites, Parody, and the First Amendment

The Internet has created an unprecedented way for dissatisfied customers to criticize companies they believe have wronged them or that engage in practices with which they disagree. In the past, customers had few outlets through which they could express their dissatisfaction—passing out leaflets is time-consuming and reaches a rather limited audience, and getting the mainstream media interested in any particular issue is often quite difficult. But the Internet has provided critics with the world's largest soapbox, by allowing anyone with only limited technical skills to create a website for all the world to see, a forum where every critical opinion can be expressed.

LEGAL ATTEMPTS TO SILENCE "CYBERGRIPERS"

In recent years, the number of critical websites has risen along with the growth of the Internet generally. And, not surprisingly, the number of lawsuits over these critical sites has risen, too. For example:

- In February 2002, the Republican Party of Texas threatened to sue the operator of a website known as EnronOwnsTheGOP .com. The site, which highlighted connections between the Republican Party and the bankrupt Texas company, used a logo in the shape of an elephant with an outline of the state of Texas and the Enron logo in the center of it. A lawyer for the Republican Party of Texas said the logo was confusingly similar to the GOP's logo and violated trademark law.[1] Ultimately, the GOP backed down.
- Starbucks filed a copyright and trademark infringement suit against a San Francisco cartoonist who created a website with a logo that had the words "Consumer Whore" in lieu of "Starbucks Coffee."[2]
- During the 2000 presidential election, George W. Bush's campaign filed a complaint with the Federal Election Commission against the operator of a site at gwbush.com, which included, among other things, cartoons of Bush with cocaine on his face.[3]
- Attorneys for the *Barney* children's television show wrote a letter to the Electronic Frontier Foundation, which hosted on its website articles from a magazine called the *Computer Underground Digest,* including one in which a writer joked about hating and wanting to kill the singing purple dinosaur.[4]

A company that is targeted by online critics—sometimes called "cybergripers"—may want to take legal steps to shut them up, but the First Amendment often provides significant protection for critical speech on the Web. Important, because a defamation claim generally requires an intentional false communication, pure opinions expressed on a critical site often are not legally actionable. And in some cases the courts have found these sites to be parodies protected by the First Amendment. But, as with so many aspects of Internet law, it is not yet easy to draw consistent and definitive legal guidance from the cases on critical websites.

PARODY AND THE WEB

Parodies are much older than the Internet, of course, and cases involving critical publications have involved some of our society's best-known icons, including Dr. Seuss, the Girl Scouts, L.L. Bean, and—in a case that reached the U.S. Supreme Court in 1994—a song by the rap group 2 Live Crew that was similar to Roy Orbison's romantic tune "Oh, Pretty Woman." (The Court said the 2 Live Crew version, about a "hairy woman," may be protected as a commercial parody within the fair use provisions of the Copyright Act.[5])

A parody, according to the courts, is a literary or artistic work that imitates the characteristic style of an author or a work for comic effect or ridicule. According to a 1999 case involving a *Barney* character look-alike, "a reference to a copyrighted work or trademark may be permissible if the use is purely for parodic purposes."[6] Interestingly, determining whether something is a parody under the law is not always easy to do, because a legal parody involves the conveyance of two simultaneous but contradictory messages: The parody must conjure up or target the work it parodies, but it must also be apparent that it is not the original. If a critical website—or any other online, or even off-line, publication—is considered a parody, it is legally acceptable (assuming other portions of it do not violate the law) no matter how offensive or harmful its target may find it; but if the site is not a parody, it may run afoul of defamation, copyright, trademark, or other laws.

For example, in a case only someone with a warped sense of humor could appreciate, the animal rights organization People for the Ethical Treatment of Animals (PETA) sued Michael T. Doughney, the registrant of the domain name peta.org, asserting claims for service mark infringement, unfair competition, trademark dilution, and cybersquatting. Though the case might at first appear to be similar to countless other domain name disputes, what made this one especially interesting—and relevant to this discussion—is the fact that Doughney created a website at peta.org with the title "People Eating Tasty Animals," an idea obviously in contradiction to PETA's mission, which includes opposing the exploitation of animals for food and clothing. Doughney's site stated that it was a "resource for those who enjoy eating meat, wearing fur and leather, hunting, and the fruits of scientific research." The site contained links to meat, fur, leather, hunting, animal research, and other organizations.

In response to PETA's lawsuit, Doughney claimed that his website was a parody, protected by the First Amendment. The district court, however, didn't buy it, granting PETA's motion for summary judgment in June 2000. The appeals court agreed, affirming the decision in August 2001 and writing:

> Looking at Doughney's domain name alone, there is no suggestion of a parody. The domain name peta.org simply copies PETA's Mark, conveying the message that it is related to PETA. The domain name does not convey the second, contradictory message needed to establish a parody—a message that the domain name is not related to PETA, but that it is a parody of PETA.
>
> Doughney claims that this second message can be found in the content of his website. Indeed, the website's content makes it clear that it is not related to PETA. However, this second message is not conveyed *simultaneously* with the first message, as required to be considered a parody. The domain name conveys the first message; the second message is conveyed only when the viewer reads the content of the website. As the district court explained, "an internet user would not realize that they were not on an official PETA web site until after they had used PETA's Mark to access the web page 'www.peta.org.' " . . . Thus, the messages are not conveyed simultaneously and do not constitute a parody.

In another case involving a controversial domain name, a court was similarly unpersuaded by a defendant's attempt to rely on the First Amendment for legal protection. In it, a man named Claude Tortora created a website at the domain name thebuffalonews.com that purported to be "a parody and forum for discussion of THE BUFFALO NEWS" newspaper. (Tortora was also the founder of a company that published an apartment rental guide that competed with a guide published by the Buffalo News.) Tortora's website contained disparaging comments about the newspaper and links to other sites with negative opinions and stories about the newspaper. It invited visitors to submit their own comments and complaints about the newspaper via e-mail. The site also contained a "legal disclaimer" link stating that it was not affiliated with the Buffalo News. Despite this disclaimer, not surprisingly, the owner of the Buffalo News filed a trademark infringement lawsuit. As in the PETA case, the court ruled in favor of the trademark owner and against the critic, calling the defendant's reliance on the First Amendment "unpersuasive."

The court focused not on the content of Tortora's website but on his selection of the domain name thebuffalonews.com:

> Had [Tortora] used a domain name other than plaintiffs' trademark, there would be little question that the content of [his] web site would be protected by the First Amendment (assuming of course it is not libelous or slanderous) and that plaintiffs would have no recourse under the trademark law to prevent [Tortora's] conduct. For example, had defendant Tortora used a domain name such as "claudetortora.com" or some derivative thereof, plaintiffs could not use the trademark laws to prevent him from criticizing The Buffalo News on his web site.
>
> Instead, however, [Tortora] chose to use plaintiffs' mark as [his] domain name in order to deceive Internet users into believing that they were accessing plaintiffs' web site. Such a use of plaintiffs' mark is not protected by the First Amendment. Use of another's trademark is entitled to First Amendment protection only when

the use of that mark is part of a communicative message, not when it is used merely to identify the source of a product.

In other words, the court indicated that a critical website that does not use a trademark owned by its target in its domain name should receive First Amendment protection. Indeed, that's exactly what happened in another case, involving a true "cybergripe" site without a controversial domain name. The court in that case decided in favor of the critic, a man who built a website called "Bally sucks" at a domain name that did not include any of the targeted company's trademarks. The site was dedicated to complaints about Bally's health club business. Bally sued the site's owner, Andrew S. Faber, for trademark infringement, trademark dilution, and unfair competition based on Faber's use of Bally's trademark. The court granted Faber's motion for summary judgment on all claims, noting that free-speech principles supported its position: "Faber is using Bally's mark in the context of a consumer commentary to say that Bally engages in business practices which Faber finds distasteful or unsatisfactory. This is speech protected by the First Amendment. As such, Faber can use Bally's mark to identify the source of the goods or services of which he is complaining. This use is necessary to maintain broad opportunities for expression."

However, in another case involving domain names and an offensive website, a court ruled against the trademark owner, discussing the relevance of (though not relying on) the parody defense. Lucent Technologies sued Russell Johnson after Johnson registered the domain name lucentsucks.com and allegedly created a website at that address containing pornographic photographs and services for sale. Although the court decided in Johnson's favor on a legal technicality unrelated to substantive issues of trademark law or the First Amendment, Johnson said the court could not rule against him without violating his rights of free speech. The court said his argument had "some merit" and that he "argue[d] persuasively that the average consumer would not confuse lucentsucks.com with a web site sponsored by [Lucent]." It added: "A successful showing that lucentsucks.com is effective parody and/or a site for critical commentary would seriously undermine the requisite elements for the causes of action at issue in this case."

CONFUSING CONCEPTS

If these cases seem confusing, that's because they are. Legally protected parody under the First Amendment was not the easiest legal concept to understand even before the arrival of domain names and trademarks, so courts are still struggling with how to apply this constitutional issue in cyberspace. Despite this confusion, though, traditional First Amendment law and the new cases interpreting online parody do provide some guidance in this area. If you are a dissatisfied customer or have some other reason for becoming a cybergriper, the most important thing to remember is that there's no doubt you can air your grievances online; the tricky question, though, is how you can do so without violating defamation, trademark, copyright, or other laws. And if your company has been targeted by a cybergriper, the most important thing to remember is that although you may feel wronged and although you may actually suffer damage, you should consider whether the First Amendment will prevent you from prevailing in a lawsuit designed to shut up your critics.

Finally, as in any lawsuit, a plaintiff should consider seriously the public relations ramifications of trying to silence cybergripers. Sometimes the attention created by filing a lawsuit will be greater—and more damaging—than that created by the cybergriper.

CHAPTER TWENTY-FIVE

HATE ON THE INTERNET

While it's a marvelous medium for education, communication, entertainment, and commerce, the Internet has a dark side, too. Hate groups have emerged from the back alleys of the past to post their hateful ideas online, in full view of everyone, where they can hide behind their anonymity while spewing their hatred for a potential audience of thousands, if not millions. Indeed, in late 2001, an employee Internet management software company reported that the number of online hate sites grew 70 percent—to more than 373,000 pages—in the preceding year.[1] The Internet is a relatively cheap and highly effective way for hate groups—as diverse as the National Alliance and the Ku Klux Klan, as well as anti-Semites, rightwing extremists, militia groups, and others—to propagate their hateful ideas.

THE SCOPE OF HATE ON THE INTERNET

The Internet has become a powerful recruitment tool for hate groups. Where the activities of these groups once were limited by geographical boundaries, the Internet allows even the smallest fringe group to spread hate and freely recruit members online by tapping into the worldwide audience that the Web provides. Technology also offers these groups the ability to post messages in chat rooms and communicate as never before.

The Anti-Defamation League (ADL), which is at the forefront of tracking this trend of hate online and exposing the phenomenon in numerous reports, has responded to several incidents where hatred and bigotry have found their way onto mainstream Internet portals. For instance, the ADL in 2000 and 2001 fielded dozens of complaints about the presence of hate "clubs" on Yahoo. Dozens of hate groups had established these clubs in plain view on Yahoo's servers. ADL and Yahoo worked together to pull the plug on these haters, resulting in the company's removal of some of the most offensive clubs because they violated of the site's terms of service agreement, which clearly prohibits hate speech.

This was one instance where it was possible to rein in white supremacist and racist groups from spreading racism and bigotry. But in the vast majority of cases, online hate speech remains protected under the First Amendment. Hate speech and the many varied forums available on the Internet for the exchange of information have opened up a new set of legal quandaries. Many of the thorniest issues surrounding hate speech ultimately will be decided in the courts.

Hate is pervasive on the Internet, and it takes many forms. Through its Internet Monitoring Unit, the ADL has documented literally hundreds of hate groups that maintain a Web presence. The ADL's report "Poisoning the Web: Hatred Online" noted that these groups have become increasingly sophisticated in their approach.[2] Many hate sites are being specifically designed to ensnare children. The virulently anti-Semitic and racist World Church of the Creator, for example, has in the past maintained a children's page complete with apparently harmless color graphics, crossword puzzles, and games. A closer look revealed the games were laced with racist and anti-Semitic themes.

The World Church of the Creator also posts membership applications and disturbing images, such as a graphic of a skinhead crushing a Hasidic Jewish man, with blood dripping from the giant fist. These hateful images are hardly an isolated phenomenon, nor are they banished to the farthest fringes of the Web. Any computer user can unwittingly land at a hate site by typing a few keywords on a search engine. Indeed, many hate sites are barely a click away, making it easier than ever for hate groups to prey on unsuspecting computer users, especially children.

While many hate sites are blatantly racist or bigoted in their approach, other sites disguise themselves as legitimate sources of information. There's one site that appears to be an examination of the life of the civil rights leader Dr. Martin Luther King, Jr. Any student doing research on Dr. King who might happen upon this site could be duped into believing it is a legitimate history. Scrolling down, the trained observer notices that it really contains racist propaganda from the National Alliance.

The Internet also has become a haven for Holocaust deniers, people who dispense anti-Semitism through distorted conceptions of modern history.

The Internet may provide some hate groups with sources of revenue. The National Alliance, a white supremacist group in the United States, purchased a nearly defunct hate music record label and revived it, taking advantage of the unsurpassed power of the Internet with a newly designed website designed to sell hate music to the masses. The Resistance Records website enables the record label to hawk its wares while spreading the word about the hate movement to a new generation of potential recruits.

THE CONSEQUENCES OF HATE ON THE INTERNET:
THE "NUREMBERG FILES" CASE

Illustrative of how a hate site can generate a charge that it is itself responsible for violence is the so-called "Nuremberg Files" case. The case, formally *Planned Parenthood* v. *American Coalition of Life Activists,* involved an interpretation of the Freedom of Access to Clinics Entrances Act (FACE), which allows a person to bring a lawsuit against anyone who

> by force or threat of force or by physical obstruction, intentionally injures, intimidates or interferes with or attempts to injure, intimidate or interfere with any person because that person is or has been, or in order to intimidate such person or any other person or any class of persons from, obtaining or providing reproductive health services.

In 1997, five doctors and two clinics that provided women's reproductive health services, including abortions, brought an action under FACE in federal district court in Oregon against fourteen individual defendants and two organizations. The plaintiffs' complaint stated that the lawsuit "seeks to protect plaintiffs . . . against a campaign of terror and intimidation by defendants that violates [FACE]." The plaintiffs sought to stop the defendants from continuing their "campaign" and, more specifically, from publishing certain documents that the plaintiffs contended were actionable as "true threats."

The individual defendants in this action were leaders and active participants in the movement to outlaw abortion, which they believed was equivalent to murder. The defendants advocated the use of violence against abortion providers and contended that the murder of abortion providers was "justifiable homicide." The leading defendant, the American Coalition of Life Activists (ACLA), was an organization that split off in 1994 from the pro-life group Operation Rescue, whose members condemned acts of violence.

One part of the case involved the "Nuremberg Files," a website that stated at the top, against a backdrop of images of dripping blood: "VISUALIZE Abortionists on Trial." It also indicated that the ACLA was "collecting dossiers on abortionists in anticipation that one day we may be able to hold them on trial for crimes against humanity. . . . [E]verybody faces a payday someday, a day when what is sown is reaped." ("Nuremberg Files" apparently was selected as the site's name by its antiabortion creators in an attempt to analogize the lawful acts performed by abortion providers to the mass murders perpetrated during the Holocaust by the Nazis, some of whom faced charges during the so-called Nuremberg Trials in Nuremberg, Germany, from 1945 to 1949.) On the Nuremberg Files site, the names of 294 individuals appeared under the headings "ABORTIONISTS: the shooters," "CLINIC WORKERS: their weapons bearers," "JUDGES: their shysters," "POLITICIANS: their mouthpieces," "LAW ENFORCEMENT: their bloodhounds," and "MISCELLANEOUS BLOOD FLUNKIES." The names of abortion providers who had been murdered were lined through in black, while the names of those who had been wounded were highlighted in gray. The site suggested that the reader "might want to share your point of view with this 'doctor.' . . ."

The plaintiffs contended that the Nuremberg Files site violated FACE because it posed a threat to them. The defendants argued that because the site did not directly advocate violence, they did not violate FACE, which, in any event, they said was an unconstitutional law because the First Amendment protects speech even if it is offensive and provocative.

After a three-week trial, in February 1999 a jury returned a verdict in favor of the plaintiffs in the amount of $107 million in damages. In conformity with that verdict, the court then issued an order permanently enjoining the defendants from intentionally threatening the plaintiffs and from publishing or distributing the documents at issue. The defendants appealed to the U.S. Court of Appeals for the Ninth Circuit, a panel of which reversed the lower court's judgment, finding that the threat was too diffuse.[3] The entire

Ninth Circuit then voted to hear the case and, in May 2002, ruled in a highly divided opinion that the defendants' actions, including the Nuremberg Files website, violated FACE and were not protected by the First Amendment, although it directed the district court to reconsider the damages award.[4]

The Ninth Circuit wrote:

> [W]e hold that "threat of force" in FACE means what our settled threats law says a true threat is: a statement which, in the entire context and under all the circumstances, a reasonable person would foresee would be interpreted by those to whom the statement is communicated as a serious expression of intent to inflict bodily harm upon that person. So defined, a threatening statement that violates FACE is unprotected under the First Amendment.

The court then went on to find that the Nuremberg Files constituted a "threat of force" because, by including the names of abortion providers on the site in the context created by the defendants, the defendants were not simply staking out a position of debate but actually threatening the plaintiffs' demise.

Interestingly, the FACE lawsuit is not the only case involving an antiabortion website. One of the men involved with the Nuremberg Files site, Neal Horsley—who was not a defendant in the FACE lawsuit—sued Geraldo Rivera for defamation after Horsley was interviewed on Rivera's CNBC talk show in 1998. The interview took place just four days after Bernard Slepian, a medical doctor who performed abortions as part of his practice, was killed while standing in the kitchen of his home in Buffalo, New York. Following the murder, Horsley added Slepian's name to a website (which may have been the same Nuremberg Files site at issue in the FACE case, although the court's opinion is not clear) and then graphically crossed it out. During the CNBC interview, Rivera called Horsely "an accomplice to homicide," which led to the defamation suit. In May 2002 (coincidentally, just twelve days after the Ninth Circuit's opinion in the

FACE case), the U.S. Court of Appeals for the Eleventh Circuit ruled for Rivera, saying that the talk-show host's comment was protected by the First Amendment because it was an imaginative and figurative expression that could not have been taken by a reasonable viewer as a literal assertion of facts. The court wrote: "When Rivera's statement is examined, as it must be, in its context of this debate, no reasonable viewer would have concluded that Rivera was literally contending that Horsley could be charged with a felony in connection with Dr. Slepian's murder. To the contrary, the record indicates that Rivera used those words only to convey the view that Horsley was morally responsible for Slepian's death."[5]

COMBATING HATE ON THE INTERNET

What should be done about the spread of hate through cyberspace? Most people, when they are presented with the scope of the problem, say, "There ought to be a law." That certainly was the reaction of Congress when it enacted the Communications Decency Act (CDA), which dealt not only with pornography but also with some extremist groups; however, as discussed in Chapter 22, the U.S. Supreme Court subsequently ruled that portions of the CDA were overly broad and therefore unconstitutional.[6] Other attempts to regulate the Internet in the United States have virtually all been struck down for the same reason. It's very hard to create a prohibition or a prescription against the free flow of information. You have to deal with hate speech in other, more creative ways.

One method available to individual computer users is to deny the bigots access to home computers. ADL has developed a HateFilter software application, which is designed for parents to use in home computers to filter out some of the most offensive hate sites.[7] The software is primarily intended for use as an educational tool by blocking access to sites and redirecting users to information about hate groups at the ADL home page.

There are legal remedies, however, when hate speech crosses the line into threats and intimidation. Under the law, some threats are not protected under the First Amendment. This applies to threats involving racial epithets or those motivated by racial animus. A threatening private message sent over the Internet to a victim, or even a public message displayed on a website describing intent to commit acts of racially motivated violence, can be prosecuted under the law. Similarly, harassing speech is not constitutionally protected because the speech in question usually amounts to impermissible conduct, not just speech. Both harassment and threats must be directed at specific individuals. Blanket statements expressing hatred of an ethnic, racial, or religious group cannot be considered harassment, even if those statements cause emotional distress.

WHAT THE FIRST AMENDMENT DOES NOT PROTECT

Another unprotected activity is incitement to violence. The U.S. Supreme Court ruled in the 1969 case of *Brandenburg* v. *Ohio*[8] that there is a line between speech that is "directed to inciting or producing imminent lawless action" and speech that is not likely to incite such action. Still, the *Brandenburg* standard is a high bar to meet. Online hate speech will rarely be punishable under this test.

Likewise, the concept of "group libel"—comments directed toward Jews, blacks, or any other religious or racial group as a whole—cannot be used as a weapon against haters who spew invective online or off. The courts have repeatedly held that libel directed against religious or racial groups does not create an actionable offensive. However, libel on the Internet directed toward a particular person or entity is actionable under the law just as are libelous remarks uttered in any public forum.

While hate speech online is not in itself punishable, it may provide evidence of motive in a hate crime case. At least forty-two states and the District of Columbia have some form of a hate crime law on the books that enables prosecutors to seek increased penalties when a victim is targeted in a bias crime. When hate speech on the Internet inspires violence, the evidence could aid the prosecution in seeking an increased penalty under the hate crimes statute. While this concept has only been applied to movies thus far, there have been an increasing number of crimes being committed by perpetrators who read hate literature online. The racially motivated shooting of blacks, Asian-Americans, and Jews in suburban Chicago over the July Fourth weekend in 1999 was carried out by a member of the World Church of the Creator, Benjamin Nathaniel Smith, who, according to law enforcement officials, has admitted to reading hate literature online. There have been similar cases where perpetrators of hate crimes have found inspiration in literature easily obtainable on the Internet.

Even with laws against intimidating speech, the anonymity of the Internet makes it difficult to track down and prosecute perpetrators of threatening messages. This proved true in a case involving a Detroit boy who received a barrage of anti-Semitic death threats in his e-mail inbox. The eleven-year-old, who innocently stumbled upon a hater while surfing through a public chat area, immediately reported the incident to his parents, who notified the local police. Not surprisingly, their investigation turned up few clues as to the source of the anonymous threats. Eventually, it was determined the source was disguised, quite possibly outside of the country, and obviously well beyond the reach of local authorities. (Chapter 23 discusses additional legal issues relating to anonymous posters online.)

Yet there have been other successful prosecutions against senders of hate mail. In one case, a student at the University of California in Irvine who transmitted threatening e-mails to Asian students was caught and convicted of a civil rights violation.[9]

THE REACTION OF INTERNET SERVICE PROVIDERS

Still, the law isn't always a panacea to hate. The best antidote to hate speech, many First Amendment advocates believe, is more speech. Public awareness of hate on the Internet, whether through reports and studies or media coverage, can go a long way to help sensitize the public, private Internet companies, and government regulators to the problem.

While most Internet access providers have policies that regulate offensive speech, most do not ban hate speech outright. Some providers cite their First Amendment rights as reason enough not to interfere with content on their servers.

For some websites, regulating content remains a work in progress. Many ISPs have clear guidelines regulating what is acceptable and what is not acceptable behavior on their servers. On AOL, for example, a subscriber can lose privileges simply because of a complaint from another user. But some ISPs have been less willing to establish firm policies against hate speech, citing the First Amendment in their defense. For example, EarthLink states in its "Acceptable Use Policy" that the site "supports the free flow of information and ideas over the Internet" and does not actively monitor the content of websites it hosts. Although EarthLink makes clear that illegal activities are not permitted on its site, that one caveat didn't stop the neo-Nazi website For Folk and Fatherland from establishing a home page through EarthLink. The website reprints Adolf Hitler's political manifesto *Mein Kampf* and more than two dozen of Hitler's speeches. It's not illegal activity, but the message is clearly hateful.

Those hate groups that do find trouble gaining access to mainstream ISPs can turn to one of a number of renegades of the Web. Since becoming the first hate site to go live in 1995, Don Black's "Stormfront" has leaped into the business of hosting extremist sites, describing itself as "an association of White activists on the Internet whose work is partially supported by providing webhosting for other sites." At least one extremist bumped from a mainstream online service has taken refuge on Black's server. Alex Curtis's "Nationalist Observer" site, once hosted by AOL, now resides at "Stormfront." The implication is clear: No matter how many mainstream Internet providers rebuff the bigots, those determined enough to establish a racist site will be able to find a willing host.

Combating online extremism presents enormous technological and legal difficulties, and the few examples provided here are only the tip of the iceberg. Even if it were electronically feasible to keep sites off the Internet, the international nature of the medium makes legal regulation virtually impossible. This lack of borders in cyberspace has created additional problems, particularly because many countries do not respect freedom of speech as strongly as the United States does. For example, in one well-publicized case, a French court ordered Yahoo in late 2000 to block the publication of certain hate-related items on its auction site, which used to allow the advertisement of Nazi and other goods.[10] (In November 2001, a U.S. court ruled that the French court's order was not enforceable against Yahoo in the United States.[11]) And Germany, which forbids the sale of Nazi merchandise, prevents Amazon.com and others from selling *Mein Kampf.* These items, while symbols of hate to most people worldwide, are protected in the United States by the First Amendment and can be advertised and sold freely.

CHAPTER TWENTY-SIX

Spam

In the United States, the legal fight to eliminate "spam"—that flood of unsolicited e-mail that crowds your in-box—has faced an uphill battle because of the First Amendment. That is, because the First Amendment guarantees people the right to freedom of speech (whether it's the spoken word or electronic text), any law that seeks to limit this right must be drafted to avoid being found unconstitutional. And any anti-spam law that's narrowly drafted may be too narrow to have a significant effect. As a result, as of this writing, the United States has passed no federal law specifically making spam illegal.

However, despite the absence of a federal anti-spam law in the United States, a number of states have passed their own laws to limit spam and there are some limits on commercial e-mail advertising, so if you're considering a spam campaign to promote your company's products or services, you'd better be careful. Also, you should seriously consider the negative backlash from a massive e-mail campaign; because so many consumers have become so irritated by "junk e-mail," your campaign could have the opposite of its intended effect, turning many people against your company.

WHAT IS SPAM?

Before exploring some of the limits on spam, it's important to know exactly what spam is.

(A little interesting background: According to a popular Internet legend, the term "spam" arose to describe mass e-mail because of a *Monty Python* sketch in which a group of Vikings sang a chorus of "Spam, Spam, Spam" and drowned out other conversation—much as too much junk e-mail can drown out important communications. Spam, of course, is also the name of a canned luncheon meat product produced by Hormel Foods Corporation. For a while, another Internet legend went around that Hormel, which owns trademark rights to the word "Spam," wanted to prevent everyone in the world from using that term to describe junk e-mail. But the truth, according to a Hormel website devoted to the food product, is that Hormel does not object to anyone using the word "spam" to describe junk e-mail, although it understandably objects to the use of its product's image in association with that term.[1] And, according to the Hormel site, the company opposes "the act of 'spamming.' " If you're still confused, either don't worry about it or read up on trademarks in Chapter 6!)

Part of the difficulty in placing legal limits on spam is in defining what spam is. "Unsolicited e-mail" seems to be a definition that's much too broad, because most people send and receive e-mail daily that is unsolicited (that is, the sender did not specifically ask the recipient in advance if he or she could send the e-mail), and they appreciate it. Without the legal right to send unsolicited e-mail, the entire electronic mail system would become useless. "Unsolicited commercial e-mail" is a more precise definition that's often used, but it, too, includes many communications that many people would not find objectionable. For example, if an Internet service provider sends an e-mail message to all of its dial-up customers that they can receive one month of free cable modem service if they sign up for a year, the message may constitute an unsolicited commercial e-mail message— many customers probably would be happy to have received it. "Bulk e-mail," another definition, gets at the massive distribution aspect of spam, but like the other definitions it may not be precise enough, because much e-mail sent in bulk is appreciated. (And what qualifies as "bulk," anyway—a message sent to a million recipients at once certainly might, but what about one hundred recipients, or even a dozen?)

The most precise definition of spam probably includes not only the attributes listed above but also those associated with the e-mail message's content and the status of the recipient. Much of what many people refer to as spam promotes fraudulent get-rich-quick schemes, weight-loss programs, sexual products, and other questionable goods and services. And most of those who receive spam would rather not. Therefore, a definition of spam as "unsolicited, bulk commercial e-mail promoting dishonest goods or services sent to recipients who have indicated a desire not to receive such communications" is much more precise. But even a detailed definition such as this raises problems, because it may violate the sender's First Amendment rights and because it may be so narrow that it fails to prevent a lot of spam at all.

THE PROBLEMS SPAM CREATES

While the issue of how or even whether to regulate spam is difficult, it is also very controversial. But, as anyone who's spent time downloading and weeding through junk e-mail knows, spam certainly can be an annoyance. And according to many anti-spam advocates, this unwanted e-mail can cause a lot of other problems, too. The following list, based on a longer list compiled by the organization known as the Coalition Against Unwanted Commercial Email (CAUCE), highlights some of these problems:[2]

- Cost-shifting. E-mail, unlike traditional postal mail, is very inexpensive—and that's exactly what makes it attractive to those who send spam. Many companies and individuals who hawk products via e-mail would never have the resources to reach the same audience via postal mail. But spam is not free. CAUCE says that "*every* person receiving the spam must help pay the costs of dealing with it. And the costs for the recipients are much greater than the costs of the sender." Internet service providers that devote precious computing time to deliver e-mail cannot use that same computing time to provide other services; or they must spend more money to increase their computing capacity to cope with the demands of spam.

- Fraud. Any good spammer knows that because most recipients don't want to receive junk e-mail, the messages should be sent in a way to avoid angry responses. Consequently, many spammers forge the headers of their e-mail messages, so the "from" line, for example, falsely indicates that the message was sent by someone else.

- Displacement of normal e-mail. Many people have had the same e-mail address for so long that they now receive more unwanted e-mail than wanted. CAUCE believes that eventually, if the growth of spam is not stopped, "it will destroy the usefulness and effectiveness of email as a communication tool."

Spam, like unwanted faxes and telemarketing phone calls, can become quite disruptive. And the legal system has found ways to deal with these problems: The United States passed a law that regulates the sending of unsolicited faxes,[3] and many states have laws that enable consumers to register for "do not call" lists that telemarketers must obey or face fines. But for a number of reasons, similar legal efforts to stop unwanted e-mail have not been very successful. And a March 2002 federal district court opinion finding that the law against junk faxes violates the First Amendment, *Missouri* v. *American Blast Fax*,[4] could mean that a federal law against junk e-mail would be equally unenforceable.

FEDERAL ATTEMPTS TO LEGISLATE SPAM

At least seven spam laws were proposed during the 1997–98 Congress, but none of them was enacted. Similarly, at least eleven were introduced during the 1999–2000 congressional session; one passed the House of Representatives, but none became law. As this was being written, seven bills on spam had been proposed during the 2001–02 session, though none had passed both houses of Congress.

An examination of one of these legislative proposals, the Unsolicited Commercial Electronic Mail Act of 2001,[5] shows the difficulty in drafting an acceptable anti-spam law. That bill, also known as H.R. 95, was introduced by Rep. Gene Green of Texas. Recognizing the obstacle the First Amendment poses to any attempt to limit spam, the bill began with the following recognition: "There is a right of free speech on the Internet," and "Unsolicited commercial electronic mail can be an important mechanism through which businesses advertise and attract customers in the online environment." However, it then went on to make findings, including the following:

- "The receipt of unsolicited commercial electronic mail may result in costs to recipients who cannot refuse to accept such mail and who incur costs for the storage of such mail, or for the time spent accessing, reviewing, and discarding such mail, or for both."
- "Unsolicited commercial electronic mail may impose significant monetary costs on Internet access services, businesses, and educational and nonprofit institutions that carry and receive such mail, as there is a finite volume of mail that such providers, businesses, and institutions can handle without further investment. The sending of such mail is increasingly and negatively affecting

the quality of service provided to customers of Internet access service, and shifting costs from the sender of the advertisement to the Internet access service."

• "Because recipients of unsolicited commercial electronic mail are unable to avoid the receipt of such mail through reasonable means, such mail may invade the privacy of recipients."

Without creating an outright ban on spam, the bill created a number of restrictions on the ability to send this type of e-mail. Specifically, H.R. 95 would have made it a crime to intentionally initiate "the transmission of any unsolicited commercial electronic mail message to a protected computer in the United States with knowledge that any domain name, header information, date or time stamp, originating electronic mail address, or other information identifying the initiator or the routing of such message, that is contained in or accompanies such message, is false or inaccurate." The bill also would have made it a crime "for any person to initiate the transmission of a commercial electronic mail message to any person within the United States unless such message contains a valid electronic mail address, conspicuously displayed, to which a recipient may send a reply to the initiator to indicate a desire not to receive any further messages." And the bill would have made it unlawful for a person to initiate the transmission of such a message in violation of a policy regarding unsolicited commercial e-mail messages that complies with specified requirements, including requirements for notice and public availability of such policy and for an opportunity for subscribers to opt not to receive such messages.

A similar bill, the CAN SPAM Act of 2001—an acronym for "Controlling the Assault of Non-Solicited Pornography and Marketing Act of 2001"—was approved by the Senate Commerce Committee in May 2002. This bill, S. 630,[6] like H.R. 95 the year before, did not create an outright ban on spam but instead would have made it illegal (civilly and criminally) to send e-mail with false or misleading headers; required unsolicited e-mail to include a valid return address so recipients could opt out of future mailings; banned the sending of e-mail to those who have requested not to receive it; and required all unsolicited e-mail to include the sender's physical postal address. Whether the CAN SPAM Act would become law—and, if so, whether it would survive a First Amendment challenge in the courts—was unknown as of this writing.

If these federal attempts to regulate spam seem confusing, that's because they are. On the one hand, some anti-spam advocates have applauded federal proposals as worthy attempts to stem the tide of unwanted e-mail. But, on the other hand, they also have criticized some of the bills for not going far enough, because they would still allow much unwanted e-mail to thrive. And, on the other side of the debate, free-speech advocates have found some of the bills too far-reaching.

If the *Missouri* v. *American Blast Fax* case mentioned above is any indication, any federal law against spam will be subjected to a 1980 U.S. Supreme Court test for evaluating whether a law regulating commercial speech—that is, a communication that proposes a commercial transaction, as most junk e-mail does—comports with the First Amendment. The test, set forth in the case *Central Hudson Gas & Electric Company* v. *Public Service Commission,*[7] states:

> At the outset we must determine whether the expression is protected by the First Amendment. For commercial speech to come within that provision, it at least must concern lawful activity and not be misleading. Next we ask whether the asserted governmental interest is substantial. If both inquiries yield positive answers, we must determine whether the regulation directly advances the governmental interest asserted, and whether it is not more extensive than is necessary to serve that interest.

In *American Blast Fax,* the court said the junk fax law—formally, a part of the Telephone Consumer Protection Act of 1991 (TCPA)— failed this test, because the government had not shown any statistical data that the TCPA actually shifted costs to fax recipients; the TCPA did not in any event advance the government's interest in reducing cost-shifting because it did not ban all unsolicited faxes; and there were less intrusive ways (such as a national "no-fax" database) to combat the problem.

STATE ATTEMPTS TO LEGISLATE SPAM

At the state level, anti-spam advocates have been more successful. About twenty states have passed spam-related legislation, though the various laws' requirements and legal enforceability is quite mixed. For example, a California law bans some sending of unsolicited e-mail for the sale, rental, gift offer, or other disposition of any realty, goods, services, or extension of credit unless certain conditions are met, such as including "ADV:" as the first four characters of the subject line (or "ADV:ADLT" as the first eight characters if the material can only be viewed, purchased, rented, leased, or held in possession by an individual eighteen years of age and older).[8] A Delaware law makes it illegal to intentionally or recklessly distribute "any unsolicited bulk commercial electronic mail (commercial E-mail) to any receiving address or account under the control of any authorized user of a computer system."[9] The Delaware law defines commercial e-mail as "any electronic mail message that is sent to a receiving address or account for the purposes of advertising, promoting, marketing or otherwise attempting to solicit interest in any good, service or enterprise." Other state spam laws are listed at John Marshall Law School professor David E. Sorkin's website.[10]

The existence of these state laws makes for a very confusing situation. Is a spammer subject to the laws only of the state from which the e-mail originates? Or is the spammer also subject to the laws of every state to which the e-mails are sent? How could a spammer know the physical location of every recipient? This confusion has led some courts to find these laws unenforceable. California's law was struck down as a violation of the Constitution's commerce clause, because it places inconsistent restrictions on interstate use of the

Internet,[11] although an appeals court later reversed that ruling.[12] And a trial court in Washington struck down a law there on similar grounds, although the Supreme Court of the State of Washington later reversed the lower court's decision and upheld the act.[13] (The Washington law, though commonly referred to in press accounts as an "anti-spam law," does not outlaw junk e-mail. Rather, the act only requires that certain "commercial electronic mail messages" sent from Washington or to state residents may not contain false information in the transmission path or misleading information in the subject line.)

As a result of the existence of numerous state anti-spam laws and their varying requirements, it is important to determine whether an e-mail marketing campaign would violate *any* of the state laws, because it is virtually impossible to limit a mailing to recipients in only certain states. In addition, it is always wise to include truthful and nonmisleading headers, a valid return address, and an easy mechanism for recipients to opt out of future mailings.

FOREIGN ATTEMPTS TO LEGISLATE SPAM

As if a hodgepodge of enforceable and unenforceable spam laws across the United States were not confusing enough, any company contemplating an e-mail campaign also should consider the varied laws of other countries, particularly if the recipients may be outside of the United States. A number of countries have adopted "opt-in" laws on e-mail that forbid the sending of unsolicited e-mail under certain circumstances except to those recipients who have previously indicated their willingness to receive it. In May 2002, the European Parliament approved an opt-in system for e-mail, faxes, and automated calling systems, requiring advance permission from users before sending them unsolicited electronic communications for marketing purposes. Some spam laws in European countries are listed on EuroCAUCE's website.[14]

USING EXISTING LAWS TO FIGHT SPAM

Even in the absence of any U.S. anti-spam law and despite the confusing status of legal attempts to regulate spam at the state level and in other countries, unscrupulous spammers may run afoul of other, existing laws.

For example, it may be illegal to send spam with false headers. This, of course, is a common tactic employed by many spammers, used to avoid the avalanche of negative feedback (and bounced e-mails) that follows any large-scale unsolicited e-mailing. U.S. trademark and unfair competition laws have been used against some spammers who identified their messages as coming from someone else. In one case, a federal magistrate judge in 2000 found that a spammer infringed America Online's trademark when he forged "aol.com" in the header of 73 million e-mail messages he sent for his adult websites.[15] The judge recommended that the spammer pay damages of more than $1.5 million.

Also, the content of many spam messages can spell legal trouble. Most "legitimate" businesses are not sending unsolicited e-mail to thousands or millions of recipients in the hope that even a tiny percentage will respond favorably. The large risk is not worth the potentially small reward. Instead, spammers consist largely of those pitching shoddy goods or false promises. Stringent advertising laws promulgated by the Federal Trade Commission address these messages. In one complaint, for example, the FTC sued a spammer who promised high investment returns, saying the promises were "false and misleading and constitute deceptive acts or practices."[16]

In April 2002, the FTC joined eight state law enforcement agencies in the United States and four Canadian agencies to tackle deceptive spam.[17] In one of the cases, the FTC said an e-mail offering recipients $10,000 in cash gifts was an illegal chain letter.[18] In another case, the FTC sued a number of people and businesses for sending spam that allegedly told the recipients they had won free Sony PlayStation 2 video game consoles or other prizes through a promotion purportedly sponsored by Yahoo; instead, the e-mail routed the recipients to an adult website via a 900-number modem connection that charged them up to $3.99 a minute.[19]

Finally, many ISPs expressly prohibit their users from sending spam. EarthLink's "Acceptable Use Policy," for example, forbids its subscribers from sending "any unsolicited commercial email or unsolicited bulk email" or using its services for activities "that have the effect of facilitating unsolicited commercial email or unsolicited bulk email whether or not that email is commercial in nature."[20] ISPs, which rely on the satisfaction of their customers and the performance of their servers, are not shy to pursue customers who breach such contracts.

PART VI

CONTRACT LAW AND HIGH TECHNOLOGY

CHAPTER TWENTY-SEVEN

Electronic Signatures and the U.S. E-Sign Act

Many people mistakenly believe that the only way two or more people or companies can enter into a contract is if they sign a piece of paper. However, a contract merely refers to whether parties have reached an agreement by exchanging promises, not whether they have signed a physical document. People and businesses enter into contracts all the time without going through the steps of creating a formal paper trail, simply by talking on the telephone and by having face-to-face discussions. These unwritten contracts are just as legally binding as written contracts, but, of course, it can be quite difficult to prove the terms of unwritten contracts if a dispute arises. (Some contracts do require a written document signed by the parties. These contracts, governed by what the law calls the "statute of frauds," apply to transactions such as the sale of real estate, services that cannot be performed within one year, and others. However, many contracts are not subject to the statute of frauds and therefore do not require a signed, written document.)

TECHNOLOGY, CONTRACTS, AND "WRITINGS"

With the rise of e-mail and other online communications, it was not immediately clear whether electronic correspondence was sufficient to create a contract. Indeed, questions about the legal validity of documents transmitted even via fax—a relatively new but now commonplace piece of office equipment—have caused problems. For example, a Georgia man by the name of Steven Earl Norris wanted to sue a construction company and the state department of transportation after his wife was killed in an accident at a highway intersection that Norris said was negligently designed, constructed, and maintained. Before Norris could file suit, though, the law required that he provide the DOT with a "notice of claim" *in writing* within twelve months after the accident. Attempting to comply with the law, Norris faxed a copy of his notice (which the DOT received *before* the twelve-month period had expired) and followed up with a copy by mail (which arrived one day *after* the twelve-month period had expired). In a 1996 ruling widely ridiculed by many lawyers, the Court of Appeals of Georgia said Norris's claim should have been dismissed because his fax did not satisfy the legal requirement that notice be provided "in writing." A fax "is an audio signal via a telephone line containing information from which a writing may be accurately duplicated," the court wrote, "but the transmission of beeps and chirps along a telephone line is not a writing, as that term is customarily used."[1] Fortunately for Norris, the Supreme Court of Georgia reversed the dismissal of his case, though it did so on technical legal grounds unrelated to the issue of whether a fax is a "writing."

The Georgia "beeps and chirps" case highlights the difficulties courts have had in applying new technologies to traditional legal transactions. In addition to the uncertainty over faxes, legal scholars have for more than a decade debated the merits of two potentially important sets of laws relating to electronic contracts—the Uniform Electronic Transactions Act (UETA) and the Uniform Computer Information Transactions Act (UCITA). UETA, approved by the National Conference of Commissioners on Uniform State Laws

(NCCUSL) in 1999, is a model statute designed for adoption by state legislatures that would apply to electronic transactions.[2] The heart of UETA states that a "record or signature may not be denied legal effect or enforceability solely because it is in electronic form." As of early 2002, thirty-eight states and the District of Columbia had adopted UETA, and seven more state legislatures had introduced the legislation.[3] The other proposed law, UCITA, also was approved by NCCUSL in 1999.[4] Unlike UETA, it does not apply to contracts in general; rather, it only covers contracts in "computer information," such as software licenses. Among many other things, UCITA provides what are known as "gap fillers"—legal provisions that would apply to contracts that do not address certain issues. As of early 2002, only two states—Maryland and Virginia—had adopted UCITA.[5]

THE ROLE OF THE E-SIGN ACT

Despite (or maybe because of) the lack of progress among the states in adopting new laws that would govern high-tech contracts (or contracts entered into via high-tech means), Congress stepped into the debate in a very significant way and in June 2000 passed the Electronic Signatures in Global and National Commerce Act, known as the E-Sign Act.[6] The E-Sign Act is similar in some ways to UETA, although it creates a single federal law whereas UETA is intended to be adopted by the states individually. (The E-Sign Act does not replace UETA. It specifically says that in any state that has adopted UETA, the E-Sign Act is preempted.)

Like UETA, the primary purpose of the E-Sign Act is to provide legal validity to contracts entered into electronically. Effective as of October 1, 2000, the E-Sign Act provides that "a signature, contract, or other record relating to [a] transaction may not be denied legal effect, validity, or enforceability solely because it is in electronic form." By "electronic," the act means any technology having electrical, digital, magnetic, wireless, optical, electromagnetic, or similar capabilities. The essence of the E-Sign Act, then, is this: Assuming a contract meets other legal requirements, it is valid even if the parties negotiated and agreed to it via e-mail or on the Web. Given the ease and speed with which companies conduct business with others worldwide on the Internet, the E-Sign Act is truly a landmark law because it grants legal validity to all of this business where uncertainty once existed. Also, the E-Sign Act is intended to be "technology-neutral," so it applies whether parties reach an agreement by exchanging e-mails, using Adobe PDF documents, or employing a more sophisticated—and often more reliable—technology such as digital signatures with encryption.

Although the E-Sign Act may be useful for many companies and many types of contracts, it does not apply to all transactions. For example, it does not apply to wills; family law transactions such as adoption and divorce; notice of cancellation of utility services; cancellation of health insurance; or product recalls. Some of these exceptions were included as a result of demands by consumer rights groups that feared electronic communications would disadvantage some people. Because of this concern, the E-Sign Act also includes language limiting its application for certain consumer disclosures. Specifically, the act says that where another law requires information to be provided to consumers in writing, consumers must affirmatively consent to electronic versions of the information and be provided with a clear and conspicuous statement informing them of a number of rights, including the right to have the information provided in nonelectronic form.

THE CONTROVERSY OF THE E-SIGN ACT

While the E-Sign Act has been mostly welcomed as a benefit to businesses, it also has generated some controversy. Consumers Union, the nonprofit publisher of *Consumer Reports,* warned that consumers should take extra precautions in light of the E-Sign Act. It issued the following list of tips in June 2000, just as the E-Sign Act was being approved by Congress:[7]

- Do not consent to an electronic contract or to receive electronic notices if you are uncomfortable using a computer or do not understand how to use e-mail.
- Do not consent to an electronic contract or to receive electronic documents until you are certain that your computer's software and hardware are compatible with the business's computer system.
- Remember that you can opt to receive documents on paper instead of electronically if you prefer.
- As with any contract, read the fine print. Don't agree to a contract that you don't understand.
- Keep backup paper copies of the electronic documents you receive, and keep a list of the businesses with which you agree to receive electronic documents.
- Notify the businesses of any changes that may affect your ability to receive e-mail, such as changing your e-mail address, your hardware, or your software.
- Close any unused e-mail accounts.
- Don't give out your e-mail address to any business if you don't want to receive e-mail notices from that business.
- Be sure to notify the business if you have any problems receiving its e-mails or opening its documents.

THE EFFECT OF THE E-SIGN ACT

Theoretically, the E-Sign Act should enhance e-commerce, because it allows people and companies to conduct business online with reassurance that their contracts will be just as legally binding as if they had negotiated and entered into them the old-fashioned way: with pen and paper. However, the act's significance is difficult to judge and is not widely used.[8] And despite the advantages that online contracting provides, there are also advantages to negotiating and signing contracts via mail or in person. For example, any lawyer knows there's no substitute for negotiations that take place with all parties in the same room. By creating personal relationships and judging body language, off-line contracting offers some benefits that the E-Sign Act cannot. And, while "Internet speed" often can be useful—particularly when an agreement has been reached and the only thing left to do is sign a document—it sometimes leaves little room for contemplation about the significance of a contract or certain provisions.

Still, the advantages of electronic contracting are obvious. Thanks to the Internet, countless companies—even those without an online presence—are using the Internet as a practical business tool. By working with a lawyer who understands the applicability and limitations of the E-Sign Act, these companies easily can conduct business with partners in faraway places without unnecessary delays.

CHAPTER TWENTY-EIGHT

WEBSITE DEVELOPMENT AGREEMENTS

Contracts are vital to the creation of any important and successful business relationship, whether Internet issues are involved or not. However, contracts for the development and maintenance of websites are especially important because they may be used to create a company's entire public presence. Just as no bricks-and-mortar company would trust a contractor to build a physical storefront or office building for it based on an informal discussion of its needs and a handshake, so, too, no company with a Web presence—either as its total existence or as a mere marketing tool—should expect to hire a website developer without a thorough contract.

In many ways, contracts for the development of websites are like contracts for the creation of physical buildings such as houses or offices. They both require significant advance planning, but regardless of the amount of detail included in the contract, the project is likely to evolve in unanticipated ways as construction proceeds. On the other hand, because websites, unlike buildings, are intangible, website development agreements raise unique issues such as those relating to intellectual property ownership.

You may be tempted to use a "form" website development agreement, either something a friend at another company has shared with you or one of those you can find on the Internet with a little searching. However, just as no two websites are identical, no two website development agreements should be identical either—so trying the "one-size-fits-all" approach is probably not a very good idea. While a form agreement may provide a useful starting point, the best website development agreements are drafted, negotiated, and redrafted multiple times to create a legally binding contract that is as unique as the company going online. Therefore, this book does not attempt to provide any forms. Instead, you should know about the following issues and keep them in mind as you work with a website developer (and ideally an attorney) to create your online presence.

STATEMENT OF WORK

Like most high-tech contracts, a website development agreement should include a detailed "statement of work," that is, a description of what the developer is being hired to create. On the one hand, the statement of work should be as detailed as possible, including a site map, mock-ups of actual pages, descriptions of any applications running on the site, and so forth. On the other hand, though, many of these details either may not be known in advance or may evolve as the development process proceeds. Therefore the contract also should include references to "change order provisions," that is, procedures for how changes to the statement of work can be made, whether the developer is obligated to accept them, and how much they will cost.

COPYRIGHT ISSUES

Amazingly, many companies fail to understand that simply because they contract with a developer to create a website, the company does not necessarily own the intellectual property rights to the website. The consequences (as also discussed in Chapter 3) can be devastating, particularly if the company and the developer later part ways and the developer wants to stop the company from using its own website any longer or contracting with someone else to update or modify it. As discussed in Chapter 2, the creator of a copyrightable work (such as a website) is by law deemed to be the owner of the copyright rights in the work unless the work qualifies as a "work made for hire" or the creator has assigned (that is, transferred) its rights in writing to someone else (such as the company). Therefore, this issue certainly should be addressed in any website development agreement. Without it, the company may wind up with only a limited license to use the website (as opposed to copyright ownership of it), preventing the company from making any changes to the site without the original developer's permission.

If a website developer creates any independently copyrightable works for incorporation into a company's website (such as graphic images or behind-the-scenes software applications), the company should be certain to obtain adequate rights to those works, too. In some instances, it may be appropriate for the developer to assign its rights in the works to the company, because the developer has no other need for the works and because the company would not want the developer to permit anyone else to use them. In other instances, particularly with software, it may be appropriate for the developer to grant the company only a broad license to use the works, because the developer will want to license the same works to other clients and because the company has no need to obtain exclusive rights.

Each party to the website development agreement also should seriously consider timing issues related to these copyright topics. In particular, if the company for whom the site is being created is going to own the intellectual property rights to the copyrighted elements, when will the assignment from the developer to the company occur? Although the company may want this assignment to happen immediately upon creation or delivery of the works, the developer may want to withhold this transfer until it has been paid for its work. By doing so, the developer creates an incentive for the company to pay promptly.

WARRANTIES, INDEMNIFICATION, AND INSURANCE

A company that hires a developer to create copyrightable elements for its website will want to include in the contract language by which the developer provides assurance that the elements are original works and do not infringe anyone else's rights. This is typically addressed in a section on "warranties and representations," such as:

> Developer warrants and represents that [describe the works] are original works of authorship created by Developer and that the works do not violate any rights, including but not limited to copyright rights, of any nonconsenting third party.

If this later proves to be untrue and the company is sued by someone else who claims to own rights to a particular work, then the developer may be held liable for breach of contract. (Similarly, the website developer will want to obtain warranties and representations from its client that the client owns the rights to any materials the client provides for incorporation into the site.) Ideally, this scenario and others should be contemplated by including in the contract adequate provisions relating to "indemnification," that is, what obligations the developer incurs in certain events, such as an obligation to pay the company's legal bills to defend itself against any claims of copyright infringement based on works created by the developer.

Of course, any company that seeks to hold a website developer liable for breach of contract or to enforce an indemnification provision will hope that the developer has adequate funds to pay any compensation that may arise. Because attorneys' fees and damage awards can become quite significant, a company should consider requiring the developer to maintain insurance that would cover such costs. The website development agreement can spell out what type of insurance the developer must maintain—and the company may even want to go further by requiring that the insurance policy name the company as an additional insured or that the developer include a copy of the policy as an exhibit to the contract.

PAYMENT AND DEADLINES

Given the dynamic nature of website development agreements and the ongoing work required for most sites, there are many ways to structure payments from the company to the developer. In many arrangements, the developer is paid a portion of the total anticipated fee upfront, and additional payments are made as specified milestones are achieved, culminating in the final payment upon the company's final acceptance of the completed site and assignment, if appropriate, of all intellectual property rights. As with any contract, the party receiving payment will want to receive as much as possible as early as possible, while the party making payment will want the opposite. Ultimately, the payment terms will have to be negotiated to a point where both parties are comfortable, often requiring some give-and-take on everybody's part.

Of course, actually determining the fee for website development work is not a simple task, and, as in many service industries, many developers prefer to charge an hourly rate because they are incapable of determining in advance how much time the project will take. A company hiring a developer, though, could incur many risks in this approach, because its expenses are unclear; what if the developer expends a hundred hours and hasn't arrived at a suitable site, yet the client's budget has been drained? In that case, the client ends up spending a lot of money and having an incomplete (and potentially useless) site to show for it. To avoid this scenario, many website development agreements include a combination of predetermined fees and hourly fees, as well as caps on hourly fees for specified projects, so everybody has an idea about the maximum costs that could be incurred.

An issue that can be tied into fees in the agreement is that of deadlines. Because a company having a website developed will certainly want or need to have the site available by a certain date, the company will want to specify completion dates in the agreement. If large fees are not required to be paid unless the deadlines are met, then the developer has a significant incentive for completing the work on time. As with construction contracts, the website development agreement may include bonus fees for early completion of the project, too. But what if a developer ultimately fails to meet a deadline and the client is not content simply to withhold payment? That, too, can be addressed in the agreement, by including provisions for what are called "liquidated damages," that is, specific amounts the developer will pay to the client for breaching its obligation to meet the deadline. However, the law limits how liquidated damages can be calculated, and in any event most developers would not agree to them. Instead, a developer would want the opposite approach: a "limitation of liability" provision that limits its financial exposure to its client even if it fails to perform as promised. It is not uncommon for an agreement to limit the developer's liability to returning the fees actually paid by the client (that is, a refund), though this may be unacceptable to the client. As with every issue in the website development agreement, this should be discussed and negotiated thoroughly until each party is comfortable, although one or both parties ultimately will incur some risk.

CONFIDENTIALITY

Because the details of many website development agreements are so heavily negotiated, the developer and/or the company for which the site is to be developed may wish to prevent the other from disclosing the terms of the agreement to anyone else. Perhaps the developer doesn't want its client to reveal how much it is charging for the work. Perhaps the client doesn't want the developer to reveal its deadlines, because doing so may tip off the client's competitors. Therefore, the parties may want to include a confidentiality provision stating that the terms of the agreement may not be disclosed except to certain people. Further, because the parties may reveal sensitive information or even trade secrets to each other during the course of the site's development, the confidentiality provision also could require them to safeguard that information, too, in addition to just the terms of the agreement itself. Because different states place different limits on the scope of confidentiality agreements, consultation with an attorney for these provisions is especially important. For reasons similar to those that motivate including confidentiality obligations, the developer's client may not want the developer to provide services for any of the client's competitors. This can be addressed by including a "noncompete" provision.

BOILERPLATE

Finally, like any agreement, a good website development agreement will include a number of "boilerplate" provisions—that is, clauses that address a number of standard legal issues. Among many other issues, these include such things as:

- Termination. What rights does each party have to terminate the agreement, when can these rights be exercised, and what are the consequences?

• Jurisdiction. Where will any legal disputes over the agreement be decided?

• Choice of law. Which state's law will be applied to interpreting the agreement?

• Alternative dispute resolution. In lieu of resolving any disputes in court, will they be decided by an alternative dispute resolution process such as arbitration or mediation, and if so, how will the process work?

• Assignment. Will either of the parties be able to assign the entire agreement to another party, for example, if the developer is bought out by someone else?

• Notices and responsible persons. To whom should notices under the agreement be sent, and who will be each party's primary contact person?

Like all of the issues discussed in this chapter, these are only some of the many legal topics to be included in a website development agreement. By discussing them in advance with each other and with their attorneys, developers and their clients can avoid many (though, unfortunately, never all) legal conflicts later.

CHAPTER TWENTY-NINE

CREATING CONTRACTS ON THE INTERNET

Doing business in a high-tech environment creates unique legal challenges, especially as companies and customers move at "Internet
speed." Not long ago, when a company wanted to enter into a
contract with a customer—such as for the sale of goods or the provision of services—each party to the contract signed a hard-copy document to indicate its agreement. Today, of course, even though high
technology has failed to create the mythical paperless office, many
transactions are conducted online between companies and customers
who never even know each other. In this environment, hard-copy
contracts are useless. Instead, they've been replaced by high-tech contracts with unusual names: shrink-wrap agreements, click-wrap agreements, and browse-wrap agreements. Though these contracts offer
many advantages over their traditional counterparts—particularly
speed and efficiency—they also pose new risks, as the courts struggle
with how (and whether) to enforce them.

SHRINK-WRAP AGREEMENTS

Shrink-wrap agreements are agreements either printed on the back of or included inside a box containing commercial computer software. The agreements often contain a number of legal terms that relate to how the software may be used. The term "shrink-wrap" arose because the agreements are often inside the shrink-wrapped plastic or cellophane that seals the box containing the software. By breaking the shrink wrap, the purchaser agrees to abide by the terms of the agreement—or so the software companies would like it to be.

If you pull out a manual or box from any software product you've bought, you'll find some interesting terms in the license agreements. Typical shrink-wrap license agreements say such things as:

- "It is illegal to make or distribute copies of this software except to make a backup copy for archival purposes only."
- "Software Company warrants only that the program will perform as described in the User Documentation. No other advertising, description, or representation shall be binding."
- "Software Company shall not be liable for any damages arising out of the use of or inability to use this product even if Software Company has been advised of the possibility of such damages."
- "You may not copy the documentation that accompanies this software."

Shrink-wrap agreements became controversial because, some believed, consumers should not be obligated to abide by the terms of an agreement they might never read, particularly if the agreement is inside the box and therefore not even visible until after the purchase is made and the box is opened. Because the law requires that every binding contract have an "offer" and an "acceptance," some people argued that shrink-wrap agreements are not enforceable because consumers never accept them. However, in one important case, this argument was largely eliminated.

The case, *ProCD* v. *Zeidenberg,* involved a dispute between a software company and a consumer who used the software in a manner forbidden by a shrink-wrap agreement. In that case, Matthew Zeidenberg purchased a copy of ProCD's SelectPhone CD software—a database of telephone directories that cost more than $10 million to compile—from a retail store in 1994. To protect its investment, ProCD included a shrink-wrap agreement in its SelectPhone software stating that it could be used only for noncommercial purposes. The agreement was contained in the printed manual that came with the CDs, and the outside of the box notified purchasers that the software came with restrictions stated in an enclosed license. Despite the restrictions, Zeidenberg used the data from the CDs to create a website that offered phone listings, for a fee—clearly a commercial use that the license forbade. As a result, ProCD sued Zeidenberg, who defended himself by arguing that the shrink-wrap agreement was not enforceable. Although the trial court agreed, the appeals court did not.

"Notice on the outside [of the box], terms on the inside, and a right to return the software for a refund if the terms are unacceptable (a right that the license expressly extends), may be a means of doing business valuable to buyers and sellers alike," the U.S. Court of Appeals for the Seventh Circuit said, in 1996.[1] The court said that although the software license was not available to Zeidenberg until after he purchased the CDs, transactions in which the exchange of money precedes the communication of detailed terms are common—such as in buying insurance (where the purchaser doesn't see the insurance contract until after he's paid for it), airline tickets (which aren't delivered until after a reservation is made and typically contain elaborate terms about travel), or concert tickets (which have licenses printed on the back limiting what the ticketholder can do at the concert, such as forbidding audiotaping or videotaping).

As a result, the appeals court ruled in the *ProCD* case, "Shrink-wrap licenses are enforceable unless their terms are objectionable on grounds applicable to contracts in general." (So if, for example, a shrink-wrap agreement inside a software package informs the purchaser that he owes an additional $10,000, or that he must give up his firstborn son, then, of course, those terms would not be legally binding.) Under this reasoning, the shrink-wrap agreement applicable to the SelectPhone software was enforceable and ProCD could pursue its claims against Zeidenberg for breach of contract.

The court's holding in the *ProCD* case is widely, but not universally, accepted. Therefore, some doubt remains about whether shrink-wrap agreements always will be found enforceable.

CLICK-WRAP AGREEMENTS

The court in the *ProCD* case recognized that not all software purchases are made at retail stores where the product is contained in a box. Even as the court wrote its opinion in 1996, the Internet was emerging as a new medium for conducting business. And, of course, it has only grown since then.

Consequently, companies that offer products and services online have employed a mechanism similar to the shrink-wrap agreement when they want their customers to agree to certain terms. You've surely encountered this mechanism if you've signed up for or bought anything online.

A "click-wrap" license is generally an online variation of the shrink-wrap license. A click-wrap license typically displays an agreement to a Web user, who must click on a link or button indicating his willingness to be bound by the terms of the agreement before he can begin downloading the software, using the free e-mail service, buying books, etc. Click-wrap agreements are commonly used by e-commerce businesses for various purposes. Here are some examples:

• The New York Times uses a click-wrap agreement on its website in its user registration process. (Users are required to register to gain access to the site's full contents.) At the bottom of the registration page, users are informed: "If you agree to the terms and conditions of our Subscriber Agreement and have completed the entire registration form, please Click ONCE to Register." The words "Subscriber Agreement" link to a document that includes the following provisions (as well as many others):

- ◦ "Copying or storing of any Content for other than personal use is expressly prohibited without prior written permission from The New York Times Rights and Permissions Department, or the copyright holder identified in the copyright notice contained in the Content."

- ◦ "You acknowledge that any submissions you make to the Service (e.g. Letter to the Editor, Review or Commentary) may be edited, removed, modified, published, transmitted, and displayed by NYTD and you waive any moral rights you may have in having the material altered or changed in a manner not agreeable to you."

- ◦ "This Agreement has been made in and shall be construed and enforced in accordance with New York law. Any action to enforce this agreement shall be brought in the federal or state courts located in New York City."

• Microsoft uses a click-wrap agreement on its MSN Internet services (such as its Hotmail e-mail service). Before completing the sign-up process, users must click a button that says "I Agree," beneath a "Terms of Use and Notices" agreement. Some of the terms in the agreement are:

- ◦ "Unless otherwise specified, the MSN Sites/Services are for your personal and non-commercial use. You may not modify, copy, distribute, transmit, display, perform, reproduce, publish, license, create derivative works from, transfer, or sell any information, software, products or services obtained from the MSN Sites/Services."

- ◦ "[Y]ou will not . . . [u]pload files that contain viruses, Trojan horses, worms, time bombs, cancelbots, corrupted files, or any other similar software or programs that may damage the operation of another's computer or property of another."

○ "Microsoft reserves the right, in its sole discretion, to terminate your access to any or all MSN Sites/Services and the related services or any portion thereof at any time, without notice."

Although click-wrap agreements are now common, they, like shrink-wrap agreements, are controversial and the subject of some legal debate as to their enforceability. This was tested for the first time in a 1998 case involving Hotmail, before the service was owned by Microsoft.[2] At the time, Hotmail Corporation provided a free e-mail service to more than ten million registered subscribers on the World Wide Web. To use Hotmail's services, a subscriber had to agree to abide by a service agreement that prohibited subscribers from using Hotmail's services to send unsolicited commercial bulk e-mail, commonly known as "spam." (For more on spam, see Chapter 26.) Despite this prohibition, a number of people used the Hotmail service to facilitate a spamming operation.

Hotmail sued the spammers on a number of grounds, including breach of contract for violating the click-wrap agreement's prohibition on spamming. The court granted a preliminary injunction against the defendants based on Hotmail's likelihood of success on various claims. In discussing the breach of contract claim, the court said Hotmail was likely to prevail on the merits because it presented evidence "that defendants obtained a number of Hotmail mailboxes and access to Hotmail's services; that in so doing defendants agreed to abide by Hotmail's Terms of Service which prohibit using a Hotmail account for purposes of sending spam and/or pornography; [and] that defendants breached their contract with Hotmail by using Hotmail's services to facilitate sending spam and/or pornography."

A number of later decisions also have indicated that click-wrap agreements are enforceable. In one case, *Groff* v. *AOL*,[3] a court enforced a clause in an America Online user agreement, saying, "[P]laintiff effectively 'signed' the agreement by clicking 'I agree' not once but twice. Under these circumstances, he should not be heard to complain that he did not see, read, etc. and is bound to the terms of his agreement." The consequences were significant, because the clause at issue stated that all lawsuits against AOL must be brought in Virginia; because the user in that case filed his lawsuit in Rhode Island, the court dismissed it.

As a result of these and a few other cases, it is now widely (though, as with shrink-wrap agreements, not universally) accepted that most click-wrap agreements are legally binding. If you are creating a website with a click-wrap agreement, you can take some comfort that, if properly implemented, the agreement will create a contract that you can enforce against visitors, if necessary. And if you are a website user, you should think twice before quickly clicking "I agree" and moving on without reading the referenced agreement, because it could affect your legal rights.

BROWSE-WRAP AGREEMENTS

A third type of high-tech contract has appeared since the introduction of the World Wide Web, something courts have come to label "browse-wrap" agreements. Generally, a browse-wrap agreement is a contract that a user may view online but need not do anything to indicate his acceptance. For example, many websites have adopted "Terms of Service" or "Terms of Use" agreements; these are often linked from the bottom of every page of a site. In another setting, a browse-wrap agreement may be displayed to a user downloading a software program, but the download proceeds without the user's having to click an "I agree" button.

Why would any website use a browse-wrap agreement? The most common reason is that every additional step presented to a user online gives him an additional opportunity to turn back. In other words, a user presented with a click-wrap agreement before downloading software may refuse to accept it, either because he's unsophisticated and doesn't understand what to do or because he is skeptical (perhaps with good reason!) of what terms the agreement may contain. Similarly, imagine what would happen if every website that now links to its "Terms of Use" discreetly at the bottom of its pages suddenly blocked access to all visitors except those who affirmatively clicked to indicate their acceptance of the terms; the drop-off in traffic would be tremendous.

By using a browse-wrap agreement instead, a website can present a contract without requiring users to take any action. While this approach may be more desirable from a business point of view, it is much less desirable from a legal perspective. At least one court has refused to enforce the terms of a browse-wrap agreement.

In a 2001 New York case, *Specht* v. *Netscape*,[4] a number of computer users sued Netscape after they had downloaded and used the software company's SmartDownload software, which supposedly makes it easier to download other files. The users alleged that the software transmitted to Netscape personal information about their file activity on the Internet, in violation of the Electronic Communications Privacy Act and the Computer Fraud and Abuse Act. In response to the lawsuit, Netscape tried to force the users to arbitrate the case (perhaps because many arbitration proceedings, unlike courtroom battles, are not public). Netscape cited a provision in the SmartDownload license agreement that required users to arbitrate most disputes. But the users argued that the license agreement did not apply because they had never agreed to its terms.

The court sided with the SmartDownload users, primarily because the software engineer who created the download application was not very smart. Instead of presenting the license agreement to users and requiring them to click on an "I agree" button before proceeding, the software only asked them to "please review and agree to the terms of the agreement"—but if the users did not do so, they could still download the software. This arrangement, the court said, created a browse-wrap agreement that "reads as a mere invitation, not as a condition." The court said, "Because the user Plaintiffs did not assent to the license agreement, they are not subject to the arbitration clause contained therein and cannot be compelled to arbitrate their claims against [Netscape]."

The *Specht* case is significant not only to Netscape and others who have designed faulty software license interfaces but to every website with "terms and conditions," which the courts may now view as unenforceable browse-wrap agreements, even though they're common in the industry. Indeed, in March 2000, a California court wrote in a dispute between Ticketmaster and Tickets.com: "It cannot be said that merely putting the terms and conditions in this fashion [without requiring visitors to click an "agree" button before using a site] necessarily creates a contract with anyone using the web site."[5] (The copyright aspects of this case are discussed in Chapter 3.)

As a result, despite their prevalence, browse-wrap agreements are probably the riskiest type of contract to use for high-tech transactions. While you may wish to consider adopting "terms and conditions" for your website, you should never assume that they will be enforceable.

TIPS FOR CREATING BINDING ONLINE AGREEMENTS

To help ensure the legal validity of any online agreement, here are some steps you can take:

• If at all possible, use click-wrap agreements in lieu of browse-wrap agreements. If you must use a browse-wrap agreement, be certain the links to it are prominent throughout your site. But still, do not rely on a court to enforce its provisions.
• Make sure no terms are obscured (such as in a smaller font) and that particularly important terms are made more prominent (such as in all-caps or boldface). Some states require that certain terms—such as limitations of liability and disclaimers—be made prominent.
• Be certain users cannot proceed without clicking the "I agree"

(or other appropriately labeled) button. Some sites have been known to allow visitors to access "restricted" content even if they refused to accept the click-wrap agreement.

• When presenting the actual agreement to users, make sure they can see all of it without altering it. Although "scrollboxes" are popular, they allow users to click "I agree" without even viewing the entire agreement—and sometimes they even allow users to change the agreement!

• Do not assume that any particularly unusual terms will be enforceable. As with any contract, courts will not uphold provisions that are "unconscionable" and may try to find a way out of enforcing a contract if the user was somehow tricked or misled.

PART VII

EMPLOYMENT LAW

CHAPTER THIRTY

CASE STUDY: AN INTRODUCTION TO EMPLOYMENT LAW IN
THE TECHNOLOGICAL REVOLUTION, *STRAUSS* v. *MICROSOFT*

During the 1990s, there was a virtual explosion in the number of companies offering goods and/or services over the Internet. These companies offered everything from books and groceries to medical advice and brokerage services. Unfortunately, many of the upstart or expanding high-tech companies that survived are ill prepared to defend themselves against employment discrimination allegations. In fact, as many of these companies have grown from only one or two employees to hundreds in a short period of time, some are not even aware of what laws apply to them or of the requirements under federal and state employment laws.

Even non-high-tech companies are feeling the impact of the technological revolution. The most obvious example is the increased use of e-mail and the Internet at more traditional, "old economy" companies. This increased use of technology has resulted in a new wave of sexual harassment claims. Particularly, e-mail messages are now providing the evidentiary basis for aggrieved employees who claim discrimination, harassment, or retaliation. For instance, in one interesting case that demonstrates the legal problems e-mail can create for employers, Microsoft faced the challenge of a gender-discrimination claim supported by a number of alleged inappropriate e-mail messages distributed by supervisors and coworkers of the plaintiff.

In that case, Karen Strauss, a former assistant editor of the *Microsoft Systems Journal,* sued the software giant claiming sex discrimination. Strauss alleged that Microsoft discriminatorily denied her a promotion to technical editor and terminated her in retaliation for her complaints regarding that promotion. In support of her allegations, Strauss offered evidence of sexist remarks and e-mail messages attributed to her supervisor and coworkers. The supervisor's remarks allegedly referred to another female employee as the "Spandex Queen" and included his offer to a temporary receptionist that he would pay her $500 if he could call her "Sweet Georgia Brown." The supervisor also allegedly proclaimed himself "president of the Amateur Gynecology Club."

Some of the most damaging evidence offered by Strauss came in the form of mass e-mail messages distributed throughout the workplace by coworkers. One such message contained a satirical essay titled "Alice in UNIX Land." Still another e-mail, forwarded by her supervisor, included a parody of a play titled "A Girl's Guide to Condoms." In total, Strauss proffered four risqué e-mail messages gathered from Microsoft's own network. Although the e-mail messages and remarks were unrelated to the promotion and termination decisions at issue, the court found that the evidence was relevant and admissible. As a result, Strauss arguably possessed the added ammunition to support her allegations of gender discrimination. Shortly after the court's decision, the parties settled the lawsuit for an undisclosed amount.

The Microsoft case illustrates the potential damages presented by the informal use of e-mail in the workplace. Although inappropriate e-mail messages typically form the basis of harassment suits, they also serve as powerful evidence in support of discrimination and retaliation suits.

Overall, many employers have seen a dramatic increase in discrimination cases. Although there is no way to completely prevent these claims, the only way a company can reduce exposure is to fully understand the parameters of the law and to take preventive steps to avoid liability. Given the breadth of the topic, an overview is necessary to put some of these laws into context. In addition, unlike many other areas of the law discussed in this book, employment law cuts across the specific federal or state laws that affect employees. These laws are Title VII, the Americans with Disabilities Act (ADA), the Age Discrimination in Employment Act (ADEA), and various state laws. The following sections introduce these laws, and subsequent chapters discuss their particular relevance to the Internet and high-tech industry.

TITLE VII

Title VII of the Civil Rights Act of 1964[1]—an employment law that is familiar to many people—prohibits discrimination based on race, color, religion, sex, or national origin with respect to hiring, discharge, compensation, or any other "terms and conditions of employment," such as training, transfer, or discipline. Title VII applies to companies with fifteen or more employees.

Title VII prohibits both intentional and certain types of unintentional discrimination. Intentional discrimination is generally proved under the theory of "disparate treatment." In a typical case, an employer is alleged to have treated a protected employee less favorably than an employee outside the protected class. For example, an African-American employee may allege that he or she was terminated for violation of a given company policy, while another employee outside the protected class was not terminated for the same infraction. In contrast, claims for "disparate impact" involve employment practices that appear neutral but allegedly fall more harshly on one protected group of employees. For example, a female may allege that a certain selection test disproportionately excludes women from consideration for employment. In these cases, proof of discriminatory motive or intent is not required.

In addition to prohibiting discrimination, Title VII also includes a prohibition against harassment based on the same protected factors. Although there are other types of harassment (such as racial and national origin), the most commonly asserted claim is for alleged sexual harassment. Finally, Title VII prohibits taking adverse employment action against an individual in retaliation for either opposing or protesting discriminatory employment practices. These cases typically arise when an employee files a charge of discrimination with the Equal Employment Opportunity Commission[2] (EEOC), or alleges that the employer engaged in discriminatory practices and then claims that he or she was treated more severely because of the protected conduct.

When Title VII was passed in 1964, plaintiffs suing under the law could recover only "equitable" relief—that is, back wages, reinstatement (or front pay in lieu thereof), injunctive relief, and attorneys' fees. These claims were tried before a judge. However, in 1991, Title VII was amended to give plaintiffs the right to a jury trial. In addition, plaintiffs now can recover compensatory damages, which cover emotional damages, pain and suffering, inconvenience, and mental anguish, as well as receive punitive damages, which are designed to "punish" the employer. Although there are limits in the law on these damages, depending on the size of the employer, plaintiffs now can recover up to $300,000 in compensatory and punitive damages alone.

AMERICANS WITH DISABILITIES ACT

The Americans with Disabilities Act[3] (ADA) makes it unlawful for an employer to discriminate against a qualified individual (an employee or applicant) with a disability. Like Title VII, the ADA applies to companies with fifteen or more employees, and claims under it are tried before a jury. Similarly, a claim must be brought, in the first instance, with the EEOC, which generally will investigate the claim before issuing a right-to-sue letter.

In general, the ADA prohibits discrimination against an individual with a "disability," which means people with impairments that substantially limit a major life activity. Not surprisingly, much litigation exists over whether conditions such as back injuries, chronic stress, repetitive-stress injuries (such as carpal-tunnel syndrome), and many types of mental conditions, such as depression and bipolar disorders, are covered disabilities.

In addition to an antidiscrimination provision, unlike the other federal employment laws, the ADA requires a company to take affirmative steps to allow people with disabilities to perform a job. This is known as making a "reasonable accommodation." That is, an employer can also violate the law if it does not make a reasonable accommodation for an otherwise qualified individual to allow that person to perform the "essential functions" of the job. A company can avoid making that accommodation only if it proves that implementing such an accommodation would be an "undue hardship."

Like Title VII and the ADEA (below), the ADA contains an anti-retaliation provision. The same types of relief that are available to plaintiffs filing Title VII claims are available to those filing claims under the ADA.

AGE DISCRIMINATION IN EMPLOYMENT ACT

The Age Discrimination in Employment Act[4] (ADEA) prohibits an employer from discriminating against an employee or applicant on the basis of age (forty years of age or older). Unlike Title VII, the ADEA applies only to companies with twenty or more employees.

Like claims under Title VII, claims under the ADEA are investigated by the EEOC. The ADEA also contains an anti-retaliation provision. In addition, ADEA claims are tried before a jury. However, unlike many other antidiscrimination statutes, the ADEA only provides relief in the way of back wages, reinstatement (or front pay in lieu thereof), and attorneys' fees. Compensatory and punitive damages are not allowed. However, if the violation is "willful," a plaintiff is also entitled to "liquidated damages," in which case the plaintiff's back-pay award is doubled.

Although there are a variety of age claims that could be alleged, high-tech employers are especially vulnerable to age "stereotyping" claims. In fact, over the last decade, many ADEA claims have been brought after comments were allegedly made regarding the need to get rid of the "deadwood" or the difficulty of teaching an old dog new tricks. Comments like these could be especially problematic to Internet employers, many of whom have managers who tend to be younger. All of this would be used as evidence of age discrimination in an ADEA suit.

STATE LAW CLAIMS

In addition to federal antidiscrimination statutes, employers also must contend with "tort" claims under state law. Although a variety of claims may be asserted, lawsuits filed by employees often include claims for defamation, invasion of privacy, intentional infliction of emotional distress, and negligent hiring or retention. Employers are seeing a number of claims stemming from electronic monitoring in the workplace. Unlike the federal antidiscrimination statutes, state law claims vary among jurisdictions. That is, what may be actionable in one state may not be a viable claim in a neighboring jurisdiction.

In addition to state tort claims, employers also should be aware of contract claims that may be brought by employees. These often arise out of alleged written or oral promises made during the recruiting process.

Contract claims also may be brought by employers against former employees for breach of restrictive covenants that the employee may have signed during his or her employment. Typically, these restrictive covenants include a covenant not to compete, which prevents the former employee from competing against the former employer for a given period of time. In addition, many employers, especially in the high-tech area, require employees to sign nondisclosure and confidentiality agreements that restrict the employees' ability to disseminate certain information learned during their employment.

Clearly, there are a number of employment laws that apply to expanding Internet and high-tech companies as well as to traditional, "old-economy" companies. Fortunately, an employer can avoid some of the potential problems through a clear understanding of the law and by adopting proactive policies and procedures. As with the Internet, knowledge is power when it comes to preventing claims under federal and state employment laws.

CHAPTER THIRTY-ONE

Sexual Harassment

Whether because of their informal work environments, the counter-corporate cultures, or other factors, high-tech companies have found themselves prime targets for sexual harassment litigation. Of course, sexual harassment claims are nothing new to employers, but not until recently have high-tech employers faced the costly legal battles associated with such claims. In recent years, several highly publicized sexual harassment claims have been brought against major high-tech companies across the country.

In addition to an increase in the number of claims against high-tech companies, employers (both high-tech and "old-economy") are seeing a change in the type of evidence used to prove sexual harassment. Although a variety of evidence exists that could be used to establish a claim, including allegations of physical touching, sexual harassment cases commonly involve allegations of verbal off-color jokes or other sexual banter in the workplace. Technology now is changing the type of evidence employers typically see in lawsuits. Instead of walking down the hall, employees are working together over e-mail or intranets. Many companies also conduct at least a portion of their business over the Internet. This increase in electronic communication has also led to a new wave of claims—"e-harassment." The risk of e-harassment claims exist for any employer that uses communication tools of the digital revolution.

WHAT IS SEXUAL HARASSMENT?

Although it is not specifically mentioned in the statute, the Supreme Court long ago held that sexual harassment is prohibited by Title VII. Starting in 1986 with *Meritor Savings Bank* v. *Vinson*,[1] the Supreme Court explicitly recognized sexual harassment as a form of gender discrimination within the scope of federal antidiscrimination laws. *Meritor Savings Bank* presented a scandalous set of facts; the plaintiff's supervisor allegedly demanded and received sexual favors from the plaintiff, over a two-year period, in return for hiring her. The plaintiff further alleged that the supervisor forcibly raped her, exposed himself to her, and fondled her and other female employees at work. Based on this factual scenario, the Court held that "without question, when a supervisor sexually harasses a subordinate because of the subordinate's sex, that supervisor 'discriminates' on the basis of sex." The Court cautioned, however, that to be actionable under Title VII, the harassment must be "sufficiently severe or pervasive 'to alter the conditions of [the victim's] employment and create an abusive working environment.' " Of course, through the years, much of the litigation in this area has focused on what conduct is "sufficiently severe" to create a hostile environment, as opposed to simply rude or boorish conduct.

Seven years later, the Supreme Court again addressed the subject of sexual harassment in *Harris* v. *Forklift Systems, Inc.*[2] The plaintiff in the *Harris* case contended that the company president repeatedly directed insulting, gender-based remarks to her, including "You're a woman, what do you know?" and "We need a man as the rental manager." In addition to these derogatory comments, the company president allegedly engaged in sexual innuendo, particularly regarding the plaintiff's and other female coworkers' attire, asked female employees, including the plaintiff, to retrieve coins from his pockets, as well as dropped objects on the ground, requiring the employee to bend over. In deciding whether the alleged conduct was actionable, the Court set forth objective considerations in determining whether a workplace is "permeated with 'discriminatory intimidation, ridicule, and insult' . . . 'sufficiently severe or pervasive to alter the conditions of the victim's employment and create an abusive working environment.' " Specifically, the Court looked to "the frequency of the discriminatory conduct; its severity; whether it is physically threatening or humiliating, or a mere offensive utterance; and whether it unreasonably interferes with an employee's work performance."

Relying upon the Supreme Court's guidance, courts across the nation draw the distinction between hostile and abusive conduct, affecting the terms and conditions of employment, and "simple teasing," discourtesy, rudeness, playful sexual utterances, offhand remarks, and isolated incidents, which fall short of establishing an actionable claim. Without a magic formula or bright-line test, courts often engage in a fact-intensive, case-by-case analysis. As a result, precise predictions of whether conduct constitutes actionable harassment are often elusive. However, as one federal appellate court has observed, sexual harassment cases decided by the Supreme Court consistently have involved "patterns or allegations of extensive, long-lasting, unredressed, and uninhibited sexual threats or conduct that permeated the plaintiffs' work environment," thereby highlighting "the intensity of the objectionable conduct that must be present in order to constitute an actionable hostile environment."

By way of example, many federal court decisions have denied recovery for merely offensive and boorish conduct. In *Shepherd* v. *Comptroller of Public Accounts of the State of Texas*,[3] the plaintiff alleged that her harassing coworker commented, "[Y]ou have big thighs," while he simulated looking under her dress. She also alleged this same coworker commented, "[Y]our elbows are the same color as your nipples." The coworker also would allegedly rub the plaintiff's arm and attempt to look down her clothing. On at least two occasions, while the plaintiff was looking for a seat during an office meeting, the harassing coworker allegedly patted his lap and remarked, "[H]ere's your seat." Although the conduct spanned more than one year, the U.S. Court of Appeals for the Fifth Circuit in 1999 found the conduct insufficient to establish a hostile work environment. By comparison, other courts have found that similar conduct is sufficient to constitute severe and pervasive harassing conduct, thereby creating a hostile work environment. For example, in *Westvaco Corp.* v. *United Paperworkers International*,[4] the plaintiff alleged a company employee sexually harassed her by staring, making telephone calls to her home, leaving messages with heavy breathing, and making "love you, baby" comments. The harassing employee also allegedly addressed the plaintiff as "foxy mama" or "foxy lady" for a year. Finally, on one occasion, the harassing employee allegedly asked for a kiss and, when denied, responded, "I am serious, I want some tongue." The U.S. Court of Appeals for the Fourth Circuit in 1999 held that this conduct was enough to state a claim for harassment.

A second broad category of claims involves allegations of *quid pro quo* harassment. In general, *quid pro quo* harassment occurs when an employee is threatened with adverse employment action if the employee does not submit to unwelcomed sexual conduct. Similarly, *quid pro quo* harassment occurs when a favorable employment decision is contingent on the employee's acceptance of such conduct. These claims can be predicated on explicit promises or threats, as when a supervisor tells a subordinate, "If you sleep with me, you'll get a raise," or "If you don't sleep with me, you'll be fired." However, some claims are brought when the promises or threats are far less obvious. For example, subtle *quid pro quo* situations may exist when a manager asks a subordinate for a date and, following the rejection of the advances, the employee begins to receive adverse performance reviews.

In prior years, in order to state a hostile environment claim, the plaintiff had to establish, among other things, that the employer "knew or should have known" of the harassment. On the other hand, employers generally were strictly liable for *quid pro quo* harassment. In the companion cases of *Burlington Industries, Inc.* v. *Ellerth*[5] and *Faragher* v. *City of Boca Raton,*[6] the Supreme Court departed from its traditional workplace harassment analysis and expanded employer liability for sexual harassment by supervisors. As a result of these 1998 companion cases, employers may find it more difficult to defend against a claim of supervisor misconduct.

Currently, sexual harassment by a supervisor, whether *quid pro quo* or hostile environment, that results in a concrete employment action (such as termination or demotion) triggers liability for the employer for which the employer has no defense.

GROWING CLAIMS AGAINST NEW TECHNOLOGY COMPANIES

A casual office environment, a relatively young workforce, close quarters, and long hours make the high-tech workplace an inevitable source of sexual harassment lawsuits. Compounding the potential problems created by informal corporate cultures, young, high-tech entrepreneurs may harbor a cavalier attitude and anticorporate perspective, rejecting the concept of formal policies and training. In fact, of nearly two hundred Internet executives surveyed by the human resources company EmployeeMatters, Inc., in 2000, only 50 percent said their companies maintained written sexual harassment policies.

As illustrated by recent filings, high-tech companies are no longer immune from high-stakes sexual harassment litigation:

• In 1999, Juno Online faced two separate suits from former employees who alleged that they were told they would be fired if they broke off their ongoing relationships with senior executives.[7] At least one employee has since settled for an undisclosed amount between $75,000 and $300,000.

• Pseudo Programs, a Manhattan-based Internet TV network, was sued in January 2000 after male employees allegedly referred to female employees as "bimbos" and forced them to look at sexually explicit material on the Internet.[8]

• Yellow Technology Services was sued by a former programmer who claimed a hostile work environment.[9] The plaintiff alleged that the programmers on her operating team made explicit and derogatory comments about women, ignored her, and refused to cooperate with her in the performance of daily tasks.

Although only a handful of cases have been reported against high-tech companies, the wave is coming, and high-tech employers should expect an increase in the number of sexual harassment claims.

E-HARASSMENT: THE USE AND MISUSE
OF TECHNOLOGY IN THE WORKPLACE

High-tech companies are not the only employers impacted by the explosion of technology in the workplace. The widespread infusion of high-tech productivity tools, including e-mail and the Internet, has had a substantial effect on how a significant portion of employers do business. These technologies also have had a significant impact on sexual harassment claims.

The vast majority of traditional companies, well aware of the increased productivity offered by a speedy and efficient form of communication, now conduct business, both internally and externally, via e-mail. E-mail is supplanting the interoffice memorandum and the formal typed letter as the preferred method of communication. In fact, many employees opt for the electronic forum in communicating with coworkers right down the hall or in the next cubicle. One survey estimated that 1.5 billion e-mail messages are sent per day.[10]

Many companies allow employees direct access to the Internet as well. It is more than just a cliché; the Internet has truly changed the way nearly all companies do business. The burgeoning technology has revolutionized human resource management, customer support, research and development, product ordering and tracking, and dissemination of information to employees and customers alike. One survey indicated that more than 88 million U.S. workers are connected to the Internet at work.[11]

These innovations have increased productivity greatly and increased the exchange of information in the workplace. These innovations also have triggered e-harassment claims. According to a 2000 survey, 27 percent of Fortune 500 companies have fought sexual harassment claims based on employee misuse of employer-provided e-mail and Internet access.[12]

E-mail

For many in the business world, e-mail has become the preferred mode of communication. Often users view e-mail as an informal, casual form of correspondence by which they may quickly compose a short message and instantly send it to any destination. Based on this perception, employees often feel free to express views that they would never commit to paper, much less speak over the phone or in a conversation by the proverbial water cooler. For instance, an employee is much more likely to forward a dirty joke through e-mail than recount the risqué humor during lunch with coworkers.

Employees often view e-mail as private correspondence simply between them and the intended recipient, and assume such correspondence will soon fade away following the transmission. To the contrary, e-mail may be more permanent than any traditional mode of communication, and records of e-mail generally exist in servers and company files long after it is generally assumed the message has been deleted. Moreover, an e-mail message can easily find its way to thousands, even millions, of unintended e-mail account holders.

For all these reasons, plaintiffs have found e-mail records to be extremely useful in establishing their claims of workplace harassment. Fortunately for employers, however, a number of cases have found that e-mails with sexual overtones do not constitute harassment. For example, in 1998, in *Schwenn* v. *Anheuser-Busch, Inc.*, a federal district court in New York found that a series of sexually graphic e-mails for a three-week period was not sufficient to create a hostile environment. The plaintiff, a brewery warehouse employee, claimed she received sexually harassing e-mail through the computer terminal mounted on her forklift truck. Specifically, the plaintiff testified that she received e-mail that said, "I want to eat you," "Meet me in Aisle 50-B," and "Don't just sit there, do your job, somebody else has to do your work for you." Although these e-mails may have been offensive and inappropriate, the court concluded that the plaintiff had not been subjected to a hostile work environment, which would give rise to an actionable claim.

Many other courts have held that a single offensive e-mail message is generally insufficient evidence to establish a hostile work environment. However, such messages, as part of a harassing pattern, can amount to persuasive evidence in a sexual harassment case. For instance, a series of "joke-of-the-day" e-mail messages forwarded to a broad distribution list of company employees can serve as the centerpiece of a sexual harassment claim. E-mail messages produce a reliable trail in cases that would otherwise boil down to a swearing contest between the parties.

The significant proliferation of e-mail use among U.S. employers all but guarantees that misuse of the technology is going to become an issue and a potential source of litigation. For example, both Dow Chemical and the New York Times Company made headlines in 2000 by firing sixty-four and twenty-four employees, respectively, after discovering widespread use of the company e-mail to receive and distribute pornographic images and offensive jokes.[13] And, in

April 2002, six employees from the Washington State Labor Department were terminated for excessive use of state-provided computers for personal e-mail, including e-mails of a sexual nature.[14]

Studies support what the anecdotes seem to suggest, revealing that more than 50 percent of employees have received pornographic, sexist, or racist e-mails at work. Approximately 46 percent of the employers in 2001 surveyed by the American Management Association reported disciplining employees for sending sexually suggestive or explicit material via office e-mail.[15] Considering these statistics, it is not surprising that employers across the country are facing allegations of pervasive e-mail-based sexual harassment.

The following is just a sampling of the traditional companies that faced claims where the main evidence is based on e-mail:

- Nationwide Insurance was sued after a supervisor in the legal department allegedly sent graphic e-mail messages to an employee stating his sexual desire for the plaintiff and evaluating her physical attributes.
- Chevron Corporation was sued by four employees based on allegations of sexual harassment via e-mail. The inappropriate e-mail messages circulated by male coworkers included "25 Reasons Why Beer Is Better Than Women." The case was eventually settled in 1995 for $2.2 million.

These cases illustrate the use of offensive e-mails as a "smoking gun" in conjunction with other inappropriate harassing behavior. In some circumstances, however, e-mail can serve as the exclusive tool of harassment.

Pervasive and prolonged misuse of an employer-provided e-mail system may result in significant litigation risks and substantial exposure, even where evidence of a hostile work environment is limited to offensive e-mail messages. In extreme cases, employers may face the specter of class-action litigation arising from a hostile work environment created through the e-mail system.

World Wide Web

As with e-mail technology, the World Wide Web's introduction into the workplace may be accompanied by a whole host of employee-employer issues and litigation liabilities. With business-related use of the Internet increasing, employers must face the increased opportunity for porn to find its way into the workplace. The problem is no longer nudie pin-ups or exploitative beach and bikini calendars, which generally have been removed from the walls of work areas since the sexual harassment revolution. Employers must now deal with JPEGs, GIFs, and MPEGs—images and audio files retrieved, stored, and displayed on company-provided equipment. Employees may somehow view such electronic media as less offensive. For employers, however, the risk of sexual harassment litigation remains the same whether the offensive material is downloaded and stored onto the hard drive of an employee's desktop computer or contained in a scxually suggestive magazine openly displayed on the employee's desk.

Unrestricted workplace access to the Internet will result inevitably in inappropriate use and access to obscene, sexually explicit pages by some employees. A 2000 Vault survey noted that 54 percent of the researched companies had caught employees browsing non-business-related websites.[16] Given the notorious availability of pornography on the Internet, it is not surprising that nearly 10 percent of U.S. employees with access to the Internet have visited inappropriate sites that display nudity and sexually explicit materials, according to a report citing from *The ePolicy Handbook* by Nancy Flynn.[17] Specifically, a Nielsen Media Research survey suggested that employees of major Fortune 500 companies, including IBM, AT&T, and Hewlett-Packard, accessed the *Penthouse* magazine site thousands of times a month.

Fortunately for employers, these rogue Internet surfers often are being caught and disciplined. In 1999, for example, Xerox terminated more than forty employees for accessing X-rated sites and downloading pornographic videos and pictures.[18] A 2001 survey conducted by the American Management Association found that approximately 36 percent of the companies surveyed had taken disciplinary action against an employee for downloading, uploading, or viewing pornographic material on an office Internet connection.[19]

Once sexually explicit pictures or jokes infest the workplace via the Internet, it is only a matter of time before allegations of sexual harassment and a hostile work environment emerge. There are a number of factual scenarios by which a coworker could be exposed to offensive materials. For example, a downloaded picture could be e-mailed as an attachment to an unsuspecting coworker, possibly only because he or she was on an extensive distribution list. Obscene images could be publicly displayed on an employee's computer, even as a screen saver or wallpaper. An unsuspecting coworker could catch a glimpse of pornographic material while casually passing by another employee's workspace. Or, a curious coworker may happen upon, inadvertently or intentionally, sexually explicit files stored on a company computer.

Employers also may risk liability simply by permitting open Internet access, on which employees could gain access to pornography. In one case, a group of librarians from the Minneapolis Public Library, dubbed the Minneapolis 12, submitted a sexual harassment charge to the EEOC.[20] The librarians claimed that by being forced to work in an environment with unfiltered computers connected to the Internet, from which patrons could access pornography, they were effectively sexually harassed in violation of federal law. On May 23, 2001, the EEOC agreed and publicly announced its finding of probable cause that the librarians were subjected to a sexually hostile work environment.

Electronic Message Boards

A hybrid of e-mail and Web technology, electronic message boards also provide a potential forum for harassing conduct. As part of an increasingly popular trend to create interactive electronic communities, many companies have started contracting with third-party websites such as Yahoo and Vault to create and manage message boards where employees can anonymously express concerns on any number of employment issues. Although the frank discussions facilitated by such a forum may be useful for company management, much of the information flowing from this process may be, at best, mean-spirited, off-topic, or "politically incorrect," and at worst, threatening, harassing, or defamatory, as also discussed in Chapter 23.

As demonstrated by a 2000 New Jersey case, electronic dialogues can generate significant liabilities or aggravate an already existing claim of harassment or discrimination. In *Blakey* v. *Continental Airlines, Inc.,*[21] a female airline pilot sued her employer, stating a hostile work environment claim under New Jersey state law based upon retaliatory and gender-based statements posted on a work-related electronic message board. Specifically, male pilots allegedly posted derogatory and insulting remarks, imputing various acts of incompetence upon the female pilot and acrimoniously responding to her prior claim of sexual harassment filed in federal court. One message suggested that two particular female pilots, including the plaintiff, were "weak pilots by reputation, and [had] alienated themselves from their peers with their boorish behavior." Another entry directed toward the plaintiff stated: "In my opinion, you are a wart (really bad choice of words with your ALLEGED problem) on the judicial system. I have zero respect for you and your kind." In evaluating the liability of the airline for statements posted by its pilots, the New Jersey Supreme Court observed that "the fact that the electronic bulletin board may be located outside of the workplace . . . does not mean that an employer may have no duty to correct off-site harassment by co-employees."

The *Blakey* case suggests that an employer, at the very least, must respond swiftly and effectively to complaints regarding inappropriate postings on business-related message boards. The most conservative approach with regard to electronic message boards supplied by employers, however, would suggest occasional monitoring of the electronic dialogues for offensive remarks and unlawful subject matter.

PRACTICAL STEPS COMPANIES CAN TAKE
TO PROTECT THEMSELVES

Although there is no way a company can completely insulate itself from sexual harassment lawsuits, there are steps that employers may take to minimize their potential risk.

• Adopt an anti-harassment policy. The first step to preventing sexual harassment, and to reducing legal liability, is developing an anti-harassment policy. The policy should require employees to report the alleged sexual harassment immediately. Companies should consider including a short list of managers to whom the sexual harassment should be reported. The policy should explicitly provide that the employee does not need to report the conduct to the alleged harasser, but can use an alternative reporting mechanism. The policy also should provide that the employee will not be retaliated against for making a report of allegedly inappropriate conduct.

• Enforce the anti-harassment policy. Employers may require that their employees sign and date an acknowledgment stating that they have read and understood the anti-harassment policy and the procedure for reporting harassment. A copy of the signed acknowledgment should then be maintained in the employee's personnel file. Employers also should post the anti-harassment policy in conspicuous locations throughout the workplace. Finally, employers should promptly investigate any complaints of sexual harassment and take appropriate disciplinary action.

• Institute training programs. Perhaps one of the most effective steps to prevent these claims is to train the workforce on sexual harassment. Training could include educating all employees on the company's anti-harassment policy and on how to report suspected incidents. Training also would be wise for managers. Managerial training could cover the harassment law, managers' reporting obligations, and how to investigate such claims. Education should reduce the occurrence of many hostile work environment claims by fostering dialogue among employees and an awareness of the issue. Interestingly, the digital revolution now has its own contributions in the area of sexual harassment education. As an example, Corpedia Training Technologies offers a Web-based program of sexual harassment training that tracks and records for its clients which of its employees have used and completed its program.

• Consider dating and nepotism policies. Employers also should consider adopting other policies to prevent situations that could lead to claims of sexual harassment. Many claims of sexual harassment come from interoffice romances that have gone sour. Accordingly, employers should consider adopting policies regarding dating of other employees. Companies also should consider instituting an anti-nepotism policy. This should minimize arguments of favoritism in the workplace that are the basis of many discrimination claims.

• Consider e-mail policies. Companies should take steps to ensure that their e-mail systems are being used for appropriate purposes. Most companies will want to limit use of this technology to business purposes. To ensure that employees follow the policy, the companies should reserve the right to review or monitor these systems. Companies also should inform employees that any passwords they have do not mean the company will be unable to review any e-mail communication.

• Consider Internet policies. Employers should also take steps to define appropriate Internet usage. In addition, employers should explicitly provide that inappropriate use of the Internet is grounds for discharge. As with use of e-mail, employers should inform employees that their Internet use may be monitored.

CHAPTER THIRTY-TWO

THE AGE DISCRIMINATION IN EMPLOYMENT ACT

Since the late 1960s, federal law has prohibited discrimination in the workplace on the basis of age. However, as the Baby Boomers get closer to retirement age, the number of age claims has increased. In fact, in the past ten years, the EEOC has received more than 170,000 charges related to the Age Discrimination in Employment Act (ADEA).[1] In 2001 alone, the EEOC received 17,405 charges— an increase from 16,008 charges in 1999. In addition, during that same period, the EEOC collected more than $417 million in damages for individuals claiming to have been the target of age discrimination. This amount does not include private settlements or jury awards under the ADEA.

Because age discrimination cases are so prevalent and costly, all employers must take steps to ensure that they do not run afoul of the statutory prohibitions. This is especially true for high-tech companies. In an era in which so many young entrepreneurs are achieving what appears to be overnight success in the Internet industry, some contend that more senior members of the workforce may not have a place in the high-tech market. Indeed, a University of California study indicates that many programmers begin to have difficulty finding work as they reach age thirty-five, which has resulted in fewer than one-fifth working in the field by their early forties.[2]

OVERVIEW OF THE ADEA

In 1967, Congress enacted the Age Discrimination in Employment Act (ADEA), which generally prohibits discrimination on the basis of age by employers against any employee who is forty or more years old. This prohibition applies to all terms and conditions of employment, including hiring, discharge, and compensation.

Also, this prohibition applies even when one employee over forty is affected by another employee over forty. In *O'Connor* v. *Consolidated Coin Caterers*,[3] a 1996 case in which a fifty-six-year-old employee was replaced by a forty-year-old employee, the U.S. Supreme Court found that the terminated employee could maintain an action under the ADEA. The Court explained that as long as the individual himself is over the age of forty, he potentially will have a claim under the ADEA if he has been replaced by someone "substantially younger" than he. However, in courts across the nation there has been considerable debate over what age difference qualifies as "substantially younger."

Often, age discrimination cases result when an employee has been the target of age-related comments. Proof of age-related comments is not an automatic indicator of an employer's liability. Instead, courts have required that employees prove that the ageist comments are related to the discriminatory employment decision. Comments deemed to be "stray remarks," which are not linked to the employment decision, have been held to be insufficient to support a claim.

Unfortunately, there does not appear to be a bright-line test to determine which comments are stray remarks and which are evidence of age discrimination. In cases in which employers have stated that they "need some young blood" or that "long-term employees have a diminishing return," or in which they have called an employee an "old soldier," these remarks were considered stray. On the other hand, when employers have stated that an employee was "too damn old to learn new technology" and that it was "unusual for people over forty to be hired," these comments were not found to be stray remarks. Rather than focusing on the statements themselves that seem to be equally offensive, courts tend to focus on the context in which the statements were made. Specifically, courts consider whether the statement was made by a decision-maker, whether the statement related directly to the employment action, and when the statement was made in relation to the challenged employment action.

Although alleged ageist comments have triggered several claims, employers are also especially vulnerable to age-discrimination suits by employees who have been laid off during a reduction in force, a practice that has become increasingly common since the Internet bubble burst in 2001. Here the argument is that age bias motivated the employer's decision about which employees would be discharged. As evidence of discrimination in these cases, plaintiffs generally rely upon statistics. However, an employer generally can escape ADEA liability by proving that a nondiscriminatory layoff procedure was followed. An employer may rely upon differences in performance, skill, or productivity levels as valid, nondiscriminatory selection criteria. Likewise, some courts have found that the "last in, first out" approach, by which the least senior employees would be discharged first, is a nondiscriminatory manner of selection.

In addition to federal protection, some states have antidiscrimination statutes that allow plaintiffs to receive an additional form of damages—punitive damages. Plaintiffs in these states will opt to bring their age claims under the state's statute because there is no restriction on the amount of punitive damages that potentially can be awarded. It is common to see very large punitive damages awards.

ADEA CLAIMS AGAINST HIGH-TECHNOLOGY COMPANIES

As high-tech companies grow in size and economic prowess, they are facing increased numbers of age-discrimination lawsuits. One such action was brought against Qualcomm Inc., a company that makes cell phones, network equipment, and Internet software, and that had the best-performing stock in the Standard & Poor's 500 Index in 2000. In February 2001, four former employees of the company filed suit in Los Angeles Superior Court on behalf of an estimated 250 former employees for alleged age discrimination and for various state law tort claims. The employees alleged that Qualcomm terminated this group of older workers "to facilitate the company's desired youthful mind-set and employee makeup." The complaint against Qualcomm seeks more than $1 billion in compensatory damages, plus punitive damages for these former employees.[4]

Similarly, in 2000, a former vice president at Oracle brought suit against the company, alleging that he was terminated because of his age.[5] The fifty-five-year-old man alleged that Oracle's CEO referred to him as "old" and made other derogatory comments about his age. The former vice president was subsequently demoted allegedly because Oracle "had decided to make a change in the leadership of [the] support [division]." Two months later, the company replaced him with a forty-year-old employee. The former vice president sought $18.5 million in lost compensation and damages.

Like old-economy companies, high-tech companies are vulnerable to age-based challenges to layoffs. Based on a reduction in force that occurred in 1993, 120 former engineers sued Unisys, alleging that the reductions had a disparate impact on employees over forty years of age. The Eastern District of New York allowed the plaintiffs to sue Unisys as a collective action, which is a lawsuit in which a number of plaintiffs sue as a group.

PRACTICAL STEPS COMPANIES CAN TAKE
TO PROTECT THEMSELVES

Employers should consider taking precautionary steps to alleviate the chances of any age-discrimination claims being brought in the first place. Failure to take the necessary precautions could result in costly litigation and negative public relations, no matter what the ultimate outcome of the lawsuit.

• Training. As with many other discrimination claims, one technique to prevent potential liability is to conduct internal training, primarily of management, regarding the ADEA. Managers and supervisors should be made aware that negative, age-related comments can become the basis of litigation.

• Antidiscrimination policy. Add a prohibition against age discrimination to the company's antidiscrimination policy and ensure that all employees are aware of the process by which they may report such violations.

• Documentation. If there is a performance problem, the employer should, as appropriate, thoroughly document the issue. These records should detail the reasons for the action so that the company's legitimate nondiscriminatory reasons for the action are documented if the employee pursues litigation. Just as it is important to keep records when terminating employees, it is also important to document all employees' performance problems. This too can serve as a valuable defense to any claims.

CHAPTER THIRTY-THREE

The Americans with Disabilities Act

The explosion of the high-tech industry has resulted in new dilemmas under the Americans with Disabilities Act[1] (ADA) while, at the same time, it has sparked renewed debate over issues that other, old-economy employers have faced for years.

OVERVIEW OF THE ADA

The ADA, passed in 1990, prohibits discrimination against employees on the basis of disability. The ADA covers employment decisions related to hiring, discharge, and other terms and conditions of employment. It protects individuals with disabilities, as well as individuals who are regarded as having a disability, or who have a record of having a disability. In addition to its prohibitions, the ADA also requires employers to take affirmative steps to ensure that an individual can perform the job. That is, employers are required to provide "reasonable accommodations" to individuals with a disability to allow them to perform the "essential functions" of the job. This facet of the ADA sets it apart from the other federal antidiscrimination laws.

Between July 26, 1992, when the EEOC began enforcing the ADA, and September 30, 2001, the EEOC received a total of 158,280 ADA-related charges.[2] In addition, during that same period, the EEOC collected more than $351 million in damages for individuals who claimed to have been discriminated against because of a disability. This amount does not include the substantial sums that have been awarded in private lawsuits under the ADA, through either jury verdicts or settlement.

Statutes in many states also prohibit disability discrimination. As a result, companies doing business in more than one location must be careful to comply with the applicable laws in each state where they conduct business. In addition, employers must be aware that many of these state statutes often provide increased coverage and protection beyond that of the ADA. For example, some states, including Alaska, Hawaii, Illinois, and Wisconsin, have laws that apply to all employers with one or more employees (as opposed to the fifteen-employee minimum of the federal ADA). In addition, although federal law also may offer protection, some states, including Kentucky, Massachusetts, and Oregon, have laws providing specific protections for people who are HIV-positive.

SCOPE OF DISABILITY

To receive the protection of the ADA, an employee must establish that he or she is a "qualified individual with a disability." Under the ADA, a "disability" is defined as "(A) a physical or mental impairment that substantially limits one or more of the major life activities of [an] individual; (B) a record of having such an impairment; or (C) being regarded as having such an impairment."

Regulations issued by the EEOC broadly define a "physical or mental impairment" to include "physiological disorders, anatomical loss, and mental and psychological disorders."[3] Many cases that have been brought against employers under the ADA turn on whether the individual is "disabled" because of an impairment.

For years, back conditions constituted the most-often-claimed impairment.[4] However, in 1997, psychiatric and mental disability claims became the most-often-cited category of impairment. In addition, the following are examples of other impairments cited in 1999 charges: depression, diabetes, heart impairments, anxiety disorder, hearing impairments, vision impairments, HIV infection or other blood disorders, and cancer. Although many conditions may be considered impairments under the act, the ADA does not cover temporary illness or other short-term impairments. For example, neither a broken arm nor side effects resulting from drugs prescribed only for a short time would be covered under the ADA.

The existence of an impairment is not enough to entitle an individual to protection under the act. The impairment also must substantially limit a major life activity. According to the EEOC, major life activities include functions such as caring for oneself, performing manual tasks, walking, seeing, hearing, speaking, breathing, learning, and working. The U.S. Supreme Court has even held, in the 1998 case *Bragdon* v. *Abbott*,[5] that reproduction is a major life activity, and the U.S. Court of Appeals for the Ninth Circuit has held, in the 1999 case *McAlindin* v. *County of San Diego*,[6] that interaction with others and engaging in sexual relations are major life activities.

In addition to identifying a major life activity, an individual seeking protection under the ADA must establish that an impairment substantially limits that activity. The EEOC defines "substantially limits" to mean that the individual is (1) unable to perform a major life activity that the average person in the general population can perform; or (2) significantly restricted as to the condition, manner, or duration under which the individual can perform a particular major life activity as compared to the condition, manner, or duration under which the average person in the general population can perform that same major life activity.[7] However, some courts have taken a somewhat more narrow view of this term.

In addition to protecting individuals who currently have a disability, the ADA also protects individuals who have a record of having a disability. This provision was designed to protect against discrimination of those who had disabilities in the past but are now recovered. Finally, the ADA prohibits discrimination against those who are "regarded as" having a disability, even if they are not, in fact, disabled.

REASONABLE ACCOMMODATION AND UNDUE HARDSHIP

If the individual is "disabled," the employer may not discriminate against that person. In addition, the employer must provide "reasonable accommodations" to allow that person to perform the "essential functions of the job." The courts have found that a job's essential functions relate to those duties that are at the core of the job and not merely tangential to the duties and responsibilities of the position. Although the ADA allows employers to define the essential functions of a job, in general, the ADA does not allow employers to mandate the manner in which the function is accomplished.

In general, the EEOC's regulations interpreting the ADA place responsibility on both the employee and the employer to determine whether a reasonable accommodation exists. Specifically, these regulations envision an interactive process between the disabled individual and the employer in which the precise limitations resulting from the individual's disability and potential reasonable accommodations are identified. It is the employee's burden to request a reasonable accommodation. This request, however, generally need not be in writing and need not use the magic words "ADA" or "reasonable accommodation."

Notably, the courts have held that there is no precise formula for analyzing whether an employer reasonably accommodated the employee. Courts have found that several alternatives should be considered, including the following:

- additional leave from work;
- reassignment to a vacant position;
- longer breaks;
- equipment modifications;
- job restructuring;
- aids such as readers and/or interpreters;
- reduced work schedules; and
- telecommuting.

However, courts consistently have held that there is no magic formula and that these alternatives or others should be considered only when analyzing whether a reasonable accommodation can be made in a given case.

Although an employer's obligation to provide reasonable accommodation may include restructuring a job to reallocate nonessential job functions, an employer is not required to either eliminate or reallocate essential job functions.

Moreover, courts have held that an employer does not have to provide an accommodation if the employer can show that the accommodation would impose an "undue hardship" on the business. "Undue hardship" is defined by the ADA as "an action requiring significant difficulty or expense," when considered in light of the following factors: (1) "the nature and cost of the accommodation needed"; (2) "the overall financial resources of the facility," the number of employees, and the impact of the accommodation on the operation of the facility (including the effect on "expenses and resources"); (3) "the overall financial resources of the covered entity," the size of the business as compared to the number of people employed, and "the number, type, and location of its facilities"; and (4) "the type of operation or operations of the covered entity, including the composition, structure, and functions of the workforce of such entity; [and] the geographic separateness, administrative, or fiscal relationship of the facility or facilities in question to the covered entity."

With the continuing arrival of new and better technology, the landscape of the ADA is rapidly changing. Topics once thought settled are again being reviewed by the courts. In addition, employers' obligations to accommodate are being reevaluated in light of existing and anticipated technological advances.

Telecommuting

The issue of whether telecommuting is a reasonable accommodation for a qualified individual with a disability has been hotly debated since the passage of the ADA. By the mid-1990s, the majority of courts were in agreement in opposing telecommuting as an accommodation. In *Vande Zande* v. *Wisconsin Department of Administration*,[8] for example, the U.S. Court of Appeals for the Seventh Circuit in 1995 held that working from home was not a reasonable accommodation. Notably, the court's holding hinged on the assumption that because of the then current limitations on technology, telecommuters were considered generally less productive than other employees:

> Most jobs in organizations public or private involve team work under supervision rather than solitary unsupervised work, and team work under supervision generally cannot be performed at home without a substantial reduction in the quality of the employee's performance. This will no doubt change as communication technology advances, but is not the situation today. Generally, therefore, an employer is not required to accommodate a disability by allowing the worker to work, by himself, without supervision, at home.

Likewise, other courts have opposed telecommuting as a reasonable accommodation, based on the fact that regular attendance and presence at work are essential functions of some jobs. In *Whillock* v.

Delta Air Lines, the plaintiff, an airline reservations agent, filed suit after Delta denied her request to work at home. She suffered from multiple chemical sensitivity syndrome, which allegedly was acerbated by a disinfectant spray used by a coworker and a perfume used by another coworker. The U.S. District Court for the Northern District of Georgia held in 1995 that if the plaintiff was unable to do her job in the workplace, she therefore could not perform the essential functions of her job, since her position required that she have access to Delta's proprietary information and equipment and that she receive "in-person training, monitoring, evaluating, and counseling" from Delta employees at work. As a result, the court held that she was not a "qualified person with a disability" and that even if she were, her requested accommodation was not reasonable. Similarly, in 2001, in *Kvorjak* v. *Maine,* the U.S. Court of Appeals for the First Circuit held that an unemployment insurance claims adjudicator could not perform his job at home. Although the court found that the employee could perform some of his duties at home, the court focused on several essential functions of the job, such as training and advising the office workers, that could be performed only at the worksite.

Generally, this view still stands, but the changing nature of the workplace is quickly leading to increased acceptance of telecommuting as an accommodation. Indeed, by March 1999, the EEOC had begun advocating the use of telecommuting as a reasonable accommodation where the essential functions of the job can be performed at home.[9] The EEOC indicated that such an inquiry should involve consideration of whether the employee can be adequately supervised at home, as well as whether the employee has the physical equipment necessary to perform the job. In cases where the accommodation might be deemed reasonable, the EEOC advised that an employer may still deny the request if it is able to provide another effective accommodation, or if it is able to establish that the accommodation will cause undue hardship.

The U.S. Court of Appeals for the Ninth Circuit in 2001 relied on the EEOC's guidance to rule that working at home could be a reasonable accommodation for a medical transcriptionist with obsessive compulsive disorder. In *Humphrey* v. *Memorial Hospitals Association,*[10] the plaintiff continually failed to arrive for work on time because her illness resulted in "obsessive thoughts and rituals," including, at times, washing her hair for up to three hours. Noting that other transcriptionists worked from home, the court reasoned that physical attendance was, therefore, not an essential function of the plaintiff's job.

Not only are the courts considering whether other comparable employees are allowed to telecommute, but they also are considering whether the same employee was previously allowed to telecommute. In *Davis* v. *Guardian Life Insurance,*[11] a Pennsylvania district court in 2000 considered the accommodation request of an insurance underwriter with Crohn's disease. Years before the lawsuit, the company had allowed the plaintiff to work at home three days a week as an accommodation. After a full year of that arrangement, the plaintiff's illness began to prevent her from working in the office on the agreed-upon number of days. When the company found out, it required her to commit to the previous schedule. The court found that the company's reason for its renewed interest in the plaintiff's scheduling was "not evident" and that, therefore, the continued accommodation, without the rigid adherence to scheduling, could be reasonable. In coming to its conclusion, the court noted the "flexible nature" of the plaintiff's earlier arrangement and the fact that her job duties remained the same during both periods of accommodation.

As the courts move toward a more general acceptance of telecommuting as a reasonable accommodation, Internet and Web-based companies could become a convenient target for disabled litigants. Because so many individuals within high-tech companies work in an independent environment, with little or no day-to-day supervision, some may argue that these positions are well suited to telecommuting. In addition, to the extent that a company already allows employees to work from home, which is likely the case in many high-tech companies, the argument on behalf of a reasonable accommodation becomes even stronger. Finally, Internet and Web-based companies may find it increasingly difficult to argue that their employees will not have the equipment to perform their jobs from home, since advances such as Web-based technologies and instant messaging allow many jobs to be done from almost anywhere.

An increasing number of high-tech positions may find telecommuting to be a reasonable accommodation. Because situations must be evaluated on a case-by-case basis, however, years may pass before the full effect is understood. In the meantime, as the workplace continues to evolve at a rapid pace, one is certain that disability advocates will carry on with their litigation strategies, in an effort to more specifically define the rights of the disabled.

Access to Websites

Although the vast majority of ADA cases against employers are for alleged discrimination in the employment context (that is, for hiring or firing decisions), employers also must be aware of their obligations to provide access to "public accommodations." Employers also are required to take steps to ensure that the public has access to their goods or services.[12] Unlike ADA provisions governing the employment context, the public accommodations provisions are not limited to employers with fifteen or more employees. Instead, these obligations apply to all "commercial facilities," which are defined as those facilities "intended for nonresidential use" and "whose operations will affect commerce."

Specifically, the ADA states that "no individual shall be discriminated against on the basis of disability in the full and equal enjoyment of the goods, services, facilities, privileges, advantages, or accommodations of any place of public accommodation."[13] To enforce this prohibition, the ADA may require an employer to do any of the following:

- change current "policies, practices, or procedures," unless it would "fundamentally alter the nature of the goods, services, facilities, privileges, advantages, or accommodations";[14]

- provide auxiliary aids or services (such as interpreters, telephone amplifiers, or closed captioning);[15] and
- make physical changes, such as installing wheelchair ramps or wheelchair-accessible lavatory stalls, widening doors, or repositioning furniture or equipment.

With the rise of the Internet economy, many high-tech and Web-based businesses are beginning to realize that the ADA's public access provisions also may require changes to company websites.

In November 1999, the National Federation of the Blind (NFB) and nine individuals, all of whom were blind, filed suit against America Online in the U.S. District Court for the District of Massachusetts, alleging that AOL's Internet service was inaccessible to the blind.[16] Specifically, the plaintiffs charged that, unlike other Internet providers, AOL's software was incompatible with the screen-access software used by the blind. The suit sought to enjoin AOL from continuing to violate the ADA and to change both the software and its website. On July 26, 2000, the parties announced they had reached an agreement to resolve the litigation. Pursuant to the terms of the settlement, AOL agreed to work with the NFB to ensure that AOL content is largely accessible to the blind and committed to release new software in 2001. AOL also reaffirmed its corporate commitment to accessibility in a formal policy, which is posted on its website.

Disability rights organizations also are exerting considerable pressure on Internet companies outside of the courtroom. In 2000, the NFB and the Connecticut attorney general approached Intuit, HDVest, H&R Block, and Gilman & CioCia after determining that the companies' tax-filing websites could not be accessed by blind taxpayers. In April 2000, all four companies voluntarily agreed to make their websites accessible to the blind in time for the 2001 tax-filing season.[17] Likewise, in 2000, a blind voter enlisted the assistance of the NFB in lobbying for accessibility to the Election.com website.[18] The Arizona woman could not vote online in the state's March 2000

Democratic primary because the screen reader on her computer could not interpret the website's information. After discussions, Election.com agreed to renovate its website to make it accessible to screen readers.

In addition to the restrictions of the ADA, there are now new requirements for companies that provide websites or software to the federal government. Disability discrimination in the federal sector is governed by the Rehabilitation Act of 1973,[19] which uses the same compliance standards as the ADA. Congress amended the Rehabilitation Act specifically to require that "[w]hen developing, procuring, maintaining, or using electronic and information technology, each Federal department or agency . . . shall ensure" that every medium of technology utilized allows disabled federal employees and members of the general public to have the same level of access to the services and information provided by the federal department or agency as nondisabled individuals.[20] The revised law applies to all kinds of technology: software applications and operating systems; Web-based intranet and Internet information and applications; telecommunications products; video and multimedia products; self-contained, closed products (such as information kiosks, copiers, printers, and fax machines); and desktop and portable computers. Although federal departments or agencies may use an undue burden defense to accessibility, the law imposes upon them the responsibility to attempt to use alternate means of providing the required access.

PRACTICAL STEPS TO AVOID ADA CLAIMS

Employers should consider taking precautionary measures to decrease the likelihood of a lawsuit under either the ADA or state law and to increase the likelihood of a defense verdict, if a lawsuit is filed. The following are suggestions that some companies have adopted to reduce the chance of litigation:

• Draft a detailed description for each job that lists the essential functions of the position. Review current requirements for all positions to ensure that each is job-related.

• Be certain that interviewers do not ask applicants questions that are prohibited by the ADA. In addition, make sure that applications and other forms do not include questions regarding an applicant's disability status.

• Establish an open-door policy for discussing disability issues with employees. Outline the company's commitment to disabled employees in written publications, such as the employee handbook, and post the required EEOC posters.

• Train management-level employees and supervisors about the ADA. Attempt to foster an attitude that is understanding and accepting of disabled workers. Implement harsh sanctions for ineffective treatment of disability-related concerns.

• Maintain consistency in the use of accommodations—do not refuse to allow employee A to telecommute while allowing employee B to telecommute, unless there is a compelling reason for the distinction.

CHAPTER THIRTY-FOUR

Noncompete Agreements and
Other Restrictive Covenants

Employers in high-technology companies rely on the expertise and innovative ideas of their employees to maintain a competitive edge. To stay ahead of the curve, companies must invest considerable resources in attracting, training, and retaining skilled employees for high-tech positions. In many cases, employers also disclose confidential and sensitive information to their employees who are exposed to aspects of the employer's business operations, including technical information, that could not be obtained by an outside observer.

Companies are competing for a small pool of high-tech talent. And, in our increasingly mobile employee culture, job-hopping has become the norm. In Management Recruiters International's fall 2000 survey of more than three thousand employers, companies reported attrition rates of 40 to 50 percent. Technology employers reported the high costs of attrition on productivity in a survey conducted by Integral Training Systems. Those employers measured annual productivity losses in each vacated position between 65 and 75 percent. One Silicon Valley employer estimated the average cost to be $125,000 when just one employee left, and another employer estimated possible sales losses of over $1 million for the departure of a single sales representative.

Many employers have attempted to minimize the risks of employee mobility and protect their investment in employee capital by means of "covenant not to compete" agreements and other "restrictive covenants," such as nondisclosure and nonsolicitation agreements. These types of agreements generally prohibit an employee from working for a competitor, disclosing the former employer's confidential information, or otherwise competing with the employer.

These agreements must be drafted with extreme care. Although courts recognize the employer's interests, courts generally view these types of agreements to be restraints on trade and on an individual's ability to earn a living. Therefore, courts will enforce these agreements only if they are properly drafted to be "reasonable," meaning that they reasonably balance the employer's interests with the employee's interests.

OVERVIEW OF TRADITIONAL STANDARDS FOR RESTRICTIVE COVENANTS

Restrictive covenants are contracts between an employer and an employee that the employer may use to protect its investment in employee capital and its confidential information. They are enforced by courts, typically through an injunction prohibiting the employee from violating the contract. Restrictive covenants come in many forms. For example, a "covenant not to compete" provision generally prohibits an employee from performing certain defined duties for a competitor or within a set geographic area for a specific period of time during employment and after termination. A nondisclosure provision prohibits the employee from disclosing or using the employer's confidential information without permission for a set period of time during employment and after termination. A nonsolicitation provision may prohibit an employee from contacting or soliciting certain of the employer's clients or customers that the employee worked with during his or her employment for a set period of time. Another type of nonsolicitation provision prohibits the employee from recruiting or attempting to solicit the employer's other employees to work for another employer for a specific period of time after termination.

State law governs whether these types of covenants are enforceable, and there are significant differences in the way courts in different states interpret and enforce restrictive covenants. Most states enforce noncompete agreements if they are reasonable. Several states, however, completely prohibit certain noncompete agreements. Additionally, some states will reject a noncompete agreement if any part or provision in the agreement is found to be too broad. On the other hand, some states will "blue-pencil" an unreasonable agreement, which means that the courts will enforce the reasonable parts of the agreement while striking the unreasonable provisions. Still other states will "reform" a contract and modify the unreasonable terms to make them reasonable.

Although there are significant differences among the states' approaches, a general scheme of determining whether an agreement is enforceable has emerged across the jurisdictions. Generally, in those states that enforce covenants not to compete, the restriction must meet three requirements:

- It must be reasonably limited in terms of the activity or future employment that it prohibits.
- It must contain a reasonable time limit.
- It must include a reasonable geographic limitation.

In most states, these three requirements apply to determine whether any form of a restrictive covenant is enforceable. In other words, many states require both a nondisclosure agreement and a nonsolicitation agreement to satisfy all three conditions. Several states, however, have found that different types of restrictive covenants affect competition and an employee's ability to earn a living. Those states impose various different requirements for different types of restrictive covenants. For example, some states may not impose a geographical restriction requirement for a nondisclosure agreement.

Reasonably Limited Prohibitions on Activity or Future Employment

In general, courts will enforce a restrictive covenant only if the agreement narrowly and clearly defines the prohibited activity. Many courts have found that the activity or future employment that is prohibited must bear some relationship to the activity that the employee actually performed for the former employer. In other words, a covenant should prohibit an employee only from performing for another employer in the same industry or field the same type of tasks, duties, and responsibilities that he or she currently performs. For example, a court likely would enforce a noncompete agreement that prohibits a computer salesperson from working for another computer sales company. A court probably would not enforce, however, a covenant that prohibits the same computer sales employee from performing other types of sales, such as office equipment or other products, or from engaging in other activities, such as computer software development. Of course, the outcome depends on a variety of factors, including the jurisdiction and the unique factual circumstances.

In fact, many courts may be reluctant to enforce a covenant prohibiting an employee from working for a direct competitor in a completely different job. A court may find that the employer's interest in prohibiting competition in general is not outweighed by the employee's right to work. However, courts consider the unique nature of an employee's role or contributions to a business. Accordingly, some courts have enforced broader restrictions where an employee played a crucial role or had extensive involvement in an employer's business or operations.

Reasonable Time Limits

In addition to narrowly limiting the activity or future employment, a restrictive covenant also must contain a reasonable time limit. Although the law will vary from state to state, most courts will strike down covenants that contain no limitation on time. Traditionally, courts have enforced time restrictions of one or two years as reasonable. However, courts will interpret what is reasonable in light of the specific business circumstances of the particular case and may enforce longer provisions.

Reasonable Geographic Limits

Finally, most courts require a restrictive covenant to contain some type of geographic limitation. Geographic restrictions can range from a specific locale, such as a metropolitan area, to an area associated with the office or territory in which the employee worked. Courts typically disfavor restrictions prohibiting a former employee from competing in an area simply because the employer conducts business in that area, and courts traditionally have disapproved strongly of and commonly have struck down overly broad restrictions or limitations that contain no geographic boundary. However, courts generally prefer the prohibited area to be related to where the employee actually worked.

In evaluating time and geographic limits, courts traditionally have looked to balance the employer's interests in protecting its investment in its employees versus the employee's right and realistic ability to earn a living. Generally, the most successful covenants are those that are drafted to restrict the employee's ability to work as narrowly as possible by using a limited geographic area where the employee actually worked and proscribing the employee from performing duties that the employee actually performed for as short a time period as possible.

APPLYING RESTRICTIVE COVENANTS TO THE HIGH-TECH AND INTERNET INDUSTRIES

These standards were developed during a time when computers were an academic curiosity, jobs were far less automated, and long-term employment and customer relationships were the norm. Now, computers and the technology employed by and sold in the high-tech and Internet industries advance on a monthly, if not daily, basis. Accordingly, the technical information that an employee may leave with loses its value quickly. Furthermore, Web-based companies market to and compete within national and global client bases, making useless the geographic restrictions appropriate to traditional local or regional businesses. Considering the changing face of commerce in the "new economy," courts may need to modify the traditional factors used to determine the enforceability of restrictive covenants to accommodate the realities of the high-tech and Internet industries.

Many courts already have recognized the imprudence of blindly applying traditional restrictive covenant principles developed to fit both businesses and industries bound by the physical realities of the old economy. The U.S. Court of Appeals for the Eleventh Circuit in *W. R. Grace & Co.* v. *Mouyal* recognized in 1993 that the factors to assess reasonableness must be redefined to maintain the law's currency and usefulness in "an age of commerce where technology enables business to be conducted across continents and oceans by electronic impulse." Accordingly, courts may become skeptical of time limits that would have been considered reasonable and enforceable under the traditional analysis. On the other hand, technology companies also may be more successful in enforcing broader geographic limitations than old-economy employers.

Reasonably Limited Prohibitions on Activity or Future Employment

When analyzing the reasonableness of the prohibited activity within the high-tech environment, courts thus far have used the same standards as in more traditional old-economy industries. That is, even in the high-tech arena, covenants should restrict the employee only from activity or from employment that mirrors the tasks, duties, or responsibilities the employee performed for the employer. Indeed, many courts have found covenants prohibiting a high-tech employee from performing an activity or job that is beyond what the employee performed for the employer not to be narrowly limited to protect the employer's business interests and, therefore, unenforceable.

For example, in *Marshall* v. *Gore,* a 1987 case from Florida, an employee who developed a formula and computer software for feeding dairy cows had signed a noncompete agreement. The agreement prohibited the employee from working for any business "involved in the development or marketing of computer software or for any business that competed with the employer." The Florida court found that, although the employer had a legitimate interest, the scope of activity restricted was overly broad and that the noncompete agreement was unenforceable as written. Specifically, the court held that because the provision prohibited the employee from participating in "any computer business," it was too broad. The employee was not in the general business of software development, but only in the bovine nutrition area. Accordingly, the court modified the provision and enjoined the former employee only from marketing and from developing software for the management and programming of dairy cow feeding programs.

On the other hand, when the restriction bears a close relationship to the employee's former job duties, courts are more likely to enforce it. For example, in *Alta Analytics, Inc.* v. *Muuss,* a 1999 case, the restrictive covenant at issue prohibited an account representative of Alta, an insurance and financial fraud detection software company, from working for any company or business "which is directly or indirectly in competition with any of the products or services being developed, sold or otherwise provided by Alta." An Ohio court found that this provision only restricted the employee from working for an insurance and financial fraud detection software company. Because the court found that the employee was not prohibited from seeking employment outside of the narrow fraud detection software market, the court enforced the provision.

The rapidly advancing nature of technology in the high-tech and Internet industries not only affects whether a particular device or method is current, but also may affect the meaning of particular words or phrases. High-tech "jargon" may become commonly used in business. On the other hand, as technology advances, commonly used technological terms of the past may take on new meanings. For example, in the 1998 case *Sprint Corporation* v. *DeAngelo*, Sprint Corp. attempted to enforce a noncompete agreement against Dominick DeAngelo, a former executive, that prohibited DeAngelo from engaging in telecommunications functions "related to long distance services" for a competitor. The noncompete did not define "related to long distance services." While employed at Sprint Corp., DeAngelo had had the title assistant vice president for internet protocol services and had supervised the development and marketing of the corporation's Internet telecommunications services in the United States. DeAngelo resigned from Sprint Corp. and accepted employment with a long-distance carrier that planned to introduce Internet telecommunications services similar to Sprint Corp.'s. The U.S. district court in Kansas found that the agreement did not provide sufficient guidance to determine whether "related to long distance services" encompassed DeAngelo's new job. In striking down the agreement, the court observed that in the three years since the parties had executed the noncompete agreement, the terminology "related to long distance services" had gained new meaning. Because the covenant did not define the term, the court could not determine whether DeAngelo's new position violated the agreement.

Reasonable Time Limits

Employers should consider the rapid rate of change and advancement within the high-tech and Internet industries when crafting time restrictions for noncompete agreements. Although courts typically have accepted time limitations of one to two years in most industries, many have found that the high-tech and Internet industries are fundamentally different. These industries yield major innovations almost overnight, and information or knowledge loses its competitive value quickly. The rapid changes in technology may impact the length of restrictive covenants.

For example, in *EarthWeb, Inc.* v. *Schlack*, a New York court in 1999 struck down a restrictive covenant because of an overly broad time restriction.[1] Marty Schlack was hired by EarthWeb as the vice president for worldwide content. During his eleven months with the company, Schlack was responsible for the content of all of Earth-Web's websites. Schlack resigned from EarthWeb and accepted a position with a competing Internet company. EarthWeb sought to stop Schlack from starting his new employment based on a one-year noncompetition agreement that he had signed. Pointing to the "dynamic nature" of the high-tech industry, the court invalidated the noncompete agreement. The court stated that the nature of Schlack's "cutting edge position . . . depended on keeping abreast of daily changes in content of the Internet." The court recognized that the unique business information and experience that EarthWeb wanted to preserve for one year would be of no value to any of its competitors well before that year passed. The court noted that "[w]hen measured against the information technology industry in the Internet environment, a one year hiatus from the work force is several generations, if not an eternity."

Similarly, in *DoubleClick, Inc.* v. *Henderson*,[2] two top executives at DoubleClick, the Internet advertising company, had access to highly sensitive information, including company revenue projections, pricing, and product strategies. DoubleClick sought an injunction prohibiting them from beginning a competitive business or from working for a direct competitor. The court in 1997 enjoined the former employees, but only after adjusting the scope of activity restriction and shortening the time restriction from one year to six months. The court noted that, given the speed with which the Internet advertising industry changes, the former employees' knowledge of the company's operations would soon lose value.

Reasonable Geographic Limits

Noncompetition agreements typically were permitted to encompass any area in which the former employee conducted business. However, courts generally were reluctant to enforce broader nationwide or worldwide restrictions. In light of the expansive reach of the Internet and e-commerce, some courts have modified this position and approved nationwide or global limits.

In *National Business Services, Inc.* v. *Wright*, for example, a Pennsylvania court in 1998 enforced a broad restriction, in part, because of the expansive reach of the World Wide Web. In this case, the former employee, Roni Wright, was the Internet distributor sales manager and national account manager for distributor sales for National Business Services (NBS). Wright had primary responsibilities for Internet sales distribution and other technical issues. As a condition of employment, Wright agreed not to compete "in any state in which NBS conducts business." Because NBS had a nationwide business, the covenant prohibited Wright from competing anywhere in the United States. The court enforced this restriction, noting that "[t]ransactions involving the Internet, unlike traditional sales territory cases, are not limited by state boundaries."

Indeed, some courts have enforced very broad restrictions in light of the reach of the Internet and the computer industry's global presence. Specifically, in *Intelus Corp.* v. *Barton,*[3] a Maryland court in 1998 upheld a noncompetition agreement containing no geographic restrictions whatsoever. Intelus, a computer software company, sold and developed support software packages for health-care organizations on a national and international basis. Bernard Barton, Intelus's former product specialist, who conducted demonstrations and helped to develop software systems, went to work for a competitor that also developed and sold software to health-care providers. The noncompete agreement prohibited Barton from working for any direct competitor for six months and had no geographic limitation. The court found that in light of Intelus's worldwide presence, the unlimited geographic restriction was reasonable. The court noted that competition unlimited by geography should be expected when the nature of the business includes computer software and information technology.

Employers may argue that in some cases, the Internet has made geography, and geographic restrictions, irrelevant. Just as the invention of the telephone marked the advent of a new era of commercial business and advancement, so the Internet has reduced communications barriers and expanded global markets. Given its broad scope, courts may, in some cases, enforce geographic limits beyond those used by old-economy employers.

ALTERNATIVE PROTECTIONS FOR CONFIDENTIAL INFORMATION AND EMPLOYEE CAPITAL

Restrictive covenants are difficult to enforce, and drafting them is often an unpredictable endeavor. Accordingly, some employers may choose to use narrower nonsolicitation and nondisclosure agreements, which provide specific protection against the solicitation of current employees and the disclosure of confidential information, or to rely on protecting their information as trade secrets. Nonsolicitation and nondisclosure agreements can be tailored to protect against specific concerns that a general noncompete agreement does not address. These restrictive covenants also may be preferable to some employers because many states impose less stringent requirements in evaluating their reasonableness.

Nonsolicitation Agreements

Reducing employee attrition and retaining talented employees, especially after investing in their training and other benefits, is often one of a technology employer's highest priorities. Although a noncompete agreement may prevent an employee from working for a direct competitor, it does not prevent a former employee from attempting to recruit from the former employer's pool of talent. A nonsolicitation agreement is designed to address that exact concern by prohibiting a former employee from either soliciting or recruiting former co-employees for a set period of time. As such, nonsolicitation agreements can provide specifically tailored protection against one of technology employers' most common complaints—high employee turnover rates.

As is the case with noncompete agreements, state law governs the enforceability of nonsolicitation agreements, and states impose varying requirements for an enforceable nondisclosure agreement. Generally, however, nonsolicitation provisions are scrutinized less strictly than noncompete agreements.

Nondisclosure Agreements

Employees in the information age have access to both sensitive and confidential information regarding their employers and their employers' clients. Protecting this intangible asset is another great priority of the high-tech employer. A nondisclosure agreement is designed to prohibit an employee from either disclosing or using the employer's confidential information. A nondisclosure agreement also can be tailored to prohibit the employee from disclosing any customer or client information with which the employee might have worked. As is the case with noncompete and nonsolicitation agreements, state law governs the enforceability of nondisclosure agreements, and state-by-state differences exist in what is required for an enforceable nondisclosure agreement. For example, most states consider nondisclosure agreements to be restraints on trade and use the same three-part test for "reasonableness" as used when analyzing noncompete agreements. Some of those states, however, recognize the strength of the employer's interest in protecting confidential information and find nondisclosure provisions without time and/or geographic limits to be reasonable.

As is the case with other restrictive covenants, the business realities of high-tech and Internet industries likely will affect what courts deem to be reasonable nondisclosure agreements. As information becomes outdated so rapidly in these arenas, more courts probably will require shorter time limits for nondisclosures. On the other hand, just as with general noncompete agreements, the national and global natures of these industries arguably justify broader geographic ranges. Even in states that do not require a time or geographic limitation, technological advances may change what information courts are willing to protect as confidential.

Trade Secrets

Certain types of unique technical or specialized information used by high-tech employers also may be protected as a "trade secret." Most states have enacted laws to define and to protect trade secrets, and, accordingly, the extent of protection will vary from state to state. Generally, a trade secret is information that

- is not commonly known to the public;
- has actual or potential economic value to the possessor because others do not know it and cannot readily ascertain it; and
- has been maintained by the possessor's reasonable efforts as confidential.

The type of information protected may include technical or non-technical data, formulae, patterns, compilations, programs, devices, methods, techniques, processes, product plans, blueprints, drawings, financial data or plans, and, in some cases, lists of actual or potential customers or suppliers. The protection generally lasts until the information becomes known through proper means.

If information satisfies the state's test for a trade secret, an employee cannot "misappropriate" it, meaning the employee can neither disclose nor use the information. Employers may seek relief for damages caused by a misappropriation or, perhaps more important, seek an injunction to prohibit the use or disclosure of the trade secret. Clearly, trade-secret protections are of great benefit to employers in the high-tech and Internet industries. They are designed to protect the type of information central to these industries' success. To take full advantage of these protections, technology employers should be familiar with their state's trade-secret protection schemes and understand their limitations and parameters.

CHAPTER THIRTY-FIVE

Privacy Issues and Employee Monitoring

Technological advances such as e-mail and the Internet are designed to make the workplace more efficient. Of course, these tools also expose employers to new types of employment law claims, including e-harassment, as discussed in the previous chapters in this section of the book. Some employers may decide to monitor the use of e-mail and the Internet to limit their exposure to discrimination and/or harassment claims. In addition, employers also are concerned about employees sharing, intentionally or inadvertently, the company's trade secrets and other proprietary or confidential information with competitors. Unfortunately, without a full understanding of the risks of monitoring, employers may open themselves up to potential lawsuits. In addition, such techniques may result in low morale among employees, who may resent being told they cannot use e-mail for personal messages and that their every move is being monitored.

Regardless of the risks, many employers have determined there is a need to monitor employees' computer usage. According to a 2001 survey by the American Management Association, nearly 80 percent of employers engage in electronic monitoring of employees' work-related communications and activities—including monitoring employees' e-mail or Internet usage, videotaping the worksite, and recording employee telephone calls.[1] This is a dramatic increase from 1997, when only 35 percent of employers monitored their employees. And while most of this monitoring is done on a spot-check rather than on a continuous basis, the fact remains that more and more employers are engaging in some form of monitoring.

Tellingly, employee surveillance software sales are estimated at $140 million a year. New technological advances also provide employers a number of options in monitoring devices. For example, SpectorSoft Corp., a Florida-based software company, released a monitoring program that takes surreptitious "screen shots" of employees' computers at selected intervals for employers to view at a later date. Another company, Content Technologies, launched software called Pornsweeper that examines images attached to e-mails and searches picture files for anything that appears to be human flesh. Computer programs also exist that monitor an employee's keystrokes and can determine what the employee has typed on his or her computer, even if the employee did not save the document.

Even prior to e-mail and the Internet, employers were forced to deal with privacy issues regarding employees in a variety of situations, such as the use of company lockers and the company telephone system. For example, in *K-Mart Corp. Store No. 7441* v. *Trotti*,[2] an employee sued K-Mart for invasion of privacy after the contents of her work locker, including her purse, were searched. The employer provided lockers to employees and locks upon request. However, when the employer ran out of locks, the employee was allowed to provide his or her own lock. In this case, the employee, with her employer's permission, had secured the locker with her own lock. On appeal, the Court of Appeals of Texas in 1984 allowed the matter to be tried before a jury because the court found that by placing her own lock on the locker, the employee had "demonstrated a legitimate expectation to a right of privacy in both the locker itself and those personal effects within it." However, in other cases other courts have come to the opposite conclusion.

Today, employees' privacy lawsuits often involve employer monitoring of e-mail and the Internet. According to the Privacy Foundation,[3] in 2001, 40 million of the 140 million workers in the United States had access to and regularly used e-mail and the Internet at their jobs. Employees have sued employers who have monitored their communications under either common-law state claims or federal and state statutory claims. Fortunately for employers, most cases have allowed employers to monitor employees' use of company e-mail and the Internet. However, the risk of litigation is always present.

INVASION OF PRIVACY CLAIMS

Most employees who have sued their employers for monitoring have done so under state invasion of privacy actions. In general, the employee must show that he or she had a reasonable expectation of privacy in the communication at issue. Because invasion of privacy is a state law claim, the standards vary among jurisdictions.

In one case, *Smyth* v. *Pillsbury Co.*,[4] an employee was terminated for sending inappropriate and unprofessional messages over the company's e-mail system. The company repeatedly had assured its employees that e-mail was confidential, that it would not be intercepted, and that it would not be used as a basis for discipline or discharge. Michael Smyth retrieved, from his home computer, e-mail sent from his supervisor over Pillsbury's e-mail system. Smyth allegedly responded with several comments concerning the sales management staff, including a threat to "kill the backstabbing bastards" and a reference to an upcoming holiday party as "the Jim Jones Kool-aid affair." Pillsbury intercepted the e-mail and terminated Smyth, who then sued the company for wrongful discharge and invasion of privacy. The court dismissed the case in 1996, finding that Smyth did not have a reasonable expectation of privacy in the contents of his e-mail messages, despite Pillsbury's assurances, because the messages had been voluntarily communicated over the company's computer system to a second person. The court went on to find that even if some reasonable expectation of privacy existed, that expectation was outweighed by Pillsbury's legitimate interest in preventing inappropriate or unprofessional communications over its e-mail system.

Some employees have attempted to argue that their expectation of privacy was reasonable because their e-mail was protected by a personal password. However, of the courts that have addressed this issue, this argument has been unsuccessful. For example, in *Bourke* v. *Nissan Motor Corp.,*[5] while training new employees on the e-mail system, a message sent by Bonita Bourke was randomly selected and reviewed by the company. The message turned out to be a personal e-mail of a sexual nature. Once Bourke's e-mail was discovered, the company decided to review the e-mails of the rest of Bourke's workgroup. As a result of this investigation, several other personal e-mails were discovered. Nissan gave the employees who had sent the personal messages written warnings for violating the company's e-mail policy. The disciplined employees sued Nissan for invasion of privacy. The employees argued that although they had signed a form acknowledging the company's policy that company-owned hardware and software were restricted for company business use only, their expectation of privacy was reasonable because the company gave the plaintiffs passwords to access the computer system and told them to guard their passwords. However, a California court in 1993 held that this was not an objectively reasonable expectation of privacy because the plaintiffs knew that e-mail messages "were read from time to time by individuals other than the intended recipient."

Similarly, in *McLaren* v. *Microsoft Corp.,*[6] the Texas Court of Appeals in 1999 dismissed an employee's claim that his employer's review and dissemination of e-mail stored in the employee's workplace personal computer constituted an invasion of privacy. The employee argued that he had a reasonable expectation of privacy because the e-mail was kept in a personal computer folder protected by a password. The court found this argument unconvincing because the e-mail was transmitted over his employer's network.

However, according to a news account of one case, a court held that an employer's use of a supervisor's password to review an employee's e-mail may have violated a Massachusetts state statute against interference with privacy. In that case, Burk Technology allowed employees to use the company's e-mail system to send personal messages, but prohibited "excessive chatting." To use the e-mail system, each employee used a password. The employer never informed employees that their messages would or could be monitored by supervisors or the company president. The president of the company reviewed the e-mails of two employees who had referred to him by various nicknames and discussed his extramarital affair. The two employees were fired by the company president, who claimed the terminations were for their excessive e-mail use and not because of the messages' content. The court denied the company's attempt to dismiss the suit and allowed the matter to be set for trial on the merits. The court focused on the fact that the employees were never informed that their e-mail could be monitored. This case illustrates the importance of informing employees that their use of company equipment to send e-mail and to surf the Internet is subject to monitoring to prevent subsequent confusion, and a possible future defense, on the part of employees.

WIRETAP STATUTORY REMEDIES

In certain cases, employees are able to pursue state and federal wiretap statutory remedies, within limits, against employers that monitor their employees' communications. In 1968, Congress enacted the federal wiretap statute, which imposes criminal liability on the use of technology to intercept and record telephone calls. The statute also provides a private right-of-action to employees who discover that their telephone calls are being monitored or recorded in violation of the statute.

Employers have two exceptions to liability under the federal wiretap statute. One is known as the "business extension exemption." Under this exception, an employer may monitor its employees' communications if the "interception device" is furnished by the telephone company in the ordinary course of business. In a typical "interception case," an employer monitors its employees' telephone conversations to evaluate business-related matters such as efficiency, productivity, and client service. For example, in *Simmons* v. *Southwestern Bell Telephone Co.,* an employee alleged that his private conversations were being monitored. The U.S. Court of Appeals for the Tenth Circuit in 1979 noted that monitoring was done both for quality control purposes and to prevent the use of monitored lines for personal calls. The court also noted that the company had provided a separate nonmonitored phone line for personal calls. The court concluded that the company's monitoring activities were reasonable and in the ordinary course of business, and thus covered under the business extension exception.

A second exception, known as the "service provider exemption," came about as a result of the Electronic Communications Privacy Act[7] (ECPA) (also discussed in Chapter 17), which amended the federal wiretap statute to include the interception of electronic communications, including e-mail. Under the "service provider exemption," a provider of communications services may access stored communications, including e-mail messages. In some cases, courts have used the service provider exemption to find that any company furnishing computer hardware and software may access its employees' e-mail files. For example, in *Bohach* v. *City of Reno,*[8] a federal court in 1996 rejected privacy claims under the ECPA raised by two police officers in Reno, Nevada. In this case, Officer John Bohach sent messages to other members of the department over the department's "Alphapage" messaging system. Several months later, faced with an internal affairs investigation based on the contents of those messages, Bohach and another officer filed suit, claiming that the department's accessing and retrieving the months-old messages violated, among other things, the federal wiretap statutes. The court reasoned that because the Alphapage messages were essentially e-mail, the officers could not reasonably have believed them to be private. In addition, the court pointed to a department order informing employees that their messages would be "logged on the network" and that sending certain types of messages was prohibited. The court found that the city was a "service provider" as defined under the ECPA, and was "free to access the stored messages as it pleased." Therefore, the court found that the city had not violated the ECPA.

Other courts have found posttransmission monitoring of e-mail not to be "interception" and thus not even covered by the ECPA. In *Fraser* v. *National Mutual Insurance Company,* the District Court for the Eastern District of Pennsylvania in September 2001 found that the ECPA does not prohibit an employer from monitoring an in-house computer system.

In addition to the restrictions, if any, imposed by the ECPA, several states as well as the federal government have proposed legislation that would require employers to advise employees that their e-mail and Internet access is being monitored. For example, proposed legislation in California would have prevented employers in that state from monitoring employee e-mail and computer files unless the employer first informed the employees in writing or electronically that their files may be monitored. On October 9, 2001, Governor Gray Davis vetoed the proposed legislation. He had vetoed similar bills in 1999 and 2000. On the other hand, at least one state, Connecticut, has enacted a law that protects employees' privacy rights when it comes to e-mail. Under that law, Connecticut employers must give employees notice of any electronic monitoring. Legislation to address electronic monitoring also was introduced in the U.S. Congress in 1993. Ultimately, the proposed legislation died in committee. But, following the terrorist attacks of September 11, 2001, President Bush signed the Uniting and Strengthening America by Providing Appropriate Tools Required to Intercept and Obstruct Terrorism Act (USA PATRIOT Act).[9] Although this antiterrorist legislation expanded the government's surveillance authority under the ECPA, the act did not expand or restrict the ability of employers to monitor their employees.

PRACTICAL STEPS COMPANIES CAN TAKE
TO PROTECT THEMSELVES

Although there is no way to completely insulate a company from these suits, employers may consider one or more of the following suggestions:

- Integrate e-mail and other policies. An employer's e-mail policy could be integrated with the company's harassment and nondiscrimination policies. If so, the policy should make clear that e-mail communications will be treated like any other business communication and that use of the e-mail systems to engage in communications that are in violation of company policy—including transmitting defamatory, offensive, or harassing messages—is explicitly prohibited.

- Limit use of technology to business purposes only. Electronic communications could be referenced expressly in any lists of "company property." Employees should be notified that all technology, including e-mail and access to the Internet, is provided by the company to assist employees in carrying out the company's business purposes. Explicitly state that employees who use company property—including e-mail, telephones, and Internet access—for personal use are violating company policy and are subject to disciplinary action.

- Reserve the right to review and monitor. To advance the argument that monitoring is appropriate, employees should be notified that the employer will treat all messages sent, received, or stored in the e-mail system as business messages, which the company is entitled to review, monitor, and disclose. The company should warn employees that if they make incidental use of the e-mail system to transmit personal messages, such messages will be treated no differently from other messages; that is, the company reserves the right to access, review, monitor, or disclose such messages. The policy should state explicitly that employees should not use company e-mail to send or to receive any messages that they wish to remain private. In addition, employers should notify employees that even though their files may be protected by passwords, such passwords do not prevent system administrators and other authorized employees from accessing messages for business purposes.

• Include notice and consent language. Include in the policy language that by using the company's electronic communications systems, the employee is, in effect, aware of and will be covered by the policy. In addition, by using the e-mail system, the employee expressly consents to the company's review and monitoring of e-mail messages as outlined in the policy.

• Strictly define appropriate Internet use. When employees are permitted access to Internet sites, provide guidelines regarding its use. For example, an employer's policy may provide that employees may access the Internet only through the employer's approved Internet access procedures. In addition, an employer may wish to restrict or to prohibit subscribing to public mail forums, discussion groups, and the like. A company must determine and incorporate guidelines for an employee's failure to comply with its Internet and e-mail policies, or the policies are useless. Determine the penalties for specific policy violations, communicate them to the employees, and then enforce them consistently. Employers may wish to obtain an acknowledgment that the employee received the policy and that the employee intends to comply.

AFTERWORD

It is impossible to write a "final chapter" on Internet law, because this subject area is constantly evolving. While some of the pillars of Internet law—such as those created by U.S. intellectual property laws and the First Amendment—are well established, the Internet and other forms of high technology are challenging them in ways once never imagined. And new laws, such as those on domain names, spam, and privacy, are emerging. As a result, unlike some other areas of the law, Internet law is undergoing a continual development.

For example, since the rise of Internet law as an identifiable legal practice in the mid-1990s, the following are just a few of the significant developments:

• The United States passed the Anticybersquatting Consumer Protection Act, in 1999, to protect trademark owners against mischievous domain name registrants who exploited gaps in existing trademark law.

• The Internet Corporation for Assigned Names and Numbers (ICANN) was created, in 1998, to oversee important governing issues in cyberspace and adopted the important Uniform Domain

Name Dispute Resolution Policy to help resolve contentious domain name battles.

• The United States amended its 1976 Copyright Act by adopting the controversial Digital Millennium Copyright Act in 1998, providing copyright owners with additional legal protections against new technological threats.

• The United States and other countries implemented and revised privacy laws for the Internet, including the Children's Online Privacy Protection Act, while also debating whether even more laws are needed to protect consumers in the digital age.

• The courts struggled to apply existing patent laws to inventions brought about by the Internet and other forms of high technology, such as software and business methods.

• The U.S. Congress passed and the courts looked skeptically on laws restricting offensive content on the Internet, creating new tensions between the right of free speech and the understandable interest in protecting children.

• Electronic signatures—a concept obviously unfathomable by John Hancock and the other signers of the Declaration of Independence—emerged as a useful but often perplexing legal tool for conducting business online, and the United States tried to give the practice a boost by passing, in 2000, the Electronic Signatures in Global and National Commerce, or E-Sign, Act.

Congress and the courts surely will continue to shape the future of Internet law, and the development of new technologies always will present new challenges. Among the many questions that lie ahead: Can spam be legally reined in? Can one country apply its laws to a global Internet company based in another country? What are the limits of speech in cyberspace? Can intellectual property laws adequately protect digital—and therefore easily copied—works online? Will lawmakers, consumers, or the high-tech industry decide the ultimate extent of privacy protection on the Internet?

Lawyers, lawmakers, and high-tech architects have for some time engaged in a philosophical debate over the appropriate role of the legal system in cyberspace. On the one hand, many of them believe that strong and numerous laws are necessary to adequately protect authors, inventors, consumers, and businesses on the Internet. On the other hand, many others believe the Internet is best left unregulated and that too many laws will stunt the Internet's growth. As with many such debates, the truth probably lies somewhere in between.

Although it may be interesting to watch this philosophical debate play out, or even participate in it, the important thing for any person or company using or conducting business online is this: Internet law cannot be ignored, and doing so could lead to costly legal mistakes, either by violating someone else's rights or by failing to adequately protect your own. As with any set of legal rules, regardless of whether you agree with the laws, you must obey them.

Certainly, an understanding of the issues raised in this book will provide any reader with a tremendous head start in conducting business in cyberspace legally. But no book can substitute for the advice of an attorney who is knowledgeable about the intricacies of the law—and, in the case of Internet law, developments that may have occurred since this book was written. Keeping up-to-date on any area of the law is demanding, but the complex and evolving issues of Internet law make doing do so a particular challenge, as well as a necessity. Along with a personal attorney, the websites listed in the appendix of this book—including, of course, GigaLaw.com—provide convenient ways to learn about even more details of Internet law and to stay abreast of the latest changes.

Even without new legislation, new technology and uncertain court rulings make Internet law a difficult topic to grasp. Many if not most of the lawsuits that could be considered to involve Internet law are based not on new laws created since the rise of cyberspace but on old laws applied to this new medium. And the medium itself is constantly changing, too, creating new legal challenges and disputes that have arisen over technology—such as peer-to-peer file sharing systems popularized by Napster—that was once unimaginable.

In law school, many professors emphasize that half of the challenge for any lawyer is simply to identify the legal issues that a particular situation presents, even if the answers are not readily ascertainable. For Internet law, this is especially true. Even after having read this book, you may not be certain in every instance whether a particular decision you make online, for yourself or for your company, is clearly legal. But simply knowing where the legal traps lie in cyberspace will prepare you well for avoiding costly problems presented by today's—and tomorrow's—technology.

Appendix: The Fifteen Essential Internet Law Bookmarks

Although a number of websites offer information about Internet law, not many of them are comprehensive, current, and completely reliable. Given the breadth and depth of Internet law, no single website can provide everything you'll ever need to know about this topic. But the following fifteen are among the most essential websites on Internet law. If you add them to your bookmarks and either visit them regularly or turn to them for research, you'll have access to the best resources on Internet law.

1. GigaLaw.com
http://www.gigalaw.com
Naturally, this book recommends the website that inspired it. But don't think that this is just self-promotional. GigaLaw.com is the most comprehensive resource online for information about Internet law. The site offers original articles by practicing attorneys, an active discussion list, daily news updates, and more. GigaLaw.com has won numerous awards and is one of Yahoo's most popular sites.

2. U.S. Copyright Office
http://www.loc.gov/copyright
The U.S. Copyright Office's website is a treasure trove of resources about

copyright law. It includes general information on copyright law as well as numerous publications about discrete legal issues, a copy of the important Digital Millennium Copyright Act, and forms for applying for copyright registrations.

3. U.S. Patent and Trademark Office
http://www.uspto.gov
The U.S. Patent and Trademark Office's website is visually unappealing but practically very important. The site allows users to search for trademark and patent applications and registrations—for free—and offers useful information about these two areas of the law vital to conducting business online.

4. Federal Trade Commission
http://www.ftc.gov
The FTC is an important federal entity in the world of Internet law, particularly in the areas of privacy, advertising, and antitrust. The FTC's website offers a wealth of resources on these topics, including substantive reports on Internet privacy and enforcement, extensive documents on the Children's Online Privacy Protection Act, and an entire subsite (http://www.ftc.gov/bcp/menu-internet.htm) on e-commerce and the Internet.

5. Cybercrime
http://www.cybercrime.gov
The Cybercrime site is published by the U.S. Department of Justice Criminal Division's Computer Crime and Intellectual Property Section. The site offers excerpts of relevant federal criminal laws related to computer crimes and information on issues including encryption, intellectual property crimes, privacy, and protecting critical infrastructures.

6. ICANN
http://www.icann.org
ICANN, the Internet Corporation for Assigned Names and Numbers, is a nonprofit corporation formed in 1998 to manage Internet addresses. The organization established the Uniform Domain Name Dispute Resolution Policy (UDRP), approved the launch of seven new top-level domains, and takes other actions with respect to Internet governance. Though often criticized, ICANN is the closest thing there is to the Internet's ruling body, at least with respect to domain names.

7. ACLU Cyber-Liberties

http://www.aclu.org/issues/cyber/hmcl.html

Well known for its advocacy of civil liberties issues, the ACLU has been an active participant in online rights. Among other things, the ACLU was the lead plaintiff in the two most important Internet lawsuits—one challenging portions of the Communications Decency Act and the other challenging the Child Online Protection Act—both of which reached the U.S. Supreme Court.

8. Electronic Frontier Foundation

http://www.eff.org

The EFF is the granddaddy of high-tech civil liberties organizations. Founded in 1990, the EFF advocates and educates on the most important Internet legal issues today, including those about intellectual property and the First Amendment. A strong proponent of free speech, the EFF's well-known "blue ribbon campaign" generates support for its causes.

9. Center for Democracy and Technology

http://www.cdt.org

The CDT's mission is "to promote democratic values and constitutional liberties in the digital age." Backed by some of the biggest names in high technology—including AOL, IBM, and Microsoft—the CDT offers a website with newsworthy and important information on many areas of Internet law, including a list of pending legislation that could affect the Internet.

10. Electronic Privacy Information Center

http://www.epic.org

EPIC is a private-interest research center that was established in 1994 to focus public attention on emerging civil liberties issues and to protect privacy, the First Amendment, and constitutional values. With a particular focus on online privacy issues, the EPIC website offers vital factual information, action items, and news about topics such as fighting terrorism, the FBI's online-monitoring program, and the intricacies of Internet privacy policies.

11. Coalition Against Unsolicited Commercial Email

http://www.cauce.org

Though unabashedly opposed to most forms of spam, CAUCE provides a website with some of the most comprehensive information about unsolicited commercial e-mail, including the latest legal news, pending legislation, and links to other important websites on this topic.

12. The Berkman Center for Internet and Society at Harvard Law School
http://cyber.law.harvard.edu
A true academic resource, the Berkman Center for Internet and Society describes itself as a research program founded to explore cyberspace, share in its study, and help pioneer its development. Established in 1997, the center provides online courses and in-depth explorations of the most important Internet legal issues, led by Harvard Law School's faculty and a dedicated panel of fellows.

13. Perkins Coie Internet Case Digest
http://www.perkinscoie.com/casedigest
Although judges' written opinions are in the public domain, access to them always has been limited—generally to physical law libraries and expensive electronic resources. However, the law firm of Perkins Coie began compiling summaries of important Internet law cases (and, where available, links to them on the Web) several years ago, just as Internet law was emerging. The site is the best one-stop-free-shop for finding cases about Internet law.

14. Phillips Nizer Internet Library
http://www.phillipsnizer.com/internetlibrary.htm
Like the Perkins Coie site, this site from the Phillips Nizer law firm offers summaries of and links to important Internet law cases. Though not as extensive as Perkins Coie's, the Phillips Nizer site offers an alternative presentation and some additional information.

15. Legal Information Institute (Cornell Law School)
http://www.law.cornell.edu
Though not a site specifically about Internet law, the LII is one of the best places on the Internet to find general information about the law—including the entire texts of the U.S. copyright, trademark, and patent laws, all of which are critical to high technology.

CONTRIBUTORS

Internet law is such a vast topic that any lawyer who professes to practice it probably is well qualified only in a subset of it. That is true of me. Through GigaLaw.com and my professional and personal contacts, I am fortunate to have met some of the smartest people in this area of the law, and I am proud to include some of their contributions in this book. Without them, this book would have been much less comprehensive.

GREG KIRSCH is the author of all chapters in Part III, on patent law. A longtime friend since we both attended Washington University in St. Louis concurrently (he in law school while I was an undergrad), Greg is a shareholder at Needle & Rosenberg, P.C.,[1] in Atlanta, a prestigious intellectual property law firm. A patent attorney who concentrates on software and high-tech issues, he is registered to practice with the U.S. Patent and Trademark Office. Greg is a charter member of the GigaLaw.com Editorial Board[2] and has served as an adjunct professor of law at Emory University and as chair of the Intellectual Property Law Section of the State Bar of Georgia.

DOUG TOWNS is the author of all chapters in Part VII, on employment law. I first met Doug soon after GigaLaw.com launched in January 2000, when he saw an important need to provide information about employment law issues for the high-tech industry and quickly joined the GigaLaw.com Editorial Board.[3] Doug practices labor and employment law as a partner at Jones, Day, Reavis & Pogue[4] in Atlanta. Doug represents employers in a variety of state and federal discrimination claims and specializes in the defense of employment class actions and high-tech employment issues. He would like to thank Joy M. Hodge, Katherine F. Glennon, Michael A. Kolczak, Kathleen G. McBride, and Kara L. Thompson, attorneys in Jones Day's Atlanta office, for their assistance with his chapters in this book.

JAY HOLLANDER is the author of Chapter 23, on message boards and anonymity. Jay, a charter member of the GigaLaw.com Editorial Board,[5] has a varied legal practice of his own at Hollander and Company LLC[6] in New York City, focusing not only on computer and Internet law, but also on real estate and general commercial matters. Among other functions, Jay serves on the International Board of Governors of the Technion-Israel Institute of Technology, Israel's largest applied technology university, and is on the United States national board of directors of the American Society for Technion, an international philanthropy benefiting the Technion. Closer to home, Jay is also a member of the New York Software Industry Association, a trade group devoted to the interests of New York's software and Internet industries.

PETER YU is the author of Chapter 19, on the European Union's privacy directive. Peter possesses the important but uncommon skill of explaining complicated legal issues in layman's terms, something he has done regularly as a member of the GigaLaw.com Editorial Board.[7] Peter is the executive director of the Intellectual Property Law Program and deputy director of the Howard M. Squadron Program in Law, Media and Society at Benjamin N. Cardozo School of Law[8] in New York City, where he also serves as an acting assistant professor of law. He is also a research associate of the Programme in Comparative Media Law and Policy at the University of Oxford.

CHRIS WOLF is the author of Chapter 25, on hate on the Internet. A partner in the Washington office of Proskauer Rose LLP,[9] he co-chairs the firm's iPractice group and leads the firm's privacy law efforts. He has litigated cutting-edge Internet issues, involving online privacy, jurisdiction over website operators, domain names, and the protection of intellectual property online. He also counsels and represents companies in a nonlitigation context on a wide range of legal issues involved in e-commerce. The first time I met Chris in person was at a meeting of the Anti-Defamation League in Washington, when he gave a thorough presentation about many of the difficult legal issues extremists pose online.

JONATHAN WINER is the author of Chapter 20, on the Canadian Privacy Act. Jonathan is a partner in the Washington office of Alston & Bird LLP[10] (the firm where I first practiced), where he focuses on electronic commerce, financial regulatory issues, and privacy. He formerly served at the U.S. Department of State as U.S. deputy assistant secretary of state for international law enforcement. In 2001, following the terrorist attacks on the World Trade Center and the Pentagon, Jonathan served as a consultant on terrorist finance for ABC Television, providing on-air commentary and analysis.

Notes

Foreword
1. http://www.law.cornell.edu/uscode/18/ch119.html
2. http://www.eff.org/Privacy/Surveillance/Terrorism_militias/20011025_hr3162_usa_patriot_bill.html
3. http://www.townhall.com/columnists/jamesglassman/jg2000725.shtml
4. http://www.fbi.gov/hq/lab/carnivore/carnivore.htm
5. http://www.kentlaw.edu/classes/rwarner/legalaspects/us_v_lamacchia.html

Introduction
1. http://www.gigalaw.com/articles/2000/isenberg-2000-01.html
2. http://www.gigalaw.com/news/index.html
3. http://www.gigalaw.com/news/index.html
4. http://www.gigalaw.com/bookshelf/index.html
5. http://www.gigalaw.com/discuss/index.html

Chapter 1: Case Study: An Introduction to Copyright on the Internet, *Playboy* v. *Sanfilippo*
1. http://www.gigalaw.com/library/playboy-sanfilippo-1998-0324.html
2. http://www.loc.gov/copyright/title17/92chap1.html#106
3. http://www.loc.gov/copyright/title17/92chap5.html#504

Chapter 2: The Basics of Copyright Law

1. http://www.wikipedia.com/wiki/Statute_of_Anne
2. http://www.loc.gov/copyright/title17
3. http://www.loc.gov/copyright/title17/92chap1.html#102
4. http://www.loc.gov/copyright/title17/92chap1.html#106
5. http://www.loc.gov/copyright/title17/92chap1.html#101
6. http://www.loc.gov/copyright/reg.html
7. http://www.loc.gov/copyright/circs/circ1.html#cr
8. http://www.loc.gov/copyright/title17/92chap4.html#401
9. http://www.loc.gov/copyright/title17/92chap3.html
10. http://cyber.law.harvard.edu/cc/dcaopinion.html
11. http://www.loc.gov/copyright/title17/92chap2.html#201
12. http://www.loc.gov/copyright/title17/92chap1.html#101
13. http://www.loc.gov/copyright/title17/92chap1.html#107
14. http://www.ca9.uscourts.gov/ca9/newopinions.nsf/
    C38AD9E9A70DB15188256B5700813AD7/$file/0055521.pdf
15. http://www.loc.gov/copyright/title17/92chap5.html#504
16. http://www.loc.gov/copyright/title17/92chap5.html#502
17. http://www.bsa.org/usa/freetools/consumers
18. http://www.usdoj.gov/criminal/cybercrime/17-18red.htm
19. http://www.loc.gov/copyright/legislation/hr2281.pdf
20. http://www.wipo.int/treaties/ip/copyright/index.html
21. http://www.wipo.int/treaties/ip/performances/index.html
22. http://www.eff.org/IP/DMCA/US_v_Sklyarov/20010707_complaint.html
23. http://www.usdoj.gov/usao/can/press/html/2001_12_13_sklyarov.html

Chapter 3: Creating a Copyright-Friendly Website

1. http://www.loc.gov/copyright/title17/92chap1.html#101
2. http://www.loc.gov/copyright/title17/92chap4.html#401
3. http://legal.web.aol.com/decisions/dlip/washcomp.html
4. http://www.gigalaw.com/library/ticketmaster-tickets-2000-0327.html
5. http://www.gigalaw.com/library/ticketmaster-tickets-2000-0810-p1.html
6. http://www.wired.com/news/business/0,1367,48874,00.html
7. http://www.nytimes.com/2001/03/23/technology/23CYBERLAW.html
8. http://www.inta.org/copyright/linkpol.shtml
9. http://www.nysd.uscourts.gov/courtweb/pdf/D02NYSC/0008118.PDF
10. http://www.eff.org/Cases/MPAA_DVD_cases/20011128_ny_appeal_
    decision.html
11. http://www.wired.com/news/politics/0,1283,52213,00.html
12. http://www.dallasnews.com/registration/termsofservice.html
13. http://www.nysd.uscourts.gov/courtweb/pdf/D02NYSC/0107482.PDF

14.http://www.newsbooster.com/?pg=lost&lan=eng
15.http://www.wired.com/news/politics/0,1283,53697,00.html
16.http://www.loc.gov/copyright/title17/92chap4.html#401
17.http://www.loc.gov/copyright/circs/circ03.html
18.http://www.loc.gov/copyright/circs/circ55.pdf
19.http://www.loc.gov/copyright/circs/circ61.pdf
20.http://www.loc.gov/copyright/forms/formtxi.pdf
21.http://www.loc.gov/copyright/forms/formpai.pdf
22.http://www.loc.gov/copyright/forms/formsri.pdf
23.http://www.loc.gov/copyright/forms/formvai.pdf
24.http://www.loc.gov/copyright/circs/circ66.html
25.http://www.loc.gov/copyright/cords

Chapter 4: The Digital Millennium Copyright Act

1.http://www.loc.gov/copyright/legislation/hr2281.pdf
2.http://www.wipo.int
3.http://www.wipo.int/treaties/ip/copyright/copyright.html
4.http://www.wipo.int/treaties/ip/performances/index.html
5.http://www.loc.gov/copyright/title17/92chap12.html#1201
6.http://www.eff.org/IP/DMCA/US_v_Sklyarov/20010707_complaint.html
7.http://www.adobe.com/aboutadobe/pressroom/pressreleases/200107/
20010723dcma.html
8.http://www.usdoj.gov/usao/can/press/html/2001_12_13_sklyarov.html
9.http://www.nysd.uscourts.gov/courtweb/pdf/D02NYSC/0008592.PDF
10.http://www.nysd.uscourts.gov/courtweb/pdf/D02NYSC/0008118.PDF
11.http://www.eff.org/Cases/MPAA_DVD_cases/20011128_ny_appeal_
decision.html
12.http://www.2600.com/news/display.shtml?id=1233
13.http://caselaw.lp.findlaw.com/scripts/getcase.pl?court=us&vol=464&
invol=417
14.http://www.321studios.com/complaint.pdf
15.http://www.loc.gov/copyright/onlinesp/list/index.html
16.http://www.loc.gov/copyright/title17/92chap5.html#512
17.http://www.loc.gov/copyright/title17/92chap5.html#512
18.http://www.loc.gov/copyright/onlinesp/
19.http://www.loc.gov/copyright/title17/92chap5.html#512

Chapter 5: Case Study: An Introduction to Domain Names and Trademark Disputes, *Electronics Boutique* v. *Zuccarini*

1.http://www.gigalaw.com/library/electronicsboutique-zuccarini2000-10-30
-p1.html

2.http://www.paed.uscourts.gov/documents/opinions/01D0083P.HTM

3.http://www.gigalaw.com/library/electronicsboutique-zuccarini2000-10-30
-p1.html

4.http://www.gigalaw.com/library/anticybersquattingact-1999-11-29-p1
.html

5.http://www.gigalaw.com/library/electronicsboutique-zuccarini2000-10-30
-p1.html

6.http://www.gigalaw.com/library/electronicsboutique-zuccarini2000-10-30
-p1.html

7.http://www.ftc.gov/opa/2001/10/cupcake.htm

CHAPTER 6: THE BASICS OF TRADEMARK LAW

1.http://www4.law.cornell.edu/uscode/15/1051.html

2.http://www4.law.cornell.edu/uscode/15/1127.html

3.http://www.net2.com/lindows/ruling.pdf

4.http://www.uspto.gov/web/offices/tac/tmfaq.htm#Basic002

5.http://www.uspto.gov

6.http://www.thomson-thomson.com

7.http://www.cch-corsearch.com

8.http://www.allwhois.com

9.http://www4.law.cornell.edu/uscode/15/1111.html

10.http://www4.law.cornell.edu/uscode/15/1125.html

11.http://www4.law.cornell.edu/uscode/15/1125.html

CHAPTER 7: TRADITIONAL TRADEMARK LAW AND DOMAIN NAMES

1.http://www.eff.org/Legal/Cases/MTV_v_Curry/94_mtv_v_curry_memo
.order

2.http://www.cmcnyls.edu/public/USCases/Planned.HTM

3.http://www.jmls.edu/cyber/cases/cardsvc1.txt

4.http://eon.law.harvard.edu/h2o/property/domain/Shades.html

5.http://www4.law.cornell.edu/uscode/15/1125.html

6.http://eon.law.harvard.edu/h2o//property/domain/Intermatic.html

7.http://www.ce9.uscourts.gov/web/newopinions.nsf/
4bc2cbe0ce5be94e88256927007a37b9/
a5277602df5a94b488256927007d87e0?OpenDocument

8.http://www.jmls.edu/cyber/cases/panavis2.html

9.http://cyber.law.harvard.edu/metaschool/fisher/domain/dncases/lockheed
.htm

10.http://www.ipcounselors.com/juno.htm

11.http://www.jmls.edu/cyber/cases/intermat.html

12.http://www.gigalaw.com/library/anticybersquattingact-1999-11-29-p1
.html
13.http://www.finnegan.com/summ/cases/nissan.htm

CHAPTER 8: THE ANTICYBERSQUATTING CONSUMER PROTECTION ACT
1.http://www.gigalaw.com/library/anticybersquattingact-1999-11-29-p1
.html
2.http://frwebgate.access.gpo.gov/cgi-bin/getdoc.cgi?dbname=106_cong_
reports&docid=f:sr140.pdf
3.http://www4.law.cornell.edu/uscode/15/1125.html
4.http://www.finnegan.com/summ/cases/morrisonfoerster.htm
5.http://www4.law.cornell.edu/uscode/15/1125.html
6.http://www.phillipsnizer.com/int-art228.htm

CHAPTER 9: THE UNIFORM DOMAIN NAME DISPUTE RESOLUTION POLICY
1.http://www.icann.org/udrp/udrp-policy-24oct99.htm
2.http://www.icann.org/announcements/announcement03dec01.htm
3.http://www.cpradr.org/ICANN_Menu.htm
4.http://www.arbforum.com/domains
5.http://arbiter.wipo.int/domains
6.http://www.eresolution.com/pr/30_11_01.htm
7.http://www.icann.org/udrp/udrp-rules-24oct99.htm
8.http://arbiter.wipo.int/domains/decisions/html/2000/d2000-0053.html
9.http://arbiter.wipo.int/domains/decisions/html/2001/d2001-0362.html
10.http://arbiter.wipo.int/domains/decisions/html/2001/d2001-0629.html
11.http://arbiter.wipo.int/domains/decisions/html/2000/d2000-1619.html
12.http://arbiter.wipo.int/domains/decisions/html/2000/d2000-1532.html
13.http://arbiter.wipo.int/domains/decisions/html/2000/d2000-0129.html
14.http://arbiter.wipo.int/domains/decisions/html/2000/d2000-1254.html
15.http://www.arbforum.com/domains/decisions/96492.htm
16.http://www.sork.com/domain/netlearning1.html
17.http://www.ca1.uscourts.gov/cgi-bin/getopn.pl?OPINION=01-1197.01A

CHAPTER 10: OTHER TRADEMARK ISSUES
1.http://www.ca9.uscourts.gov/ca9/newopinions.nsf/
04485f8dcbd4e1ea882569520074e698/
4d113518c149b6a388256952007578b9?OpenDocument
2.http://www.irconnect.com/goto/pages/news_releases.shtml?d=8016
3.http://www.insd.uscourts.gov/opinions/AIB950O8.PDF
4.http://news.com/2100-1001-212931.html

5. http://news.cnet.com/news/0-1005-200-4314233.html
6. http://www.wired.com/news/business/0,1367,38898,00.html
7. http://news.cnet.com/news/0-1006-200-2378098.html
8. http://www.zdnet.com/zdnn/stories/newsbursts/0,7407,2776086,00.html
9. http://www.siliconvalley.com/docs/news/tech/024088.htm
10. http://lw.bna.com/lw/19990504/9856918.htm
11. http://www.terriwelles.com/order_01.htm

CHAPTER 11: CASE STUDY: AN INTRODUCTION TO PATENTS ON THE INTERNET, *AMAZON.COM* v. *BARNESANDNOBLE.COM*
1. http://www.uspto.gov
2. http://patft.uspto.gov/netacgi/nphParser?Sect1=PTO1&Sect2=
   HITOFF&d=PALL&p=1&u=/netahtml/srchnum.htm&r=1&f=G&l=50
   &s1='5,960,411'.WKU.&OS=PN/5,960,411&RS=PN/5,960,411
3. http://eon.law.harvard.edu/h2o/property/patents/AmazonInjunction.html
4. http://serv5.law.emory.edu/fedcircuit/feb2001/00-1109.wp.html
5. http://news.com.com/2100-1017-854105.html

CHAPTER 12: THE BASICS OF PATENT LAW AND PROTECTION
1. http://www4.law.cornell.edu/uscode/35/1.html
2. http://www.uspto.gov
3. http://www.european-patent-office.org
4. http://www.eapo.org
5. http://www.oapi.wipo.net
6. http://www.aripo.wipo.net
7. http://www.wipo.org/treaties/ip/paris
8. http://www.wipo.org/pct/en

CHAPTER 13: PATENTS FOR SOFTWARE AND INTERNET BUSINESS METHODS
1. http://www.lawstudents.org/copyright/cases/797F2D1222.html
2. http://www.lawstudents.org/copyright/cases/982F2D693.html
3. http://caselaw.lp.findlaw.com/scripts/getcase.pl?court=us&vol=409&
   invol=63
4. http://caselaw.lp.findlaw.com/scripts/getcase.pl?court=us&vol=437&
   invol=584
5. http://www.gigalaw.com/library/diamond-diehr-1981-03-03-p1.html
6. http://www.fedcir.gov
7. http://www.lawstudents.org/copyright/cases/982F2D693.html
8. http://www.ca1.uscourts.gov/cgi-bin/getopn.pl?OPINION=95-1793.01A
9. http://www.loc.gov/copyright
10. http://patft.uspto.gov/netacgi/nphParser?Sect1=PTO1&Sect2=

HITOFF&d=PALL&p=1&u=/netahtml/srchnum.htm&r=1&f=G&l=
50&s1='5,794,207'.WKU.&OS=PN/5,794,207&RS=PN/5,794,207
11. http://patft.uspto.gov/netacgi/nphParser?Sect1=PTO1&Sect2=
HITOFF&d=PALL&p=1&u=/netahtml/srchnum.htm&r=1&f=G&l=
50&s1='4,528,643'.WKU.&OS=PN/4,528,643&RS=PN/4,528,643
12. http://www.patents.com/ige/order.htm
13. http://www.law.emory.edu/fedcircuit/nov2000/991324.wp.html
14. http://www.gigalaw.com/library/statestreetbank-1998-07-23p1.html
15. http://www.uspto.gov/web/offices/com/hearings/software/analysis/
computer.html
16. http://www.uspto.gov/web/offices/com/speeches/00-22.htm
17. http://www.uspto.gov/web/menu/busmethp/index.html

CHAPTER 14: EXPLOITING AND ENFORCING PATENTS
1. http://www.zdnet.com/eweek/stories/general/0,11011,2336665,00.html
2. http://www.iipi.org/eng/viewpts/Toronto.htm
3. http://www0.mercurycenter.com/svtech/news/indepth/docs/price011001
.htm
4. http://www.hp.com/hpinfo/newsroom/press/04jun01c.htm
5. http://www.bannerwitcoff.com/press/press_3.htm
6. http://www.xerox.com/go/xrx/template/019e.jsp?id5NR_2001Dec20_
Patent_Infringement
7. http://patft.uspto.gov/netacgi/nphparser?Sect1=PTO1&Sect2=
HITOFF&d=PALL&p=1&u=/netahtml/srchnum.htm&r=1&f=G&1=
50&s1='5,596,656'.WKU.&OS=PN/5,596,656&RS=PN/5,596,656
8. http://www.prnewswire.com/cgi-bin/micro;ubstories.pl?ACCT=
153400&TICK=PALM&STORY=/www/story/12-21-2001/
0001638062&EDATE=Dec121,12001
9. http://patft.uspto.gov/netacgi/nph-Parser?Sect1=PTO1&Sect2=
HITOFF&d=PALL&p=1&u=/netahtml/srchnum.htm&r=1&f=G&I=
50&s1='4873662'.WKU.&OS=PN/4873662&RS=PN/4873662
10. http://www.techlawjournal.com/courts2000/bt_prodigy/200001213com
.asp

CHAPTER 15: CASE STUDY: AN INTRODUCTION TO PRIVACY ON THE INTERNET,
FEDERAL TRADE COMMISSION v. GEOCITIES
1. http://www.ftc.gov
2. http://www.ftc.gov/os/1998/9808/geo-cmpl.htm
3. http://www4.law.cornell.edu/uscode/15/41.html
4. http://www4.law.cornell.edu/uscode/15/45.html
5. http://www.ftc.gov/os/1998/9808/geo-ord.htm

6.http://www.ftc.gov/opa/1998/9808/geocitie.htm
7.http://www.internetnews.com/bus-news/article/0,,3_24421,00.html
8.http://docs.yahoo.com/docs/pr/release321.html
9.http://www.ftc.gov/speeches/muris/privisp1002.htm
10.http://www.ftc.gov/os/2002/04/sb2201muris.htm

CHAPTER 16: INTERNET PRIVACY LAWS AND PRIVACY POLICIES
1.http://www4.law.cornell.edu/uscode/15/41.html
2.http://www.ftc.gov/ogc/coppa1.htm
3.http://www.revisor.leg.state.mn.us/cgi-bin/getbill.pl?session=ls82&version=latest&number=SF2908
4.http://www.eff.org/Privacy/Surveillance/Terrorism_militias/20011025_hr3162_usa_patriot_bill.html
5.http://www.eff.org/Privacy/Surveillance/Terrorism_militias/20011031_eff_usa_patriot_analysis.html
6.http://lcweb2.loc.gov/const/const.html
7.http://www.louisville.edu/library/law/brandeis/privacy.html
8.ftp://ftp.cpsr.org/cpsr/privacy/law/video_rental_privacy_act.txt
9.http://www.junkbusters.com/ht/en/amazon.html#FTC
10.http://www.ftc.gov/os/closings/staff/amazonletter.htm
11.http://www.junkbusters.com/ebay.html#feb
12.http://news.com.com/2100-1017-863294.html
13.http://help.yahoo.com/help/us/privacy/privacy-23.html
14.http://www.wired.com/news/privacy/0,1848,51461.00.html
15.http://cs3-hq.oecd.org/scripts/pwv3/pwhome.htm
16.http://www.w3.org/P3P
17.http://www.gigalaw.com/articles/2002-all/cranor-2002-04-all.html
18.http://www.gigalaw.com/articles/2002-all/harvey-2002-02-all.html
19.http://www.ftc.gov/os/2000/07/toysmartcmp.htm
20.http://www.ftc.gov/opa/2000/07/toysmart.htm
21.http://www.epic.org/privacy/internet/etour.html
22.http://www.truste.org
23.http://www.bbbonline.org

CHAPTER 17: GENERAL PRIVACY LAWS
1.http://www.epic.org/privacy/financial/fcra.html
2.http://www4.law.cornell.edu/uscode/18/ch119.html
3.http://www.infoworld.com/articles/hn/xml/01/04/27/010427hnalexa.xml
4.http://www.epic.org/free_speech/cyberp_v_aol.html
5.http://pub.bna.com/eclr/997885.htm

6. http://www.phillipsnizer.com/int-art229.htm
7. http://www.hhs.gov/ocr/hipaa
8. http://www.hhs.gov/news/press/2001pres/01fsprivacy.html
9. http://www.ftc.gov/privacy/glbact/index.html

CHAPTER 18: THE CHILDREN'S ONLINE PRIVACY PROTECTION ACT
1. http://www.ftc.gov/ogc/coppa1.htm
2. http://www.ftc.gov/os/1999/9910/64fr59888.htm
3. http://www.ftc.gov/ogc/coppa1.htm
4. http://www.gigalaw.com/library/coppa-1999-11-03-p1.html
5. http://www.ftc.gov/os/1999/9907/agenda.htm
6. http://www.gigalaw.com/2000/articles/isenberg-2000-07a.html
7. http://www.gigalaw.com/articles/2000/winer-2000-10.html
8. http://www.ftc.gov/opa/2001/04/girlslife.htm
9. http://www.ftc.gov/opa/2002/04/coppaanniv.htm
10. http://www.ftc.gov.os/2002/04/ohioartcomplaint.htm
11. http://www.ftc.gov.os/2002/04/ohioartconsent.htm
12. http://www.ftc.gov/opa/2002/04/coppaaniv.htm
13. http://www.ftc.gov/opa/2001/05/truste.htm
14. http://www.ftc.gov/os/2001/02/caruletter.pdf
15. http://www.ftc.gov/privacy/safeharbor/esrbapprovalltr.htm
16. http://www.ftc.gov/privacy/safeharbor/shp.htm

CHAPTER 19: THE EUROPEAN UNION'S PRIVACY DIRECTIVE
1. http://europa.eu.int/eur-lex/en/lif/dat/1995/en_395L0046.html
2. http://lcweb2.loc.gov/const/bor.html
3. http://www.export.gov/safeharbor
4. http://www.export.gov/safeharbor/SHPRINCIPLESFINAL.htm
5. http://www4.law.cornell.edu/uscode/15/45.html

CHAPTER 20: THE CANADIAN PRIVACY ACT
1. http://www.privcom.gc.ca/legislation/02_06_01_e.asp
2. http://canada.justice.gc.ca/en/news/nr/1998/attback2.html
3. http://www.privcom.gc.ca/index_e.asp

CHAPTER 21: CASE STUDY: AN INTRODUCTION TO FREE SPEECH ON THE
INTERNET, ZERAN V. AMERICA ONLINE
1. http://www.jmls.edu/cyber/cases/zeran.html
2. http://www.gigalaw.com/library/zeran-aol-1997-11-12-p1.html
3. http://www.loc.gov/copyright/legislation/hr2281.pdf

4.http://www4.law.cornell.edu/uscode/47/230.html
5.http://www.eff.org/Legal/Cases/Stratton_Oakmont_Porush_v_Prodigy/
stratton-oakmont_porush_v_prodigy_et-al.decision

CHAPTER 22: SEX, THE FIRST AMENDMENT, AND THE INTERNET
1.http://www.epic.org/cda/cda.html
2.http://www4.law.cornell.edu/uscode/47/223.html
3.http://www4.law.cornell.edu/uscode/47/223.html
4.http://www.eff.org/Censorship/Rimm_CMU_Time
5.http://www.gigalaw.com/library/reno-aclu-1997-06-26-p7.html
6.http://www.aclu.org/court/cdacom.html
7.http://www.aclu.org/court/cdadec.html
8.http://www.aclu.org/court/renovacludec.html
9.http://www.eff.org/Censorship/Internet_censorship_bills/1998_bills/
s1482_hr3783_1998.bill
10.http://www.eff.org/Legal/Cases/ACLU_v_Reno_II/HTML/19981120_
tro_order.html
11.http://www.eff.org/Legal/Cases/ACLU_v_Reno_II/HTML/19990201_
injunction_order.html
12.http://www.ca3.uscourts.gov/indexsearch/oop/qfullhit.htw?
CiWebHitsFile=%2Fopinions%2F991324%2Etxt&CiRestriction=
reno&CiBeginHilite=%3Cstrong+class%3DHit%3E&CiEndHilite=
%3C%2Fstrong%3E&CiUserParam3=/indexsearch/opinions
.asp&CiHiliteType=Full
13.http://www.supremecourtus.gov/opinions/01pdf/00-1293.pdf
14.http://www.supremecourtus.gov/opinions/01pdf/00-795.pdf
15.http://www.paed.uscourts.gov/documents/opinions/02D0415P.HTM
16.http://www.usdoj.gov/ag/speeches/2001/080801childpornography.htm
17.http://www.usps.gov/postalinspectors/NRReedy.htm
18.http://www.fbi.gov/pressrel/candyman/candymanhome.htm
19.http://www.customs.ustreas.gov/hot-new/pressrel/2002/0320-00.htm
20.http://www.nap.edu/catalog/10261.html?onpi_newsdoc05022002
21.http://www4.nationalacademies.org/news.nsf/isbn/0309082749
?OpenDocument

CHAPTER 23: MESSAGE BOARD MISCONDUCT AND ONLINE ANONYMITY
1.http://supct.law.cornell.edu/supct/html/93-986.ZO.html
2.http://supct.law.cornell.edu/supct/html/96-511.ZS.html
3.http://www.judiciary.state.nj.us/opinions/A2774-00.htm
4.http://www.eff.org/Legal/Cases/PrePaid_Legal_v_Sturtz/20010712_
proposed_order.html

5. http://www.eff.org/Cases/2TheMart_case/20010427_2themart_order.html
6. http://www.healthfreedomlaw.com/Court%20Documents/
Rosenthal%20SLAPP/Rosenthal%20Ruling.pdf

CHAPTER 24: CRITICAL WEBSITES, PARODY, AND THE FIRST AMENDMENT
1. http://www.enronownsthegop.com/news/cease.htm
2. http://www.law.com/cgi-bin/nwlink.cgi?ACG=ZZZWOAIIQ8C
3. http://www.nytimes.com/library/tech/00/04/cyber/articles/18bush.html
4. http://www.eff.org/Censorship/SLAPP/Intprop_abuse/20010706_eff_
barney_response.html
5. http://supct.law.cornell.edu/supct/html/92-1292.ZS.html
6. http://www.ca5.uscourts.gov/opinions/pub/98/98-11003-cv0.htm

CHAPTER 25: HATE ON THE INTERNET
1. http://www.websense.com/company/news/pr/01/112901.cfm
2. http://www.adl.org/poisoning%5Fweb/introduction.html
3. http://www.ca9.uscourts.gov/ca9/newopinions.nsf/
761F198CBF88F75988256A1D005E8ED1/$file/9935320.pdf
?openelement
4. http://www.ca9.uscourts.gov/ca9/newopinions.nsf/
A3AC4A8F164DA30288256BBA0080B31D/$file/9935320.pdf
?openelement
5. http://www.law.emory.edu/11circuit/may2002/01-15821.opn.html
6. http://www.aclu.org/court/renovacludec.html
7. http://www.adl.org/hate%2Dpatrol/info/default.htm
8. http://caselaw.lp.findlaw.com/scripts/getcase.pl?court=us&vol=
395&invol=444
9. http://news.cnet.com/news/0,10000,0-1005-200326457,00.html
10. http://www.gigalaw.com/library/france-yahoo-2000-11-20.html
11. http://www.cdt.org/jurisdiction/011107judgement.pdf

CHAPTER 26: SPAM
1. http://www.spam.com/ci/ci_in.htm
2. http://www.cauce.org/about/problem.shtml
3. http://www4.law.cornell.edu/uscode/47/227.html
4. http://pacer.moed.uscourts.gov/opinions/STATE_OF_MISSOURI_
EX_REL_JEREMIAH_W_NIXON_ATTORNEY_GENERAL_V_
AMERICAN_BLAST_FAX_INC_ET_AL-SNL-79.PDF
5. http://frwebgate.access.gpo.gov/cgi-bin/getdoc.cgi?dbname=107_cong_
bills&docid=f:h95ih.txt.pdf
6. http://thomas.loc.gov/cgi-bin/bdquery/z?d107:s630:

7.http://caselaw.lp.findlaw.com/scripts/getcase.pl?court=us&vol=447&invol=557

8.http://www.spamlaws.com/state/ca1.html

9.http://www.spamlaws.com/state/de.html

10.http://www.spamlaws.com

11.http://www.techfirm.com/briefs/emailo.pdf

12.http://news.cnet.com/news/0-1005-200-8365021.html

13.http://www.courts.wa.gov/opinions/opindisp.cfm?docid=694168MAJ

14.http://www.euro.cauce.org/en/countries/index.html

15.http://legal.web.aol.com/decisions/dljunk/webcomm.html

16.http://www.ftc.gov/opa/1998/9803/ibb.htm

17.http://www.ftc.gov/opa/2002/04/spam.htm

18.http://www.ftc.gov/opa/2002/04/universaldircmp.pdf

19.http://www.ftc.gov/opa/2002/04/btv.htm

20.http://www.earthlink.net/about/policies/use

CHAPTER 27: ELECTRONIC SIGNATURES AND THE U.S. E-SIGN ACT

1.http://law.gsu.edu/gsuecp/Act/DSTF/07_14_98_Meeting/BeepsandChirpsMemo.htm

2.http://www.nccusl.org/nccusl/uniformact_summaries/uniformacts-s-ueta.asp

3.http://www.nccusl.org/nccusl/uniformact_factsheets_uniformacts-fs-ueta.asp

4.http://www.nccusl.org/nccusl/uniformact_overview/uniformacts-ov-ucita.asp

5.http://www.nccusl.org/nccusl/uniformact_factsheets_uniformacts-fs-ucita.asp

6.http://frwebgate.access.gpo.gov/cgi-bin/getdoc.cgi?dbname=106_cong_bills&docid=f:s761eah.txt.pdf

7.http://www.consumersunion.org/finance/digitaldc600.htm

8.http://news.com.com/2100-1017-884544.html

CHAPTER 29: CREATING CONTRACTS ON THE INTERNET

1.http://www.law.emory.edu/7circuit/june96/96-1139.html

2.http://eon.law.harvard.edu/h2o/property/alternatives/hotmail.html

3.http://legal.web.aol.com/decisions/dlother/groff.html

4.http://www.nysd.uscourts.gov/courtweb/pdf/D02NYSC/01-07482.PDF

5.http://www.gigalaw.com/library/ticketmaster-tickets-2000-03-27.html

CHAPTER 30: CASE STUDY: AN INTRODUCTION TO EMPLOYMENT LAW IN THE TECHNOLOGICAL REVOLUTION, *STRAUSS V. MICROSOFT*
1. http://www.eeoc.gov/laws/vii.html
2. http://www.eeoc.gov
3. http://www.usdoj.gov/crt/ada/pubs/ada.txt
4. http://www.eeoc.gov/laws/adea.html

CHAPTER 31: SEXUAL HARASSMENT
1. http://caselaw.lp.findlaw.com/scripts/getcase.pl?court=us&vol=477&invol=57
2. http://caselaw.lp.findlaw.com/scripts/getcase.pl?court=us&vol=000&invol=U10433
3. http://www.ca5.uscourts.gov/opinions/pub/98/98-20171-cv0.htm
4. http://www.law.emory.edu/pub-cgi/print_hit_bold.pl/4circuit/mar99/981601.p.html
5. http://caselaw.lp.findlaw.com/scripts/getcase.pl?court=us&vol=000&invol=97-569
6. http://caselaw.lp.findlaw.com/scripts/getcase.pl?court=us&vol=000&invol=97-282
7. http://news.cnet.com/news/0-1005-200-1474996.html
8. http://www.siliconalleydaily.com/issues/sar01062000.html
9. http://www.kscourts.org/ca10/cases/1999/07/97-3387.htm
10. http://news.cnet.com/news/0-1007-200-2924978.html
11. http://www.internetmanager.com/pdf/Cyberliability_White_Paper.pdf
12. http://www.post-gazette.com/businessnews/20000319emailethics1.asp
13. http://www.post-gazette.com/businessnews/20000319emailethics1.asp
14. http://www.usatoday.com/life/cyber/2002/04/25/racy-email.htm
15. http://www.amanet.org/research/pdfs/ems_short2001.pdf
16. http://www.post-gazette.com/businessnews/20000319emailethics1.asp
17. http://www.epolicyinstitute.com/about/bio.html
18. http://www.epolicyinstitute.com/disaster/stories.html
19. http://www.amanet.org/research/pdfs/ems_short2001.pdf
20. http://pqasb.pqarchiver.com/sptimes/main/document.html?QIID=000000073959276
21. http://lawlibrary.rutgers.edu/courts/supreme/a-5-99.opn.html

CHAPTER 32: THE AGE DISCRIMINATION IN EMPLOYMENT ACT
1. http://www.eeoc.gov/stats/adea.html
2. http://heather.cs.ucdavis.edu/itaa.real.html
3. http://caselaw.lp.findlaw.com/scripts/getcase.pl?court=us&vol=000&invol=U10195

4. http://www.zazona.com/ShameH1B/Library/Matloff/Qualcomm.htm
5. http://news.cnet.com/news/0-1007-200-1863780.html

CHAPTER 33: THE AMERICANS WITH DISABILITIES ACT

1. http://www.usdoj.gov/crt/ada/pubs/ada.txt
2. http://www.eeoc.gov/stats/ada-charges.html
3. http://frwebgate.access.gpo.gov/cgi-bin/get-cfr.cgi?TITLE=29&PART=1630&SECTION=2&TYPE=TEXT
4. http://www.eeoc.gov/stats/ada-resolutions.html
5. http://caselaw.lp.findlaw.com/scripts/getcase.pl?court=us&vol=000&invol=97-156
6. http://www.ca9.uscourts.gov/ca9/newopinions.nsf/04485f8dcbd4e1ea882569520074e698/d3a9a4d2e67b223d882569580069b072?OpenDocument&Highlight=2,McAlindin
7. http://frwebgate.access.gpo.gov/cgi-bin/get-cfr.cgi?TITLE=29&PART=1630&SECTION=2&TYPE=TEXT
8. http://www.kentlaw.edu/7circuit/1995/94-1884.html
9. http://www.eeoc.gov/docs/accommodation.html
10. http://www.ca9.uscourts.gov/ca9/newopinions.nsf/ABD495F0E26FA48E882569F200608B6B/$file/9815404.pdf?openelement
11. http://www.securitymanagement.com/library/Davis_guardian0401.txt
12. http://www4.law.cornell.edu/uscode/42/12181.html
13. http://frwebgate.access.gpo.gov/cgi-bin/get-cfr.cgi?TITLE=28&PART=36&SECTION=304&TYPE=TEXT
14. http://frwebgate.access.gpo.gov/cgi-bin/get-cfr.cgi?TITLE=28&PART=36&SECTION=302&TYPE=TEXT
15. http://frwebgate.access.gpo.gov/cgi-bin/get-cfr.cgi?TITLE=28&PART=36&SECTION=303&TYPE=TEXT
16. http://www.nfb.org/BM/BM01/BM0102/bm010203.htm
17. http://www.nfb.org/bm/bm00/bm0006/bm000601.htm
18. http://www.thestandard.com/article/0,1902,16236,00.html
19. http://www.eeoc.gov/laws/rehab.html
20. http://www4.law.cornell.edu/uscode/29/794d.html

CHAPTER 34: NONCOMPETE AGREEMENTS AND OTHER RESTRICTIVE COVENANTS

1. http://www6.law.com/ny/stories/99/10/102999a1.htm
2. http://august1.com/courses/cyber/cases/Doubleclick.htm
3. http://www.linowes-law.com/h_uphold.htm

CHAPTER 35: PRIVACY ISSUES AND EMPLOYEE MONITORING
1. http://www.amanet.org/research/pdfs/ems_short2001.pdf
2. http://www.marquette.edu/law/course/priv_98/kmart.htm
3. http://www.privacyfoundation.org
4. http://www.epic.org/privacy/internet/smyth_v_pillsbury.html
5. http://www.loundy.com/CASES/Bourke_v_Nissan.html
6. http://normative.zusammenhaenge.at/faelle/mclaren_v_microsoft.html
7. http://www4.law.cornell.edu/uscode/18/ch119.html
8. http://www.privacyfoundation.org/legal/case/show.asp?id=22&t=2
9. http://www.eff.org/Privacy/Surveillance/Terrorism_militias/20011025_
   hr3162_usa_patriot_bill.html

CONTRIBUTORS
1. http://www.needlerosenberg.com
2. http://www.gigalaw.com/about/gregkirsch.html
3. http://www.gigalaw.com/about/dougtowns.html
4. http://www.jonesday.com
5. http://www.gigalaw.com/about/jayhollander.html
6. http://www.hollanderco.com
7. http://www.gigalaw.com/about/peteryu.html
8. http://www.cardozo.yu.edu
9. http://www.proskauer.com
10. http://www.alston.com

INDEX